MW01624406

Made with Words

POETS ON POETRY

David Lehman, General Editor
Donald Hall, Founding Editor

New titles

Josephine Jacobsen, *The Instant of Knowing*
Charles Simic, *Orphan Factory*
William Stafford, *Crossing Unmarked Snow*
May Swenson, *Made with Words*

Recently published

A. R. Ammons, *Set in Motion*
Douglas Crase, *AMERIFIL.TXT*
Suzanne Gardinier, *A World That Will Hold All the People*
Allen Grossman, *The Long Schoolroom*
Jonathan Holden, *Guns and Boyhood in America*
Andrew Hudgins, *The Glass Anvil*
Kenneth Koch, *The Art of Poetry*
Martin Lammon (editor), *Written in Water, Written in Stone*
Carol Muske, *Women and Poetry*

Also available are collections by

Robert Bly, Philip Booth, Marianne Boruch, Hayden Carruth, Fred Chappell, Amy Clampitt, Tom Clark, Robert Creeley, Donald Davie, Peter Davison, Tess Gallagher, Thom Gunn, John Haines, Donald Hall, Joy Harjo, Robert Hayden, Daniel Hoffman, Weldon Kees, Galway Kinnell, Mary Kinzie, Richard Kostelanetz, Maxine Kumin, David Lehman, Philip Levine, John Logan, William Matthews, William Meredith, Jane Miller, John Frederick Nims, Gregory Orr, Alicia Ostriker, Marge Piercy, Anne Sexton, Charles Simic, Louis Simpson, William Stafford, Richard Tillinghast, Diane Wakoski, Alan Williamson, Charles Wright, and James Wright

May Swenson

Made with Words

Gardner McFall, Editor

Ann Arbor

THE UNIVERSITY OF MICHIGAN PRESS

Copyright © by the University of Michigan 1998
All rights reserved
Published in the United States of America by
The University of Michigan Press
Manufactured in the United States of America
∞ Printed on acid-free paper
2001 2000 1999 1998 4 3 2 1

No part of this publication may be reproduced, stored in a retrieval system, or transmitted in any form or by any means, electronic, mechanical, or otherwise, without the written permission of the publisher.

A CIP catalog record for this book is available from the British Library.

Library of Congress Cataloging-in-Publication Data

Swenson, May.
Made with words / May Swenson ; Gardner McFall, editor.
p. cm.—(Poets on poetry)
ISBN 0-472-09658-3 (alk. paper). — ISBN 0-472-06658-7 (pbk. : alk. paper)
1. Swenson, May—Authorship. 2. Poetry—Authorship. 3. Poetry. I. McFall, Gardner. II. Title. III. Series.
PS3537.W4786Z47 1997
818′.5408—dc21 97-39284
CIP

Much of the material in this book is taken from the May Swenson Papers, Washington University Libraries, in St. Louis, Missouri. Unless otherwise noted, the pieces collected here are reprinted with the kind permission of the Literary Estate of May Swenson. Every effort has been made to trace the ownership of all copyrighted material and to secure permission for its use. Publication acknowledgments appear at the bottom of the first page of each text.

Acknowledgments: I am indebted to many individuals who answered questions and provided information as this volume took shape: Dana Gioia, Henri Cole, Tom Bevan, Wynn Handman, Jane Mayhall, Pearl Schwartz, Peter Davison, Lee Hudson, Jane Shore, Cathy Clarke, and Alfred Corn. Kevin Ray and Anne Posega at Washington University Libraries in St. Louis, Missouri, facilitated my work in providing copies of manuscripts and information about the May Swenson Papers. I am grateful to David Lehman and LeAnn Fields, for their editorial judgment and encouragement; and Virginia Fay, Carl Luss, and Jennifer Samet, for help with typing and proofreading. Finally, and most especially, my thanks go to Grace Schulman, for helping me "get to know May," and to the indispensable R. R. Knudson, for her generous enthusiasm, permission, and insights. —G. M.

Epigraph: May Swenson Papers, Washington University Libraries.

In Consideration of Writing Prose

What do I have to say before I die? It is something no one else has said or can say because since each one of us is one of a kind, what I will say is important coming from me. . . . True, each person is different from all others, but, equally true, all persons in a sense are the same—not identical but similar. . . . Will you in your message emphasize individuality and difference or commonality and similarity with others? Do you want to show how you are like others and they like you or how you deviate? Perhaps both? Is not all art a cry of "Look at me! Learn from me! Listen!" . . . Does not the artist crave understanding of self in equal measure as he insists on exploring, teaching, imposing his ideas and standards on others? . . .

What of an un-self-centered attitude—one aiming not at seeking understanding for himself, not self-revelatory and self-obscuring at once, but with the object of understanding his audience and revealing *it* to itself and himself. Not "Look, here I am!" but "See, there you are."

May Swenson, 1950

Contents

Introduction

Gardner McFall

At the time of her death, in 1989, May Swenson had produced eleven books of poetry and received almost every major poetry award in the United States. She also wrote prose (fables, stories, criticism, and plays), kept a record of her dreams, entitled "Chapters of the Night" as well as a daybook, and wrote hundreds of letters to family, friends, and other writers. Her reviews of books by significant poets (Anne Sexton, John Hollander, H. D., Muriel Rukeyser, W. D. Snodgrass, and others) appeared in the *New York Times, Poetry,* the *Nation,* and *Southern Review.*

This book is a miscellany of May Swenson's prose, culled from abundant material that she left, some published during her lifetime, some unpublished, and arranged in four sections: Fiction, On Poets and Poetry, The Floor (a one-act play), and Letters to Elizabeth Bishop. While Swenson corresponded with various poets (Howard Moss, Maxine Kumin, Alicia Ostriker, Irving Feldman, Mary Oliver, William Meredith, and Diane Ackerman, among others), the breadth and depth of her twenty-nine-year correspondence with Bishop make it a singular prism through which to view Swenson's poetry and prose alike.[1] It functions as a kind of constant, a backdrop against which to consider her life and work.

Born in 1913, Swenson kept a diary as a young girl. Her

1. May Swenson's correspondence and manuscripts are deposited at the Washington University Libraries, St. Louis, Missouri. Unless otherwise indicated, quotations in this introduction, including those drawn from Elizabeth Bishop's letters to Swenson, are taken from the May Swenson Papers, Washington University Libraries.

juvenilia, while not included here, show that she wrote both stories and poems. These efforts and a paean to Edgar Allan Poe from the 1940s entitled "Genius" suggest that, like her literary hero, she ambitiously planned to write in several genres. In 1928 her prize-winning story "Christmas Day" was published in the Logan (Utah) High School newspaper, the *Grizzly*. It relates the protagonist's memory of his parents' death on Christmas when he was a boy and reveals Swenson's early fascination with death and the relationship between dream and reality. Her 1933 story "Mirror," published in her college literary magazine, presents a fragmented narrative wherein a woman's inner voice interweaves with outer events to reveal her poignantly repeating her mother's life of domestic drudgery. Curiously, both stories begin with the portrayal of expectant, happy youth and end with that of old or middle age, haunted by horror in one case and regret in the other.

Evidence indicates that Swenson assembled a collection of twelve stories for possible publication in the mid-1960s. Four of the stories in that collection's table of contents are included here: "Mutterings of a Middlewoman," "Appearances," "The Power and the Danger," and "From the Window" (alternately titled "Seventeen Acts on One Set"). The poet and editor Howard Moss, who published Swenson's poems in the *New Yorker* from 1954 on, included "Mutterings of a Middlewoman" in his anthology *The Poet's Story* (New York: Macmillan, 1973).

Like many of her poems, Swenson's stories are drawn from the ordinary, daily occurrences of life. Swenson's friend, the poet Jane Mayhall, recounts that once, when visiting their mutual friend Josephine Herbst on her Pennsylvania farm, Swenson flung herself in the wild grass and lay there all day, rather like the narrator in "The Power and the Danger." "Mutterings of a Middlewoman" grows directly from her experience working as a secretary on Wall Street in the early 1950s.

Swenson's stories resonate with her poetry on thematic levels as well. Her 1951 "Appearances" (whose setting resembles Yaddo, the artists' colony that she first visited in 1950) sounds a note found again in "The Power and the Danger": "the mystery and lavish power" of nature. In "Appearances" Swenson defines the character of the artist as being that of an explorer, receptive to sensual experience and the physical world, embracive of good, evil, and inner fears most reasonable people (as represented by the doctor in the story) struggle to repress. This drive to fathom the hidden reaches of the heart and mysteries of nature fueled Swenson's poetry throughout her life.

At times the prose stands clearly in service of the poems. Her highly descriptive "From the Window," a "nonstory" as Swenson called it, enacts a drama of the eye, Swenson's favorite sense. In a letter of November 5, 1956, to Katharine White, an editor at the *New Yorker,* she described it as "a sort of diary in eighteen short entries, at the same time the account of a drama in eighteen 'acts,' in which the materials of the city scene are the actors, the plot and movement being furnished by the weather, the changing season, and the shift of mood in the observer's mind." Strikingly, it also contains imagery and strategies found in "At Breakfast," "By Morning," and "East River" in *A Cage of Spines* (1958), written at about the same time. Even Swenson's "Fables of Things," modeled after Aesop and La Fontaine, which at first glance might appear to be a digression from her path, in fact issues from the same impulse that is behind her riddle poems ("Hypnotist," "Seven Natural Songs," and "Living Tenderly," among others). Both depend on a question/answer paradigm, or, more broadly, a statement and response, whether the response is given in words at the end of a fable or evoked by them in the course of a riddle poem. But for Swenson the proper response to a question is not so much an answer as a creation, to "try to place, relate, and name" ("Her Management").

This alignment between her fiction and poems does not discredit the prose but, rather, points to a unified, artistic sensibility underlying Swenson's efforts in both. In Swenson's writing we encounter an integrated, unique consciousness, which without premeditation or self-awareness (for Swenson herself claimed, "one is not conscious of one's own consciousness") marks whatever genre it operates in. The integrity of the unconscious, which Swenson prized above any formal training, is apparent in her criticism.

When she writes about Emily Dickinson in " 'Big My Secret, but It's Bandaged,' " she does so with a sensitivity and acuity that stem from a source tied deeply to her own poetry. She approaches Dickinson purely as a poet, as contrasted with Adrienne Rich, who adopts a feminist approach to the same subject in her 1975

"Vesuvius at Home: The Power of Emily Dickinson." Though Swenson claims in an interview to have been "a feminist at age three-and-a-half," she embraces Dickinson's genius rather than the political obligation to expose the conventional, patriarchal appraisal of her. In her discussions we decipher the connections between Swenson and Dickinson (the love of riddle, attention to the everyday, and use of unconventional syntax and grammar) even as we see Dickinson come alive.

Perhaps one of the paradoxes inherent in Swenson, as revealed in her interviews and statements about poetry, is her disavowal of traditional learning or influence. Four months before her death she wrote in response to a query from Austin Straus, poetry editor of *West/Word:* "The best poetry has its roots in the subconscious to a great degree. Youth, naivety, reliance on instinct more than learning and method, a sense of freedom and play, even trust in randomness, is necessary to the making of a poem."

Yet Swenson read widely, even if she refused to claim any mastery of the tradition. Her one-act play *The Floor* suggests the influence of Samuel Beckett, with its cyclical structure, paired characters, and nonsensical wordplay. A letter to Elizabeth Bishop on April 24, 1962, confirms this suspicion, when her account of birdwatching ends with a pun on "Godot": "We were waiting for Godwit but he didn't show up." The Beckettian elements in *The Floor* are understandable inasmuch as Beckett's sensibility, as revealed in his plays, would have struck a chord in Swenson with her love of invented form and language play.

By reading widely and throwing off tradition, Swenson repeatedly arrived at something fresh and original in her poetry, which she did not do in *The Floor* or her fiction. Though her fiction evolved from linear, representational stories to those with more open, creative forms, it remained full of observation, rumination, and discussion rather than plot—a poet's prose. The evolution of her prose and simultaneous evolution of her poetry illustrate, but do not explain, why the genre of poetry was a more felicitous, natural mode of artistic expression for Swenson.

Swenson's letters to Elizabeth Bishop, spanning the years 1950 to 1979, reinforce this view. Swenson and Bishop met at Yaddo in Saratoga Springs in October 1950, and Swenson invited Bishop to visit her in Greenwich Village over Christmas. In a letter of December 12 Bishop declined the invitation, but that letter begins a vast correspondence and sets in motion a dynamic marking their entire exchange: that between supplicant and master. Their correspondence consists of more than two hundred letters, the majority written between 1954 and 1965; only fifteen of Bishop's letters to Swenson are contained in Bishop's letters *One Art* (New York: Farrar, Straus and Giroux, 1994). Included here are Swenson's first extant letter to Bishop and forty subsequent ones, edited to highlight their literary discussions and friendship.

From the letters it is evident that Bishop and Swenson admired each other's work. "Mutterings of a Middlewoman" made Bishop "hysterical with mirth" (May 20, 1955), and she encouraged Swenson to write more fiction, not only because, as she expressed it in a letter of June 11, 1955, she felt Swenson had "gifts for it" but because "it is one way of filling in the spaces between writing poems and also *making money* that doesn't do harm to and may even help, the writing of poetry." It is common to find in their correspondence one offering comments on the other's work; it is rarer to find them acting on proffered suggestions, perhaps because they went about making poems so differently. There are instances, of course: Swenson recommends to Bishop that her third book be titled "Questions of Travel" rather than "January River," and Bishop counsels Swenson on revisions to her third book, *To Mix with Time.* But many suggestions go unheeded, as when Swenson suggests changes to "The Baptism" and "The Sea & Its Shore" (December 11, 1953) or when Bishop raises objections to phrases and images in "Hypnotist" and "The Engagement" (March 17, 1955). The Vassar-schooled Bishop took Swenson to task over Swenson's unorthodox punctuation and "low-brow" use of grammar. She told her in a letter of September 19, 1953: "I am against anything being strange unless it absolutely forces itself to be." When Bishop complained that there were too many verbs in "The Centaur," such that the reader stopped "visualizing" the poem (February 18, 1956), Swenson kept them nonetheless.

In the main the letters reveal that these differences never impeded their regard for each other. Bishop repeatedly sponsored Swenson for a Guggenheim, and, when Bishop was in Brazil, Swenson offered to be her "representative in the States"

(March 10, 1953), probably never guessing that this would involve being Bishop's "personal shopper." Over the years Swenson mailed Bishop whatever she requested and reimbursed her for: a radio, Scrabble set, Levi's blue jeans, magazines, books, jazz records, perch scrapers, a cheese grater, jigsaw puzzles, Japanese lanterns, spectacle wipers, binoculars, and even a Saks bathing suit, which Bishop had seen advertised in the *New Yorker*.

Though, initially, Bishop's stance, as revealed in the letters, is that of the older, more experienced poet and Swenson's that of the grateful apprentice, Swenson quickly gains ground, and for all of Swenson's self-effacing tone, a tone absent from Bishop's side of the correspondence, their dialogue, fairly soon into their exchange of letters, becomes that of equals. On August 14, 1959, after receiving a copy of the Academy of American Poets' *Poetry Pilot*, which Swenson had guest edited, Bishop wrote to her: "How you have been heaping up the biography since I left the U.S.A.—it is astounding."

Swenson and Bishop shared similarities in small matters (they both loved cats) and larger ones: they were lesbian; they shared a lapsed religious practice, Bishop as a Baptist and Swenson as a Mormon; they were both committed to their work. But in that work Bishop was adamant about what she considered to be adequate punctuation, "accuracy," and diction that does not shock the reader. Swenson was, by comparison, too quirky and unorthodox for Bishop's tastes, Bishop's claim that Swenson's poems made her "green with jealousy" notwithstanding.[2]

Like her poems, Swenson's stories, plays, criticism, interviews, and letters are all, in her phrase from "A Note about Iconographs," "made with words," the raw material of her art. In the last volume of poetry Swenson published during her life, *In Other Words* (1987), prose manifests itself overtly in her poems. "From a Daybook," with stanzas divided by dates and attention given to the weather (Swenson remarked that her daybook was full of descriptions of the weather), points to her prose effort behind the poem much as "Dear Elizabeth" in *Half Sun Half Sleep* (1967)

2. Pauline Hanson, in *Remembering Elizabeth Bishop: An Oral Biography*, ed. Gary Fountain and Peter Brazeau (Amherst: University of Massachusetts Press, 1994), 121.

grows from her correspondence with Elizabeth Bishop[3] or "To Make a Play" in the same volume stems from her work on *The Floor.* But, beyond that, prose and verse lines intermingle in "Rainbow Hummingbird Lamplight" and "Banyan." The two streams of her writing life—poetry and prose—converge in her last book, culminating a process that can be discerned throughout her career.

Although she may not have realized it at the start, Swenson's practice of prose was inextricably intertwined with her poetic process and development. What she did realize was that writing was a constant effort at creation and her chosen discipline. She wrote her father on May 29, 1951, fifteen years after her arrival in New York and three years before the publication of her first book of poems:

> I'm sending you a copy of a poetry magazine that just came out, with a poem of mine in it. . . . I often wonder, and have doubts about whether what I write has any significance for you. I don't suppose it does—for your life is so full and active that you have no need for the playthings of art. Your creative urge is spent directly in living—in shaping people through your influence, in cultivating growing things—not in trying to capture sensations through the medium of art. The word "art" is contained in the word "artificial," the opposite of natural. Well, it is that—a sort of rebellion against life perhaps, or an attempt to control or equal it with a synthetic creation of one's own rather than riding *with* life, giving into it, immersing oneself in it, and resigning oneself to being but a particle in the process.

Swenson's poems are her masterwork; her prose, collected in this volume, will add to readers' appreciation of her whole artistic effort and oeuvre.

A Note on the Text May Swenson's unpublished prose and letters to Elizabeth Bishop have been edited to reflect standard spelling and punctuation; brackets indicate that a word, date, or ellipses has been supplied for the sake of clarity (Swenson's

---

3. Richard Howard has commented on the correspondence relating to this poem in *Paris Review* 31 (summer 1994): 171–86.

ellipses appear without brackets). Since Swenson signed her letters "May" or, occasionally, "May and Pearl" (May lived with Pearl Schwartz from 1950 to 1966), her name has been omitted until the last one. All of the texts, except for "In Consideration of Writing Prose," "Foreword," and the letters, which have been cut, appear as May Swenson wrote or published them.

I
Fiction

Mutterings of a Middlewoman

It fascinated and horrified me at the same time. Well, actually, the fascination came first. Because had it been repulsive rather than attractive (in appearance, I mean, and when quiet) I would have left it alone, I would have gone away.

I had taken off its hood and was sitting in front of it, touching various levers and keys, trying to find the one that turned it on, when Sandra came in. She was the other girl in the office; I was the new girl. Mr. Cobb was in his office dictating onto his Talk-a-Belt already. He had been there when I arrived (ten minutes before nine, because I hadn't known how long it would take to get to my new job from home). Mr. Robert L. Roberts, the head of the firm, hadn't come in yet.

This place is in mid-town on Fifth Avenue, in that building with the square archway that looks like it's made of big gold ingots. It's only brass, of course, but very swank. From across the street it looks like the entrance to a giant safe, people instead of money rolling in and out. Or closer to it would be to say, a beehive, with workers and drones trooping through it, and a queen bee once in a while, in mink, getting out of a cab and dreamily tottering over its threshold. The worker bees are mostly male and the drones female. That is, the former go and come as they please, in their process of gathering honey (money) to be fed to the queen, while the latter stay in the hive (safe) from nine to five, to take care of things and make the wax. Coincidentally, this *was* a wax products firm I was employed in: the Robert L. Roberts Company, Paraffin, Ceresin and Micro-Crystalline Waxes.

Now where were we? Oh, yes, at the point where Sandra

Originally published in *Discovery,* no. 5 (1955).

comes in. But let's not have her come in just yet. Because I want to explain how I felt about IT—the personal, subjective relationship there seemed to be between me and it—even while it stood humped there silent, cool, and asleep. I turned on the blue cathode light over it. It was huge, rugged, squarish, but with rounded edges, of light-gray pebbled steel with chrome trim. Cleanly molded, sturdy, smug-looking. It had all kinds of attachments beside the four-deck keyboard: buttons, triggers, and various-shaped switches marked with abbreviated names.

There I sat on the specially made stool affixed to it (like a jockey's saddle? a pilot's cockpit?). Anyhow, a seat of importance and adventure. Its name was inscribed on it: the Atom-atic Typer.

Only a typewriter. All right. That's its function. But think of a peasant's plow (a wooden handle, a single blade) as against a Bulldozer tractor with all its appendages: cultivator, mower, thresher, baler, loader. See now what I mean about a *difference?* And it was handsome! Nice to look at, and to touch. It thrilled my fingers wandering over it while it was still cool and unconscious. Like sometimes you come to a big smooth rock in the woods that's so solid, calm, and confident feeling. So dependable and simple looking. But what's going on inside, if you could be aware of its atoms whirling? Remember, everything in the universe is in motion, in rotation; nothing is static; *nothing ever stops.* It's an awful thought, in a way, but there's a necessity for it, I guess. You may as well assume that the way things are is the way they should be.

O.K., so here was this machine, a rock, or the opposite of a rock, in the woods of commerce, and I was to run it. I only had to find out how to turn it on, to see what it would do, what it would make. I adjusted the little microphone in my ear, I put my feet on the pedals, and my fingers on the keys. I was all ready, when Sandra came in. And she immediately showed me that the switch was hidden under the right-hand edge of the Atom-atic. I touched it, and the little window there flashed the word *on* in red. There was a low humming.

Now, don't be mad if, in this story, nothing happens really. Nothing terrible, nothing exciting. I know it might sound as if, the way I've told it up to now, we're going to another world, me and this strange contraption. Or that I'm trying to say it's a symbol for something psychologically wacked-up about our metropolitan way of life, the industrial age, or the gadgeteering craze, or whatnot. I don't mean anything like that. What happened was just what happened inside of me, I recognize that, and nobody even knew about it but me. The place didn't blow up or anything; I didn't disappear, didn't discover a new dimension.

It's just that I'm a typist, and a good, accurate, fast one. Now, ordinarily, when you hit a key it prints a letter, and the speed with which the letters appear on the page depends on how often your fingers hit the keys; each letter appears *after* you hit its corresponding key, and the carriage shifts when and/or *if* your hand rises to the jigger, there, and pushes it. In short, your hands control the machine. On the Atom-atic, however, my fingers were barely posed above the keys, getting *ready* to touch them, when they began to type, at unbelievable speed. Those keys made my fingers fly at their pace, and I had to keep up with them; they jolted my fingers into action, instead of the other way around. And when we got to the end of a line (which took a fraction of a second) my left pinky finger was nudged, lightly as a breath, by a shift key that tossed the carriage to the beginning of the next line. Hickety-dickety-ho—a line; hickety-dickety-ha—another line. As swift as that.

Effortless. Nice. Maybe I should only give into it, go along with it? But the darn thing didn't care what it typed, whether it matched with the words coming through the microphone in my ear or not. Those were Mr. Robert L. Roberts's words, and he expected them to appear on his desk, in neat block form on his very white water-marked bond, six onion skin copies to each original, plus the Yellow file sheet, each letter (with copies) attached with paper clip to addressed envelope, and another clip attaching this to the file folder containing previous correspondence to the addressee, with a typed slip noting the cross-reference files, as well as any file changes he might dictate in connection with adding or removing wax product prospects to, or from, the various files, according to the incoming correspondence as it indicated what particular lines of wax and wax products they might be in the market for; also, if in the course of dictating a letter, he thought of points of discussion to be taken up with these prospects at lunch or at a sales conference, these were to be typed on small sheets of Pink paper and appended to the correct file; and incidentally, would I remember to water the plants in the reception room the minute I came in each morning: "Ask Sandra for a key to the office in case you're the first one in In fact it would be a good idea to try to *be* the first one in The cactus plant not to get *too* much water Don't flood it The begonia to get a full glassful And while I think of it ask Sandra to explain to you how each night before closing up everything goes underground That is nothing left on tops of desks Everything in drawers The machine covered and be sure to turn it *off* as we can't have the generator running all night and please wipe off your desk with a piece of Kleenex so it looks shipshape for next morning and no butts left in ashtrays please Put these instructions on a Blue slip and initial it please and pass it to me and I'll initial it and pass it back to you for your own personal file to be kept in your lower left hand drawer then we'll understand each other O.K.? From time to time I'll give you further instructions to add to your personal file Now back to letter to Zigoni of Dappletan Wax in Rochester It says: Further to our letter of April 28 This is the second paragraph Oh by the way this should go on the Specialty stationery for the original instead of the All-Purpose stationery I said at the beginning of the belt Ask Sandra to explain when we use one and when the other so you won't waste paper or time doing letters over O.K.? All set now? Paragraph Further to our letter of April 28. . . ."

The Atom-atic wasn't recognizably typing any of this, although we were already near the bottom of the page, my fingers still going lickety-heck. Well, here, and there, you could make something out, like "our letttttr of Aprl 2888/" and "We ould deee plyap pppreciate/y our frwdg us alistof y ourr equi rements/" The thing to do was to back-track to the beginning of the belt, start all over, on Specialty stationery this time, and take it slow and careful. If possible.

Also, I had already learned that the placing of the alphabet, the numerals, punctuation marks, and other signs on the Atom-atic weren't in all cases the same as on an ordinary typewriter and that the back-spacer was where I was accustomed to finding the tabulator key. Or was it that my fingers were put on wrong? It did seem as though it would feel more familiar if I crossed my hands, as when, occasionally, you'll see a pianist playing the bass with the right hand, while the left runs into the treble. The troubling thing was that I couldn't, for the moment, lift my hands to try this. The machine went on, and my fingers dithered up and down with the keys, receiving their impulses, which felt like little electric pricks and ticklings. Not unpleasant, except for the compulsion to accelerate the speed. I did wish I could remove the little finger of my right hand, which seemed perversely lazy and tried to sit down on the ?and/ key, so that the slant bar got printed at the ends of some of the words. I curled it up like a bird's claw in flight, but this made my other little finger curl too, and then all the *a*'s dis ppe red from the copy.

I was trying to imagine I was holding a teacup in my right hand, so as to cause my pinky finger to crimp (which ought to work, as I rarely hold a teacup in my left hand; it would be on the same principle as thinking of squeezing lemons makes your mouth water) when Mr. Robert L. Roberts came in.

In a way I was glad I was going great guns; I certainly looked busy. He and Sandra exchanged breezy greetings, and he said to me:

"Well, Gal, how's it going?"

Sandra saw my embarrassment at not being able to stop to say Good-morning, and she reached around from her desk and turned off the machine. My hands plonked down, dead as dropped marionettes, on the keyboard. That mesmeric humming was gone. It should have been a relief, but it wasn't. I felt acutely uncomfortable with my hands still and my spine settling down onto the stool and having to turn my neck from its forward-march position to look up at Mr. Roberts.

I did say, "Fine, thanks," and managed a grin, but I felt it freeze on my face and stay there, even after he'd swished around into his office and closed the door. The buzzer on Sandra's desk sounded, and *she* went into his office and closed the door.

Naturally, I pulled the eight atrocious sheets out of the machine, tore them across, and slid them into the wastebasket under the desk. Sandra popped back out.

"Mr. Roberts wants all correspondence on the first belt on his desk by ten, and in the meantime wants me to show you how we handle the phones so you can take his and Mr. Cobb's calls whenever I'm out. Now, these little buttons here are the connections with the two offices. This one's for holding the call while you announce who's calling. For that you switch to the Local button, see? And the buzzer, which is a slightly different tone from the phone (please don't get it mixed up with the phone because I did when I first came and he got very annoyed), well, when it rings *once* you go in, and when *twice* it means he wants to talk to you on his connection, and, if it rings two times and then a little pause and then a third ring, that means Mr. Cobb wants you in his room to pick up a belt. Always do Mr. R.'s dictation first, no matter how Mr. C. stomps around. But they both like all their mail out by five, nothing hanging over for the next day. Sometimes when it's a heavy day, rather than ask you to put on more speed, Mr. R. will let you stay late to finish up (he can be very sweet that way), but he'd rather we all leave when he does. Now, the way he works is, he always does tomorrow's belts today, so there'll be some for you to start on when you come in in the morning. In case he gets in late. Sometimes you'll get stuff on the belt about doing shopping for his wife on your lunch hour. Now, on that, you can pass it on to me because I love to shop, and I'll do it when I go out for coffee, and you can take care of the phone. If Mr. R. ever asks where I am, and it's not my lunch hour, tell him you couldn't find whatever it is his wife wants at Altman's or wherever he said and that I offered to go to Bloomingdale's for it. It'll be too much for you to have to take care of the shopping with everything else you'll have to do. OK.?"

I hate to shop, so I said, "Thank you." Then the phone rang.

"You take that," Sandra suggested. "Let's see how you make out."

I'm not going to go into that. My fumbles on the phone would make any receptionist reading this brand me a nitwit. It wasn't a switchboard, only a dinky little intercom system. Nothing unpredictable about it like the Atom-atic. But I'm just a typist. A good typist. I've never been a receptionist.

I felt my main relationship was with that machine: my job was to run it, or learn how to give in to it—it felt like *that* was the secret. So we could turn out perfect and immediate letters together. Plus, of course, all those other incidentals: notes, agendas, file changes, reminders, and things on the colored sheets. I hate to have things sloppy myself, and I admired Mr. Roberts's organization of all the innumerable details a head of a business (and a home) must have on his mind.

So when I made errors on distinguishing the sounds of the buzzers and bells and rushed into his office when the phone rang or picked up the receiver (first I had to rip the microphone off my ear and unhitch myself from the seat and lunge over to Sandra's desk) to say "Robert L. Roberts Company Wax Wax Wax Goodmorning" when it was only Mr. Cobb buzzing to have me pick up a new belt; or forgot that Mr. R. was *never* in to Mr. Claridge, so that when that gentleman appeared at the reception window I opened Mr. R.'s door and, professionally for once, showed him right in, I didn't let the consequences disturb me greatly. Except to tell myself that it was pretty decent of Mr. R. to keep giving me one chance after another to do it right the next time, considering the number of errors I made in one morning.

Truth is, it was only my mistakes on the Atom-atic that cut deeply with me. I like to be precise in my typing, and I generally am, on an old-fashioned standard machine.

But, by lunch time—I could hardly believe it—I'd made tremendous progress. It was a matter of keeping your fingers just the right smidgin of an inch *above* the keys (like playing the Theremin, probably) and sensing with your fingertips how to respond to the electrical pulsations. You free your hands from the current by whipping them up and off. Hard to do, because that machine, while on and humming, sounded so ambitious, as if it wanted to, *had* to, be making something. Its energy and eagerness were contagious.

I used all my will power, however, and my performance did improve. Sandra showed me the newest method of erasing. You use a piece of chalk over the rubber erasure to whiten the spot. But then you have to induce the keys to strike your fingers *hard* to make the impression match the rest of the copy in blackness, and with several carbon copies to be erased too, that slows you up, so the best is to concentrate on no errors. Lifting a finger a little higher above the key makes it strike harder, but, if you lift it too high, it stabs a hole through all the copies. Now, there *is* a way to correct that, even. Mr. R. invented it himself (showing how close he is to the grass roots of his business)—then, too, of course, he hates to have his paper wasted. You use a little dispenser of RLR Liquid-Quick-Adhesive-Paper-Patching-Wax. But this is a heck of a chore requiring an absolutely steady hand and lots of practice.

I didn't get time to catch on to that. I could have, though, if the Buried, the Unforeseen, the Incalculable, hadn't cropped up. Because I'm a very determined person.

I guess I should have described Mr. Roberts and Sandra before now. Mr. Cobb wouldn't matter. He's just a husky sort of voice on the Talk-a-Belt—slow, uncertain, rather easygoing. Kind of a blimp. Can't imagine him "stomping around," as Sandra put it. Now Mr. R. is a different proposition. I'd like to call him the newest model in executives: unlimited power and drive, engineered for action, free-wheeling. He has an eel-smooth voice, rich, vibrant, that *glides,* never gallops; a voice that has all these superb features, plus the ability totalkfastersaymoregetmorestuff onaTalk-a-Beltinlesstimethanyou'dthinkhumanlypossible. I describe him chiefly in terms of voice because that's how I knew him best, in our brief but intimate association. You do feel close to a person whose actual words, hot off the tongue and onto that red strip of plastic, come directly into your ears, with all their cunning nuances such as sneezes, snorts, cigar suckings, chuckles, or parenthetical exclamations like "Oh H——" or "Shoot" or "Forget that letter, that s.o.b.'s in Bermuda chasing a piece."

As to what he's like in *person,* well, when I'd go into his office, answering his ring, I'd be so confused, usually, that there was a sort of haze in front of me, and all I saw, behind a long, flossy mahogany desk, was a head squeezing a phone receiver against a shoulder, and a cigar oscillating at the corner of a mouth. Sometimes, though, when he'd jet out of his office to squat down at the file cabinet beside my machine, I'd get a closer look. He has a strato-power chassis, with great road-hugging stability, a slab-sided fender line, and a bold front snorkel. But his clothes, I'd say, really type him as a sports convertible.

The few seconds he'd be parked there on a level with my knees, riffling through a file, I'd make a slew of mistakes and have to do a lot of scrubbing with the eraser and chalk. I'm sure I was only projecting, but it *felt* like he was looking at my calves, down there only three inches or so from his face; and I know it's crazy, but the idea came into my head he might bite me. I guess it was just that he was in a position to and *could* have. Being more objective, it was probably that the Atom-atic tended to act up whenever Mr. R. was in its vicinity. As if it got an extra charge out of him. Or maybe it resented him as a competitor, which would be only natural. Or their respective electronic wavelengths were incompatible. I don't know much about these mysteries. Shouldn't be expected to. I'm only a typist.

About Sandra. She was all *right.* A real little crackerjack, Mr. R. called her, and so do I. She looked like a Receptionist. Everybody knows what that is. Like if someone says "chair" it isn't necessary for them to add "a seat, a back, and four legs," although they might want to be specific and say "lounging chair." And carrying it further, in Sandra's case, they might say a Floating-Comfort Lounging Chair. With a long, blond, pageboy bob.

By 12:15 I felt like an old member of the firm already. Sandra gave me the kind nod to turn off the Atom-atic; it was time for lunch. I got up and took the key to go to the Ladies Room. Couldn't understand why I felt so bushed. My feet would hardly move along the corridor, which seemed to be tilting uphill. An optical illusion absolutely, because, when I came back to check in the key and get my coat, it tilted uphill *again,* running the opposite way. It was too bad I had to walk so slowly, since I had only thirty minutes and really needed to sprint to get to the cafeteria, eat, and get back by one.

I was the only one getting into the elevator from my floor, the forty-fifth, next to the top, and the boy must have recognized me because he gave me a nice smile. It made me feel as if I belonged. To be friendly in return, I asked him if he liked his job. I was scrunched up in a corner of the car holding onto both handrails, swallowing quickly with my eyes closed, as we plunged.

"It has its up and downs," he said, and I thought that was cute.

"I've never been in one that goes sideways," I said, trying to be clever too.

But it was no joke. The elevator was scudding along horizontally, simultaneously with dropping vertically, according to my stomach. In a few floors, though, it accumulated enough people to keep me bolstered upright; and going through the lobby and along the street for three downtown blocks, around the corner East to the nearest cafeteria, the crowd was so solid that, fortunately, I couldn't fall down. With the lunch time mob shoulder to shoulder moving at a lope, half one way and half the other, I felt like that little knob in the middle of a roulette wheel, smothered among clumps of chips all whizzing past me counterclockwise.

I looked up at the sky, and that helped. It was astonishingly empty, and as flannel-soft and blue as a newborn baby boy's blanket. Jabbing up into it, way above the other buildings that made a V-shaped wedge of the avenue (like the configuration on a business graph or fever chart) was the Empire State. That example of sovereign and enduring priapism that symbolizes, for me at least, the superior vigor and stamina of this, our fair city, the greatest on earth. A volt of vicarious pride, mixed with humility, suffused me. As if that great hypodermic tower had injected a shot of No-Doze into my blood. And I was able to straighten up, adjust my shoulder bag resolutely, and wriggle through traffic like a scroll-saw through soft pine.

I crammed myself into the revolving doors of the cafeteria, collected a tray and hardware at the counter, snarled my order (Swiss cheese on rye, butter, lettuce, *and* pickle), slid the tray down the nickel rods, and accepted a half-full cup of coffee in a brim-full saucer, instantly poured and handed to me by a girl who could see by my manner that I was in a hurry. I jostled my way expertly to the only table with one chair empty (in the back between the Rest Room entrance and the kitchen).

Three other girls at my table, office workers by their conversation, were nearly finished with their seventy-cent sandwiches, chewing awfully fast, talking a blue streak, combing their hair, applying fresh lipstick, and smoking their cigarettes all at the same time. And without my noticing it, or tasting anything, not even the pickle, I found I had eaten my lunch and was all through the same time they were. They got up and left, and I was alone at the table heaped with dirty dishes. I looked at my watch. Only 12:35. I could relax for a whole quarter-hour almost! After getting out the right change for the check, I lit a cigarette and crossed my legs.

Since this was the first time my spine had touched the back of a chair and my hands had been still since morning, it should have been lovely to lean back and ruminate about my new job and its future behind the gauze of my first cigarette. So what the heck was the matter? My crossed leg jiggled up and down, my hand went to the back of my neck and around to my forehead and down my face and over my chin, and I felt a little muscle there, making my mouth go twitch-twitch-twitch without my wanting it to. I guess it was all the other people in my line of vision, with their jaws chomping, and the noise they made trying to be heard by one another above the cloudburst of silverware and crockery slamming into trays, the Musak playing La Paloma, the bus boys prowling through it all with their wagons and pyramids of saucers sliding off and smashing on the floor, not to mention the traffic frisking past me in and out of the Rest Room, phone booths, and kitchen.

But this was *natural* to me, a typist, who always ate in crowded cafeterias. It had never brought itself to my attention before. Far as I was concerned, I never *heard* noise unless I chose to listen or saw what was going on unless I deliberately *looked*. Now, for no reason I could think of, in these few minutes I should be tranquilizing both my psyche and soma (I had made a practice of this during lunch hour on past jobs) so as to go back to the Atom-atic refreshed and single-minded, I was over-alert and all involved with everything around me. I found myself examining the stuff on the table as closely as if it were a Still Life in a museum. Or, as if I were boning for a test and had to memorize every object there. Besides the plates and cups with their left-over blobs of food, the filled ashtray in which was a wet teabag, the soggy napkins on the table, was a Lazy Susan bolted to the center, and on it was a mustard pot with a wooden dip, ketchup and chili bottles sticky around their tops, sugar dispenser, salt and pepper shakers . . . and in the middle of *that,* a foot-high bud vase containing an artificial pink sweet pea, with real laurel leaves wired onto its stem. Peeking out from under the edge of the Lazy Susan was a dried dollop of gum, with teethmarks in it.

All the tables were accoutered in this way, but I had to make *sure.* So my eyes flicked from table to table, taking note of the bud vase (like a flagpole or lighthouse) planted on each one. It disturbed me that I couldn't see around to the front where all the rest of them were. I wanted to get up, take a few steps, and check that part of the cafeteria too, but I restrained myself. Then I noticed that the wallpaper, which was pink and black, with ballroom couples dancing, some upside down and some rightside up, hadn't been pasted together correctly on the wall across from me, so that some of the dancers were chopped in two. I wondered if the missing strip was under the overlap, and I wanted to go over there and see if there wasn't something I could do to fix it. I felt I'd be more comfortable if I could set it right.

I looked at my watch, and it was 12:40, and I just couldn't *stand* it anymore. The best thing to do was to go back to that quiet neat little office, and my big new beautiful machine, where I could concentrate on just *one thing,* the main thing, really. And, with that thought, I felt *so* much better. We'd learn to understand each other, the Atom-atic and I, before the day was over. We'd be real buddies, and nothing else would matter.

As I opened the grain-glass door (without having to knock, even) with the light behind it outlining in simple purity the words, ROBERT L. ROBERTS CO., I did sort of hope Mr. R. would notice I was back early. But Sandra said he had gone to lunch. She was eating hers, having had it sent up, and spread on her desk were several current magazines: QUICK, SLICK, FLICK, CHIC, SNICKER, and PIC, among others. I turned on the machine and wanted to get right to work; there were six new belts, plus the one I'd left unfinished. But Sandra wanted to talk while she ate and read, and I didn't think it would be polite to not listen. She said she was getting married in two weeks and that then (had Mr. R. told me?) I'd have to take over *her* job along with my own for a while, until I got a new gal trained. Therefore, I'd better familiarize myself with all the procedure of the firm and get some practice in it, so that not only could I teach it to the new gal but show Mr. R. that I was capable of being his Gal Friday, which was the position *she* held, so that if he decided, after a year, say, to promote me to that title, he'd be convinced I was worth the raise. I didn't like to ask what the raise might be. Some firms are touchy about employees discussing this, especially behind the boss's back. So I just asked her the best way to learn about the business. And she took a thick folder out of the file marked: BACKGROUND & OFFICE PROCEDURE, and said I could take it home and absorb it after hours.

I couldn't help, out of curiosity, starting to read it while she went on talking, and I gathered roughly that RLR was a sort of middleman, or, specifically, a broker *for* middlemen in the Wax Industry; the middlemen being promotion and sales representatives (not *sales*men, that's something else) between manufacturers and wholesalers, or wholesalers and retailers. As we know, manufacturers sell to wholesalers, who sell to retailers, who sell to the ultimate consumer. Or this is how it used to be, when merchandising was in its infancy. *Now,* in between these buyers and sellers are the subsidiary outfits, the middlemen—and in between them comes a firm like RLR & Co., which, obviously, doesn't handle the product itself but does so figuratively, that is, on paper. And this is a very important function in the total merchandising process, as it largely determines the prices and costs of production as well as distribution.

So what did that make me? What little link was I in the chain? I asked myself. Because I believe in trying to orientate myself in a new job and find out just where I fit. I looked at my Atom-atic crouching there so seemingly self-sufficient, purring energetically to itself.

I was the mid-woman between the mid-middleman and the machine.

By no means a dispensable or expendable link. Because, as yet, the Atom-atic could only transcribe and not interpret Mr. R.'s words; especially in view of his spontaneous and dynamic way of dictating, with everything coming wrapped up in something else, having been incorporated inside the first thing, which might be a letter or long memo, so that sometimes the beginning of the beginning thing at the beginning of a belt would have the commencement of the final conclusion several belts later; and then the P.S.; and often the cancellation of parts or of the whole—that is, the outer shell (while the inner layers, consisting of other unrelated bits and pieces, were to remain) would come a couple of belts further on.

Now, machines are durable and inexorable, more so than the human mind, but they are not elastic, adaptable, and selective, and that's why I'd never have to worry about having a job of some kind, no matter how the marvels of technology multiplied and improved—at least while I had my youth.

Mr. Cobb came out of his office to go to lunch, with a shy smile for both of us, as he deepened the crease in his hat and put it on, and I took this as an excuse to start typing. Right after that Mr. R. catapulted back with a brilliant smile, for Sandra. And a tail end of it left over for me.

The machine and I spanked along like pretty much of a team that afternoon. Although I still had to do frequent erasures and got fouled up with the different colors and grades of stationery that were specified and then unspecified, by and large, I (or I should say *we*) coordinated to turn out clean, dark, accurate copy, manifestly did it faster and faster. The problem of editing came up, as for instance, when Mr. R. used *appreciate* four times in two paragraphs, and I asked Sandra if I should maybe change one of them to *would be very glad if*. She said:

"Ask him, if you want. I wouldn't be in a position to know. But if I were you I wouldn't. He doesn't like to have you make as if he isn't always entirely right. But if he calls *you* on it, asks you why you repeated yourself—what's the matter with your vocabulary—just say you're sorry, and *then* change it."

As I say, we zipped along famously until 3:30 or so, and I found I didn't want to do anything else. It was so sort of satisfying and secure-feeling to entrust myself to, and fall in with, the romping rhythm of the machine. If I'd stop for a minute with the idea of lighting a cigarette, I'd feel all jittery and tense and functionless. I found I felt stable as long as my fingers were constantly and rapidly drinking up those electric vibrations transmitted to them from the keys, and my ears were sorting out RLR's versatile and magnetic sizzle of words. I even regretted having to stop and go to the Ladies Room when it was time. There was too great a contrast between sitting with feet on pedals and hands on console, being *carried* in smooth momentum, and then stumbling under my own puny power through that uphill hall, with a sort of heavy stagnant silence pouring into my head. When I came back, I must have been pale, because Sandra said:

"You look like death warmed over. Why don't you punch the Tune-Tonic key? It'll give you a lift."

I thought she was ribbing me, but, as I climbed onto my stool, my eye was simply *guided* to a kidney-shaped button on the uppermost deck marked T.T. I had thought it was the Touch Control and hadn't bothered with it. Sandra was watching me, so I couldn't put it off and make the discovery in secret. Pretending I knew all about it, I . . . pushed.

Well, for Pete's Periwinkle! Music, just like Muzak! A rippling tune with an imperious percussive beat funneled into my ear just behind Mr. R.'s voice. A kind of private serenade to flatter the typist out of her blues—how *sweet,* really.*

As I mentally adjusted my goggles, tested the flaps, started the propellers, taxied to the end of the strip, gave her the gun, pulled on the stick, and took off like a scalded cat, I noticed that the rhythm of the Tune-Tonic began to accelerate just a wee bit over the speed the Atom-atic was setting for my fingers, and, when we'd synchronized with that, it accelerated just a *wee* bit more. The arrow on my m.p.h. dial pinged around to the right. Next thing I knew I was over Schenectady.

And the *next* thing I knew, I was home in bed with a 103 degree fever; my pulse was 120 and my blood pressure 205. The doctor had just left. My body was a boat—an old rowboat, not a yacht or a cruiser even—all alone in the middle of a choppy lake, and I'd lost one oar; and inside of me green bilge water was sloshing, mounting higher inch by inch. I wished I had a can to bail with. The doctor had left a basin on the bed table—*kidney shaped*—reminded me of something. I used that to bail with, but it wasn't big enough. Things started coming back, but backwards, like backtracking on the Talk-a-Belt (aha, another clue).

Well, face it. I'd have to reconstruct the crime in order to prepare my defense. (To myself, understand. Everything that happened, as I said before, happened inside myself. It was my own fault—I'm not blaming anything or anybody.)

I backtracked. I'd just got off the Fifth Avenue bus. There lay Washington Square, comparatively somnolent in the afternoon sunlight. My feet were rounded on the bottoms, like old-fashioned desk blotters. No, they were long and curved like on a rocking chair. No, I have to amend that once more: they were ice skates (and I can't skate), and the two blocks between me and home was a flashing stretch of ice; its thick slickness continued up the stoop, into the foyer, and coated the stairs of my three-floor walkup.

---

*Interesting footnote: The Sunday after I wrote this down, I found the following bit in the paper: "A California bee keeper has been regaling his bees fourteen hours a day with broadcast music. Result: More honey from his 1200 hives. The bees like the music so much they get restless and swarm if it is turned off."

Next (backtracking another strip), I was in the subway station at Forty-second and Fifth, where on one side the trains go to Queens and on the other to Times Square. One was coming in and the other going out. Now, there's a peculiar sensation you get, even under normal circumstances (if you're sensitive) when one roaring projectile is swooping toward you on one side and an identical one streaming away on the other, and you're stationary in the middle. When the trains are gone, there are two long black silent trenches that seem to *widen,* swiftly narrowing the platform between them to a rail, to a tightrope, to nothing! That's why I had to climb back up to the pavement and take a bus instead.

I backtracked some more. I was getting to the awfullest, the most shameful part (or so I thought *then,* in my state of partial amnesia). I was standing in front of The Lions, waiting for a bus to stop that had room on the step to fit a toe into. The ones that were not full surged by in the middle of the street and the ones that were jammed piled up at the curb like elephants trunk to tail. The bulbous cars crept uptown, downtown, and crosstown so close together a ballet troupe could have done Swan Lake on their tops, and yanking in and out between the blacks, cobalts, and grays of chauffeur-driven motors were the yellows, mauves, peaches, vermilions, magentas, cerises, and checkered black-and-greens of cabs and private cars. Why couldn't they be made of rubber, I thought, so when their bumpers collided and their fenders swiped, there wouldn't be that noise? The eight-million-headed rush-hour mob coiled by me endlessly, like a monster made of congealed molasses. There, above it all, serene in the blue, soared, leapt, projected, reared, ejaculated (take any one of them), the Empire State. And I caught myself commanding it (out loud, but no one let on they heard me) to contract, deflate, narrow, shrink, dwindle, shrivel, wither, wizen, crumple up, collapse, drop dead.

Now, how I could harbor such a wish within me even for one unbalanced moment, let alone voice it, fills me with guilt. It bares the deep dichotomy in my soul, I guess, but honestly, I didn't, I don't now, really mean it. I know it resembles a terribly significant symptom, and every girl is supposed to suffer with it, unconsciously at least. But I've *never* wanted to deny that women are, well, secondary, to men. I believe every active principle necessarily has its passive component and that Man constitutes the former. I do, I do, I do, and nobody's going to make me say I don't, even with a lie detector. It would also seem to show an unconscious desire not to go to work. But I *want* to work, and I need to work, and I'm a *good* typist. I have always agreed that "only through work does the individual achieve wholesome social contacts, express his creative interests, make a contribution to society, and achieve status in his community."*

The word *work,* the shape and sound of it, like an anchor pitched into the lake of my recapitulative daydream, jolted me back to the present. I looked at the clock. It was 10 A.M. of the next morning. . . . I hoped it was only the next. There were great gaps in my recollection still, but my roommate must have called the doctor before she left for her office . . . I must have moaned something to her. . . . Never mind that now, I had to get Sandra on the phone.

I managed to reach it on the bed table and dialed the number. My heart felt like a whale's having coronary thrombosis as I waited for her to say: Robert L. Roberts Company Wax Wax Wax Goodmorning. When I'd made her understand it was me (my voice was quavery and hoarse from the fever), she gave an explosive pop to her gum and said:

"You certainly left me in a spot. I had to promise Mr. R. to postpone my honeymoon a week. And the *goons* that've been trooping through this office from the Agency. They just won't *do.* They refuse to learn the machine. Mr. R. is giving birth to bulldogs."

Jeepers, Joseph, and Harry! that meant I was out of a job. What terrible thing had I done? It almost came into consciousness, and I grabbed for the bailing can.

"Want me to put Mr. R. on?"

"No, please!" I started to plead. "*You* tell him how sorry I am, and that I'll always remember his . . ."

But it was too late. Mr. Roberts was already talking into my ear. My left hand went out to twist the dial on the Talk-a-Belt to Slow—an empty gesture.

"It's a little early in the game to be taking sick leave don't you think? Now you didn't work the whole day yesterday or it would

---

*Same paper, same Sunday, Editorial Page.

have been $12 even gross Now the deduction for Withholding is $2.43 Old Age 58¢ Disability 20¢ State Payroll Tax 24¢ and that leaves just enough to pay for cleaning the rug. I'm explaining this to you in detail in case you're quitting and expect a check. I warn you don't go to USES and say I fired you I never fire anyone And remember you have a key to the office I'd like it back if *you're* not coming back I will say this I had great plans for you I'm a shrewd judge of character and when the Agency sent you over I had a hunch yours was the right temperament for the job. You and the Atom-atic would get on nicely in time It's a new whimwham Aren't many like it around Too many firms reluctant to move up to date. RLR is one of the few in the forefront It's a continual shove-shove-shove to stay there but I mean to do it. There are only a few operators as yet *built* for a sensationally efficient machine like the Atom-atic They have to be shock resistant and I sensed that you were one of them. Now I'd consider putting you on contract for say ten years By the way how old are you now? and somewhere along in there I shouldn't be surprised if you'd become useful to me. You take the day off and think it over Without pay but next time you're sick after six months and not exceeding one day I'll pay you half-time Fair enough? So long now be good see you in the morning Or send back the key."

"Yes, Mr. Roberts. Thanks . . ." I whispered. But he'd hung up.

"See you in the morning" or "Send back the key" See you in the morning or send back the key Seeyouinthemorning or Sendbackthekey. I depth-dived into blissful sleep. Those codeine pills are really wonderful. Just before my blunt nose touched the roiling bottom, I remembered how I'd thrown up about 4 P.M. on Mr. R.'s dark blue Blodroom—no, Broadloom rug, while he was in confab with three important prospects and all. He'd buzzed for me to bring in copies of the agenda on Pink paper.

Now it's late in the afternoon. I'm awake, sitting up, and feel better. I decided to tinker around with my roommate's portable (a Quiet De Luxe) just to see how it feels. It feels pretty odd—clumsy, slow, like going back to the plow. A one-handle one—not even an ox in front of it.

It's kind of peaceful though. Makes queer, subversive ideas come into your head. What if everything were to stop? (Just what-if. What-if isn't a crime, is it, as long as it's only in your head and you don't try to do anything about it?) All the cars that look like refrigerators with their round-angled, substantial, yet rocket-shaped contours, their dazzling trim, their clean flowing lines, their superior maneuverability; and the refrigerators that look like cars—what if they were to stop? There are so many other objects I could work into this, but I'll just cite those two for examples. What if the whole colossal business were to stop stock-still right where it is and grow green hair. And the city would be covered up after a while with moss and fern. And people be turned into furry animals (say, rabbits—they're so gentle) nestling in the green.

Now, that's retrogressive thinking, the worst kind, and I know I'm still sick or I wouldn't be typing these things. But, *inertia.* It's such a nice word. Try saying it. Like letting your breath out in a happy sigh.

Should inanimate things be made to move? What if scientists had never found out that a rock has molecules and that all atoms in molecules vibrate and that each vibration has a particular frequency, just as a tuning fork emits a note of a particular pitch?*

On the other hand (and that makes me wonder whether, if I only *had* one hand, and one hemisphere to my mind, I could make it up more easily), what about my beloved Atom-atic, with its luxurious superstructure, its wondrous power and supersonic speed, the potentialities for accomplishment it had begun to instill me with? Why not move into the future? *With* it—as part and parcel of it. Financially, it wouldn't make any difference whether I stayed with the plow in the backwash of progress or not. And rightly so, because eventually, once you'd adjusted to it, the Atom-atic was *easier* to operate. No pushing and shifting, no muscular effort involved—simply a matter of teaching your blood, bone, tissue, and nerves to *give in* to its dominating current and tool along.

As a woman, I was peculiarly adapted to this role in the technological scheme—with my smaller, biologically more nim-

---

*Same paper—Science Page.

ble fingers, my more malleable nature, and my greater longevity. There *was* the hazard that one might reach what seemed an ultimate speed limitation, and hence frustration. But, surely, future engineering would remedy that. For a small office like RLR's, where there was no competitive factor, such as a lot of other gals at other machines to furnish added incentive, maybe an attachment like Cineramic Television could be developed. You punch the C.T. key and a small 3-D screen, but panoramic, with stereophonic sound, would give you a forest of typists at a forest of Atom-atics, in full color, operating at a frequency or two faster than you.

Here I am, belly-whopping off the deep end again, this time at the opposite extreme (I can't swim, either).

"See you in the morning or send back the key."

Which?

Appearances

"After all, we are no longer children," the doctor said, with reference to the conversation that had gone before. He hitched the ladder-back rocking chair closer to the round-bellied stove, and, drawing up his seersucker trousers slightly at the thighs to preserve their creases, he crossed his legs. He was a small-boned man, with neat hands and feet, his straight sandy hair brushed flat to his head above a long, pale brow.

"On the contrary, I believe that we are all still children," said his host, a dark-skinned man in a purple shirt, yellow corduroy jacket, and rumpled earth-stained pants. He sat by the bare table in the center of the room, straight-backed and alert, yet with a relaxed, somehow Indian calm. His cropped hair was the color of tobacco ash, his hazel eyes so intensely white around their irises that they gave off a bluish sheen. As he talked, his nostrils, eye shaped and almost as large as eyes, widened and narrowed above his beveled mahogany lips.

Chinks of red glinted behind triangular vents in the stove's gray body, giving it the look of a seated animal, panting rhythmically, showing its bright rippling tongue.

The weather was still warm in September here on the estate, but the evenings were chill. At this time of year there were few guests at the mansion where the doctor was quartered, and he was glad to make the acquaintance of this new arrival, an artist, who had moved into one of the cabins, which had been converted into a painter's studio by their mutual benefactor, the owner of the estate. Although crude and barnlike, with its unshaded bulb dangling from the steep skylight (through which the night looked immense and very black), the cabin seemed a

---

Originally published in *New Directions in Prose and Poetry* 13 (1951).

welcome place, especially since it contained the means of making a fire. The munching sound of the flames over their meal of dry logs tore comforting slits in the layers of silence that the thick pine forest wrapped around the cabin.

"The unknown makes us, and keeps us, children in one way or another—and who knows but what that is best," the painter said with a spread-lipped smile. "For instance, my adventure of today . . .

"Soon after I arrived this morning, I went walking. I chose a leopard-pelted trail of light and shadow leading away from the cabin. I had no idea, nor did I want to know, where I was going. Some people find maps a necessity. They wish to know at every step where they stand in relation to their starting point and their destination. The possibility of *getting lost* fills them with guilt as much as fright. They expect landmarks of course, and if there aren't any, they set about making them. They're avid to learn the history of everything encountered on the way; if there's a stone tower, they must establish whether a duchess was born in it; an especially old tree will interest them only if, for example, a murderer was hanged there. Then the location of gates and shelters is a matter of anxious concern for them, in case a storm should come up. And, of course, a prime objective is the finding of trophies or mementoes of one kind or another, to bring back with them."

"That's most normal and natural," the doctor said. While listening rather indolently, from behind his glasses he let his eyes wander over the whitewashed walls but found them featureless except for a small chalk drawing in an alcove, which he could make little of. However, the colors were gray, yellow, green, and black.

"Very normal," the painter agreed. "But hardly natural, I think."

The doctor thought of some of the guests who fitted the painter's description, and remarked: "They are a proper and quite-to-be-expected product of our age—meticulously self-adjusted implements for the reception or rejection of specific phenomena, said phenomena having been selected for them by other highly organized 'implements' whose superior wisdom they justifiably take for granted. . . . But do go back to your 'leopard-pelted trail' through the forest."

The painter's forehead, which had bunched into a knot, leveled again to its habitual smoothness. "I had no idea how large or small the forest was, nor of its configuration," he went on. "I quickly lost direction, as was my unconscious purpose, I suppose. The trail undulated up, down, in and out, and was closely grown—first with birch and hemlock trees and then with tall pines. The area was large and involved, and each bend in the path presented a new vista. Everything my eye brushed over was a surprise to me, every perspective a first discovery. From their hidden leafy ledges high in the trees, the birds seemed to be calling news of my progress to one another, and when I stopped and stared, trying to detect one of them, he would become motionless and silent. Then, standing there, my feet no longer snapping twigs and crunching leaves, I became conscious of the sounds of myriad insects in the air, as if sewing on some crepuscular, all-enveloping fabric; and of creeping things beneath the humus, creating the sensation of some vast unraveling. And these two processes were fused in a continuous husky whisper, which, while walking, I had perceived as the absence of sound."

How minutely he describes a perfectly ordinary experience, the doctor was thinking. As if he were the first person hereabout to have taken such a walk and to have felt these sensations. He talks well, no doubt of that. A tendency to overembellishment, but very observant. He rocked back and forth, smiling at his host, who was saying as if in apology:

"You will understand that, living in the city as I do, this experience with nature is an unfamiliar one, and my impressions are apt to be the exaggerations of a novice. But it was the same with vision. Where, at first, looking at a thick hedge—simply leaves and more leaves—just a restful repetitive design—I would suddenly see clustered on the twigs blue and gold scarabs that I had mistaken for drops of sunlight and shadow; and on the ground, apparently, a resilient carpet of uniform gray, there unaccountably appeared, as soon as my eyes had accustomed to the gloom, spots of intricate embroidery—colored mushrooms and mosses of the richest texture."

"I remember experiencing comparable effects on my first visit to the city," the doctor replied. "Noises were strange and upsetting to me until their source was disclosed in the subways and the sirens, but after a time they tended to sink beneath consciousness into inaudibility. Faces of people cramming the streets at first looked all alike, a doughy mass, until my sense of being a foreigner abated, and I began to discern their features. As individuals, they were no longer frightening. It is an old story that the unknown inspires a mixture of awe and menace, of reverence and fear."

He felt his point had been rather well made, and, taking out his pouch, he rewarded himself with a fresh pipe full of tobacco, of which unfortunately there was little left. He made a mental pact with himself to write his tobacconist in the city before he retired, a chore he had been putting off day after day. This country leisure made one lazy even in the maintenance of the most important personal necessities.

The artist had the impulse to point out the discrepancy rather than the similarity between his guest's description and his own—to say that the former seemed to come to terms with the unknown by means of a contraction of his senses instead of their expansion—but he merely took up the doctor's concluding statement, and exclaimed: "Oh, not fear! At least not yet. Of surprise first, then of beauty . . . and then, of power—a mysterious and lavish power veining everything in nature, spilling free and raw from every stone and leaf."

His dark supple hands resting on his knees. . . . What did they suggest? the doctor asked himself. Sleeping animals, perhaps. . . . They were hound brown in color, and there was an attentiveness in their very stillness, as if they might rise at a signal and move unerringly on the scent of something.

"Emerging from the pine forest," the painter went on, "I came upon a fresh unclouded lake, with a steep slope rising from it, and a conical stone tower which might have been an abandoned mill. The stones of the structure were clothed with an ardent green vine; the slope from which it rose was padded with delicate and brilliant grass. Small warted frogs looked at me with their crystalline eyes as I dipped water into my mouth from the spring that fed the lake. . . ."

Lulled by the warmth in the room and the recitative cadence of the artist's voice, the doctor rocked and smoked without further interrupting his host. When the beguiling tale was finished, with whatever philosophy or fantasy behind it laid bare, he would no doubt be asked for comment, he thought.

"I ate my lunch sitting on the coping of a bridge," the tale continued, "suspended in sunlight, held safely in that protective element as if in a large benevolent hand, feeling myself part of the scene, one of its happy and unselfconscious details; free to pause here as long as I wished, or leave when I wished, like the marvelously patterned dragonflies which entered the broad bowls of the lilies on the water below and, for an immobile moment, let their green and aluminum bodies be recharged with warmth and light, then rose and shot away.

"I left the place by the path I had come. After a short distance it turned into a pair of grassy ruts which climbed upward. I ducked my head to pass beneath a partly fallen tree that straddled the road, and somewhat farther on I blundered into a wild orchard and ate some apples that lay on the ground. They were dewy and cool from their beds of shadow in the grass, and their tart crispness made my tongue curl with appreciation.

"On the other side of the orchard I entered another pine forest and was gradually led into the thickest shade. Here the floor of the forest was as springy as a circus net. My feet hardly sank beneath the millions of reddish-tan strands of which this net was densely woven; instead, I was bounced by it, as I strode with long, noiseless, twining steps, grasping the pines like poles as I whirled around them. But soon I had to shorten my steps. The spaces between the pines narrowed, their tops closed together above me . . . and the increasing shadow felt as if veil after cool veil were being drawn over my body, heated and tingling from my foolish acrobatics of a moment ago.

"I lay down on the mat of pine bristles. It was clean and shining. My palms began somnolently to stroke the rough, tawny hide of the forest. The forest was a great leopard sleeping and I a small invisible creature resting among his dark markings. High above me, through his tangled fur, I could see the sky as only tiny sparkling lozenges of blue. Under my ear I could feel the great leopard breathing in his long and languid sleep. His inhaling breath was an interminably building wave, which, before it broke into exhale, would cover and exceed my little lifetime on his back.

"I lay on my side and felt no inclination to shift position in the intact stillness. My mind slipped into that halfway state between sleeping and waking. How long it remained there I do not know. . . .

"I felt something move against my chest. A tender, flickering, and yet confident pressure.

"Two impulses sprang up in me. The first was acceptance, the impulse to remain still—for the touch I felt was friendly—in fact, provocative, exciting. The second was recoil and rejection, because of the unexpectedness of the touch and its ambiguity. My body was quite ready to enjoy the closeness of this other living body, which had somehow become aware of me, been bold enough and trusting enough to come to me; while I, up to now unconscious of it, for all that it could know, might be suspicious or scornful of its approach . . . but . . ."

The painter's voice had become halting and nearly inaudible. The doctor noticed, with an uncomfortable quiver, that his eyes had changed expression. There was a queer reckless craving, yet cringing, look in them. Was he going to make a confession? And, if so, would it be one of the wildest, demonic love or of the filthiest guilt? Or both, since one did not preclude the other? The doctor's knees had gone to sleep, one hooked over the other as they were, and he wanted more than anything just now to recross them the other way. He moved the inside of his hand against the slick, still-warm bowl of his pipe, and this relaxed him somewhat. His companion was going on, thank God, in a firmer voice:

"But my mind reacted oppositely. So I obeyed the second impulse. I violently squirmed away. For a simultaneous moment my body and the other writhed on the ground in an identical dance of panic, awkwardly lurching away from each other. Then I stood up, shaking—my blood in turmoil—wanting to run crashing through the woods. Not because anything had hurt me—not from the actual experience of danger—but simply to escape my own fear.

"However I stood still and watched the snake (for that's what it was) blindly zigzag a few feet. Then he stopped and made himself into a curve to look at me. He was quite small, about three feet long, if one were to straighten his kinks; gray and yellow striped, mixed with slivers of green, and with a head like a dark polished flint. His tongue whirred in and out as smoothly as a hummingbird's wing. I felt sure he wasn't poisonous, and suddenly I wanted to capture him. Was it in order to make friends with him and repent of my former distrust? I moved my foot, and he unhurriedly slid toward it. I reached for my empty lunch kit and placed it in front of him, but the noise of the lid being opened made him retreat. I waited tensely for him to come back and investigate. He seemed disinterested and merely flowed aimlessly about over the pine needles. I moved the kit a little closer. The clanging of the lid this time made him look up and ripple forward again. . . .

"But I lost the game, for in the course of our flirtation he happened to glide beneath some dead branches which were the exact color of his skin, and, although I stared and stared, I could no longer distinguish him from his hiding place. I could not cover the whole area with my gaze—the middle of the scramble of twigs as well as all the orifices around the edges from which he might emerge; and as my eyes left one exit, I imagined him oozing from another. I stood there a long time, unable to tell whether he had left or not. At last I went back to the open kit, half-expecting to find him doubled into it, waiting for me to close the lid and carry him with me.

"Had I had him safely locked in my kit, all would have been well. But since I didn't know where he was, I felt, for some obscure reason, that I had to leave the place at once. Now I pitched through the trackless forest impatiently, wanting to get out. The birds had begun their comments again, which sounded insidious and mocking. I was scratched and disheveled, puffing and hot, when I finally reached a road. I hurried along. For the first time the path seemed familiar. Sure enough, soon I came to the fallen tree, whose slanting trunk I had ducked under just before entering the wild apple orchard earlier in the day. I *wanted* a sense of direction now. I felt I would promptly get back by this road on which I had noted a landmark. I laid my hand affectionately on the trunk's gray ribs as I bent and passed beneath it.

"But the trail swerved, and, again, all around me looked new. I could not recall facing this particular prospect before. I trudged on, simply because there was nothing else to do. Then, through the enigmatic screen of tree trunks and foliage to my left, I made out a structure of sepulchral stone, a low square tower of grizzled blocks, with a vaulted door on which was a rusty knocker of iron and ornamental hinges muffled in cobwebs. I was glad to see this habitation so steady and definitely placed among the shifting green. But, although it was quite close, I had a hard time approaching it, for it sat in a low gully that was clotted with thorny vines. The closer I came, pushing my way through the tough undergrowth, the gloomier, more sunken, the place appeared. No sun could reach this hollow; it was damp and smelled of rot. It crouched in a green-brown shade such as lurks on river bottoms, through which glide the brown ghosts of fish, themselves only muddy shadows submerged in a browner dusk. I had a strange revulsion to the place—at the same time, I was determinedly trying to get to it.

"Well, I got to the door, my shoes covered with slime from the marshy ground, and there was a gray metal plate nailed to it, which seemed to have been put there recently. Painted on it was a very conventional warning: DANGER! KEEP OUT! But, as usual with such warnings, no hint was given of the kind of danger. And here I was, at the very jaw (or so it felt) of something sinister and nameless, and not able to retreat very easily. I felt my hand go up to bang the knocker or press the latch. It was the next thing to be done, now that I was here. But my hand came down as though it realized, before I did, that there was no use trying to enter. I stood there looking and listening, and I knew somehow that the tower was empty; that, furthermore, the door would be locked. The danger wasn't in it; it was inside of me. And it was *that* tower—the shadowy tower of my own fear—I was being told to keep out of.

"But if the door to it was locked and the hinges rusted, that meant I hadn't revisited that sunken place for a long time. Must be a corpse of myself inside there. Either that, or a half-grown child standing, just as I had abandoned him, fresh-skinned, smiling—just fixed there; a child I had locked up and forgotten, still standing, asleep, waiting for me to come back, to lay his hair off his forehead and put my hand under his china-round chin and say: 'Come along. We'll go right on from here.' I would melt into him, and I'd walk out of the tower as a boy again. And things would be set back a bit, in their former places, but adjusted a little differently than I had felt them up to now. I'd live over again going through life at just a slight tangent to the path I had taken, and everything would be new—completely new—on account of that imperceptible deviation at the hub, the beginning, of things.

"Or maybe there was the partly decomposed body of an old man in there. Thin, in rotted clothes, his beard and hair the only part of him alive, running like living silvery vines from his brown mummified head and face, where the features had shrunken, become vague and shapeless like charred wood. And the mouth like a ragged black gap in the wood; the eye sockets suggesting a mask of frail material, something like a wasp's nest, which would fall apart, become ashes if you touched it. As for that old man, I thought, maybe it would be just as well for me to break into the tower now and poke my finger into his eyes and, becoming him, help him to descend to dust all at once, instead of letting him wait those intervening years before slow nature settled him into her rich mixture of rot. Because, that way, things would be speeded up for me; I'd the sooner arrive at the turning hub of another wheel. I could get a head start maybe, on becoming something else—whatever I was going to be—perhaps an entirely new kind of creature, a thing different from, yet grown out of, man; a thing there wasn't yet a name for, whose shape and intellect I couldn't yet imagine.

"Still my hand wouldn't rise to that iron latch. Something held it rigid. So I backed away from the door. And turned around. And in front of me there was a path—narrow, walled in by growth—but definitely rising, winding out of the ravine.

"I started up the path, full of energy and calm now, feeling realistic, amused at myself. At the top of the gully was a level sunny meadow. The path flared out, bordered by long grass that was being slowly tumbled by the wind. The sky was full of little, fleecy, rapidly changing clouds, all marching one way—the way I was striding. I heard in my mind the voice of an old teacher of mine, the way she used to say my name when the roll was called in the morning at school. 'Present!' I answered aloud and kind of chuckled to myself."

The painter's lips had spread, his teeth glinting in a mysteriously grateful smile. The very same, the doctor thought, as must have come to his face at the age of eight with the teacher's pronouncement of his name. Even then, of course, his peculiar propensity for egoistic daydreaming had kept him busy making shining mountains out of mud-gray molehills. But no doubt it was this very propensity that shaped the artist's temperament. Here before him, in this man, was illustrated the well-known theory of compensatory illusion springing from early frustration (in this case, the special nature of the latter would remain undefined unless the patient were fully analyzed, but the general trend was substantially clear)—this tendency to illusion nurturing an often deceptively healthy and lustrous growth of the imagination, which, in turn, might throw off a by-product called Art. And that by-product, the doctor reminded himself, was a phenomenon that he took genuine pleasure in; it was, in fact, one of his hobbies, in the form of landscape gardening.

He uncrossed his legs and leaned back in the rocker. In the morning he would suggest a walk through the formal gardens with this artist. It would be interesting to converse with him on a number of aesthetic topics, on which his, the doctor's, knowledge was by no means sparse.

While this diagnosis and the resultant resolution took place, the painter's story went on, until the doctor's attention was snaffled by these words:

"Just then I saw a gleaming object in front of me on the path. My lifted foot would have stepped over it and walked on, had I not happened to be looking down. Carved in angular stillness, loosely stretched out yet stern, hard, stonelike. A queer contrast to the giddily blowing grass, the flowing tops of the trees. It was so motionless and finished in its shape. Like an artifact, rather than a living changeable thing. Its colors were glazed, more permanent than the surrounding leaves and twigs on which the sun played, for around the deep ochre, blue-gray and black, the light seemed enfolded like a crystal film that vibrated somberly over each symmetrically whittled scale.

"It was my snake. The very same one. Was it possible he had followed me all this winding way? Had he waited behind me outside the old square tower; had he been undulating through the grass at my side, his movement one with the lisping grass? His head was lifted just a little from the ground, as if watching me, but there was no curious tongue whisking in and out.

"I passed around him, and looked back. No movement. *Was he dead or alive?* I couldn't bear to poke him with my foot. He lay too perfect there; a fixed jewel, he seemed, that could not except with difficulty be pried from its setting. How beautiful he was! I remembered how different his beauty had been in motion. The smooth, quick, yet languid twist of his body making successive graceful curls as he slipped over the ground like water. A simple form yet subtly complex—a spiral—his head merely an extension of his body; no arms or legs, no details to him, except the sinuous designs on him—darkly vivid on top; pale, vulnerable, tender hued on his underside. If he were dead, it seemed to me I had killed him.

"An unreasonable grief welled up in me, as if something irreplaceable might be lost. And, if lost, this was my unconscious fault. I would be punished then; not for an act of sin, not for an aggression, but for some omission; a failure at a certain crossroad somewhere behind me to recognize some sign . . . a sign with a double meaning . . . and I had turned down the broad and level way instead of up the steep way. . . . But maybe he was not dead. His beauty was so eloquent, it burned and chilled my blood at once, as if lightning were leaping from his shining scales into my pores.

"I circled him several times with whispering steps. His head did not follow me, but, as I went on around a bend, looking over my shoulder, I thought that he began to ripple very slowly in my direction.

"I hurried along now, swinging my kit in order to make a noise louder than the incessant mutterings of leaves and insects. Would I ever get out of this endless forest? As a matter of fact, around the next turn, through a slash of leaves, I saw tall gates with shorn lawn behind them. As though I'd been lifted up onto someone's shoulder, who took much longer steps than I could, I was all at once set down in the familiar landscape in front of my own cabin."

The doctor, who had been listening with an interest and tension that he realized might have been too openly displayed and for which, he reflected, in view of the abrupt and obvious end to the story, there had been inadequate reason on his part, laughed shortly and remarked:

"Well, you have certainly proven that *you* are a child, but not exactly, do you think, that all of us are?"

The dark man let his hands come together now. They caressed, clasped, and explored each other affectionately, like long parted playfellows. "Well, I haven't finished the story. Although maybe I'd do myself a favor not to add what came later. It will make me appear very foolish in your eyes.

"This evening at dinner in the mansion, I mentioned something about my walk in the woods to one of the guests—one of the 'map carriers' I was telling you about. I remarked on what an apparently wide and varied area I'd covered, having been out since early morning; about the profusion of roads and branching paths; how these paths, dipping and rising, take so many turns; how their ends and beginnings are obscured by trees and thick growth as well as the contours of the land. I told him how confusing it all was and what a lot there seems to be to learn before one can find one's way about easily.

"I watched a rather irritated smile begin on his face. I knew he was anxious for me to stop talking so that he could begin his exact and detailed explanations. But I went on and told him about the snake; how it had followed me all that winding way, for all I knew, slithered through the gate behind me, and might be waiting there by my cabin right now. How, if it were, I meant to make a pet of it, as I was sure it was harmless.

"Then I told him about passing under the fallen tree, once going out and once coming back, so that I knew there was one path, at least, that I'd crossed twice that day. And then I made quite a story out of the 'old mill' beside which I ate my lunch; how beautiful, sunny, and tranquil it was there, with the green turf sloping up to the silvery white stone and the stained glass window in the top of the round tower throwing color like delicious notes of music from out of the ivy around it. As a contrast to this, of course, I related the story of that grizzled old square tower in the hollow on the other side of the wood and the fantasies that the damp and darkness, and my own insecurity, had called up in me.

"Well, here's what he said about it all—and in a few controlled, well-chosen, factual terms, too. For that I have to give him credit, because from his point of view he certainly had the laugh on me. Maybe he pitied me a little for being such a child, was afraid ridicule would bruise me; or maybe he decided I was 'touched,' and he had better not cross me. Anyhow, he unfolded a pocket map of the region and showed me that, since only a limited portion of it was heavily wooded, and since, by my description, I had been scrambling through that part most of the day, I had really been moving within a relatively small maze, and must have walked the same paths countless times. Their apparent difference in scenery, of course, was occasioned by the changing angles of approach and the multiplicity and variety of the objects confronting me. He worked it out from my story that there must have been two fallen trees, each on a separate trail, and he pointed to the fact that trees fall in every heavy storm, so that this would hardly constitute a reliable landmark or one of permanence.

"He located for me, on the map, both the high conical stone building and the squat stone one, where not a duchess but someone equally important had died or been born—I forget which. It is situated quite close to the main gates, just down the hill to the right, if you approach it from the front. In that case you get a lovely view from beside the lake, looking up a grassy incline, with the round, ivy-clad tower silhouetted against the blue and white sky. An extension to the tower is built square in the back, I learned—a section added later around the top, its foundation conforming to the brow of the hill there. The place is left rather uncared for in the back, and to get to the entrance from that direction one has to cross a swampy ravine. The gardeners store their tools inside and so keep a sign on the door to discourage trespassers."

"Oh," the doctor exclaimed, blinking. "There was but one tower then! I see. Two fallen trees, rather than one. One tower instead of two!" An inadvertent guffaw left his lips. Really, this fellow was a classic subject for analysis. A monograph written around this story of his, a patent fantasy constructed over a few sticks of fact, would make an interesting contribution to one of the Psychological Monthlies. The tale was as full of significant symbolism as a dream. The paper could perhaps be called "Parallelism in Prevaricative, Creative, and Dream Emblemology, Indicating Displacement of the Surrender-to-Reality Impulse into the Infantile-Exhibitionistic Sphere."

"And the snake?" the doctor asked. "Were there one or two of them?" Or none? he amended to himself.

"Well, it turned out that a snake had been killed near the tower that day by one of the gardeners, who acted on the assumption that any reptile, poisonous or not, should be disposed of, because it would make the guests apprehensive," the painter said. "Since there are two species of snakes having a good deal the same markings, one of which is venomous, the map man couldn't tell for sure whether the one killed was innocent or not. There was the possibility that the two snakes I encountered were one and the same. On the other hand, they might have been different, for all their identical size and appearance."

"Your story is most revealing," the doctor said. "It only goes to show . . ." but he paused. "By the way, I might add my assumption (although it is only that, since I am not an authority on forest lore; my province, as you know, is the wilderness of the human mind) that the reason this snake you say you met cuddled up to you in this intimate fashion was simply that, being of reptilian blood, it would constantly be seeking warmth, and it sensed that this object, yourself, which accidentally lay in its path, would furnish temporary 'fire and shelter,' so to speak. But, what strikes me most forcibly in your story is the contrast between you and this other man, the map man (I am well acquainted with him, incidentally), who knows exactly where he is and where he is going at all times, because he has taken the trouble to study his locale and make use of the knowledge experts have gathered for him. To him the world is a safe and sane place, and small enough, because of his information about it, to manage comfortably without fear."

"Yes," the painter said. He arose and stretched, letting a full yawn have its way without any gesture toward muffling it. The pliant fingers of one muscular hand fooled with the cord dangling from the bulb in the skylight. "There is much to what you say, except for the fact that my informant admitted he had never been beyond the gates himself and would not think of entering the forest, particularly alone, small as it is, considering the dangers of poison ivy, for instance, and—other things—which he did not enumerate."

The doctor drew on his pipe, while thinking of an answer, but found it had expired so that he received only a sour mouthful of whistling air. He became aware that the fire had died in the stove, leaving the cabin drafty and empty seeming. A sort of echo of the silence outside rang against his eardrums, which had the effect of making him slightly dizzy and unable to clarify his mind to present the logical reply that certainly waited there in readiness. He wished all at once that he were back in his own comfortable quarters at the mansion and cringed inwardly at the dark strip of forest he must cross to arrive there.

"There was one point of uncertainty in the map man's explanation that gave me the greatest relief and pleasure," the painter was saying, softly, confidentially.

What was that? the doctor knew he was expected to ask. But there was a really odd grin on his host's face. The corners of his mouth had taken on the contour of a sharp new moon lying on its back in the sky. His very white teeth and his very dark eyes were gleaming in his mahogany-skinned face.

The doctor arose from the rocker rather suddenly, so that his stiff knees gave him a painful twinge. He had the impression that his host was going to pull the cord and turn off the light. "A most interesting evening," he managed heartily, holding out his hand, with his upper body already swiveled in the direction of the door. "Thank you so much for inviting me in."

The painter was still grinning—whether affably or gloatingly, the doctor could not decide. He stepped forward and gripped the doctor's hand, much too hard, leaving the light bulb swinging a jerky arc behind him.

"I'll tell you what it was," he pursued in an intense, husky whisper, fixing the doctor's eyes (which were leaping from left to right behind his glasses) with his own direct and disconcerting gaze. His pupils, large, shining, and bottomless, seemed to contract and dilate to the rhythm of the pendulous bulb, which made the squatting shadows in the room, those of the stove, the rocker, and the table, expand and shrink, upon the walls.

"It was the doubt as to whether the two snakes, the dead one and the live one, were the same. Maybe *my* snake is still alive in the forest and is the evil one."

From "Fables of Things"

The Cup, the Plate, the Knife, the Fork, and the Spoon

"I am deep," said the Cup.

"I am wide," said the Plate.

"But I am sharp," said the Knife.

"I am more clever," said the Fork.

"I am neither deep, nor wide, nor sharp, nor clever," said the Spoon, "but my portion exactly matches the desire of the mouth."

Moral: *Not what you are, but what you've got to offer, counts in this world.*

From May Swenson Papers, Washington University Libraries. Swenson wrote a series of fables at her 23 Perry Street address in the mid-1950s.

The Power and the Danger

I awake this morning, and it is raining. Although the blind is undrawn, the room is as dark as evening. I can barely trace, through slashes of rain outside the window, the shape of the tree. This tree, a catalpa, twists up in the little space between this building and the next, and, because of it, that unpaved rectangle of clay out there is called garden. The tree resembles an old, rheumatic arm, bent at the elbow, with muscles wrung into tough coils. Its upper branches clutch, as if in a half-open fist, a few large draggled, yellow leaves, which the rain and wind are beating and pulling apart. In the city one feels sorry for natural things;—they are captives, imprisoned in the wrong world and uncompanioned by those of their kind. I even feel sorry for the rain, which has to fall on indifferent brick and pavement. It probably enjoys dumping itself upon these few precarious leaves, but need it be so violent? But then, pushed by wind and trapped between the buildings, perhaps the rain cannot help punishing the tree. Or it could be that I mistake for pain what is pleasure for the catalpa; maybe it enjoys the rain and wind, has even enticed them to this wrestling match. Has the tree, in fact, *caused* this chilly, stormy day, by some sorcerous gesture to heaven with that wicked arm?

My mood about the tree has turned inside out in the space between two thoughts. It is because we do not *know* Nature, I say

---

Originally published in *Women Feminist Stories by Nine New Authors with a Photographic Essay* (New York: Eakins Press, 1972). A shorter version of the story, entitled "Eclogue," appeared in the *Paris Review,* no. 10 (fall 1955). The *Paris Review* had asked her to cut the story, but, since Swenson was "not sure it constituted an improvement," the longer version is included here.

to myself, though we think we are her cleverest child. Existing within her, a tiny part of her, we envision her mysterious outline, become afraid . . .

And now, a curious memory half-formed, wavering, arises like a fume to the surface of my mind: It seems to me, when I was an infant, my mother's hands holding me felt like parts of myself. I was angry when they weren't there, astonished that I had no power over them. They came, and they went away; and that was sad, but I recognized I couldn't help it. It was still later that I found it was not they, alone, that came but a greater creature whose shape I could not clearly see, that loomed above me. It handled me, and I could not tell what it might do with me. It was then I first knew helplessness and fear . . . Until I came to trust the arms that lifted me, because they brought me to a breast—first one and then another—each the size of my own head. And these two became the first "other persons" that I recognized beside myself. But, since I craved them, I felt that they belonged to me; somehow I had created them! and I soon proceeded to dominate them, to practice my ego upon them along with my greed. And was it not true that later, when my mind like my sight had come to focus and I knew and loved my mother (having had to give up the supremely satisfying notion that only I existed and that whatever I touched or that touched me through my senses was somehow an extension of myself or invention of mine), I felt guilt at having used my mother's body selfishly, carnivorously?

Gray rain rushes past the window, slantwise like whips. The branches of the tree are writhing. On usual days the tree huddles in its narrow place, tame and humble, like a crippled hand asking for pennies of sun.

There, my mood has turned again. All at once, the rain so copiously falling makes me want to cry. Tears film my eyes as the rain films the window. But why am I crying? Because it is autumn in the city. Autumn is bad enough, but in the city . . . The city is bad enough, but in autumn . . . Two terrible losses together . . . too much.

The country in the summer. Country and summer: do they not equal my mother's two hands? or her two breasts? And now I remember something else, an incident that has to do with all this . . . another day as beneficent as this one is cruel. I will turn from this dark panel to that bright one: that day I was content to be an infant that does not discern its mother's face but only feels itself being handled. I will pretend to myself that it is happening again and that I am there:

The property must belong to someone: I come upon berry patches and fruit trees in the general wildness and tracks of cattle in the boggy grass by a stream, but there are no fences, and the last farmhouse I passed was a mile away. The ground mounts gradually, a mosaic of sun and shade, up slabs of rock, over tuffets of moss; the sky is a steady blue; the wind barely breathes in the treetops; only a sleepy chirp or a rustle, now and then, filters from above. There is such a spell of green-gold stillness on the afternoon that I, too, move without sound.

With sneaking steps I go up the shallow staircase of rocks and enter one of the many doorways of the trees. I do not feel like a trespasser but like a belonger to the place, as if I had once grown here long ago, as a bush or tree, or been one of these dark, inscrutable stones imbedded in the hillside.

I come to a flat green spot full in the sunlight. I undress entirely and stretch out, my cheek on a pad of moss, my body pressed into the warm, pricking grass. Beneath me I feel knobs of stones and spines of tree roots—the earth's skeleton under its supple flesh. The sun, a great gold brush, comes down on my back, and a ground breeze whisks over me softly. I feel myself being woven back into the fabric and contour of nature. It seems I can hear, under my ear, ants dancing, the foreheads of worms pushing, and the seeds of all growth gnawing upward through the sod. My hand, flung out, touches the smooth, ringed trunk of a birch, its skin as white as mine. Should any human being pass, it seems to me, I would not be noticed where I lie. My clothes are a disguise I have abandoned, and my nakedness is suitable and comfortable as bark to a tree, as his well-fitting hide to an animal. Face down, hugging the earth, I am secure, invisible, sunk in the landscape.

When my back is saturated with sun, I turn over. And now I absorb a new sensation: gaping, roofless blue above me, my body white as a fallen statue in the open green, I am all at once vulnerable, exposed. So an animal must feel, forced upon its back, its grip with the earth broken, its soft underparts bare to attack. But when caressed or scratched on these parts, of which the nerve tendrils are so sensitive, the animal relaxes in a kind of ecstasy; and this I do as the sun repossesses me with its burnishing stroke.

The strong light weights my eyelids, and I close them. I am suspended in a great copper sphere, whose dome turns first to yellow—the yellow of dying daffodils—then green, the green of an old album cover of stiff plush that I remember from earliest childhood—then blue, metallic, and flashing as the neckfeathers of a mallard—and, at last, a soft and secret purple, the folds of a king's robe in an ancient illustration once brooded over in some lower recess of childhood. If I lift my eyelids a splinter, the dome springs to grinning orange—a lion's mouth, a furnace doorway, an upsidedown abyss of pure frightening light. The sun now wraps me, layer over layer, with such heat that I lose consciousness of my body's weight and shape; I am formless, transparent, afloat. Invading every pore, the sun seems to reach my veins, thickening my blood, almost halting it. Closing the cups of my eyes, I let the purple light eclipse to black. I am again sealed from sight, an object colored and textured with its background. Solid now, heavy as a magnet into which a myriad particles of power have gathered, I settle to the bottom of the sphere. I am dimly aware, during a long enthralled doze, of the sun's slow glide around its arc and, later, of scarfs of shade being drawn, one by one, over my body.

When I awake it is to coolness, a thinning of the air, a hollowness in the still-blue sky, while the foliage around me has become denser where shadows have massed between the leaves. There is a listening mood to the wood now; birds utter one-syllable cries and make quick swoops in the upper branches where the sun is still yellow. I awake to the sound of grass being cropped and the slow, meandering stomp of cattle, out of sight a little way beyond the clearing. I can hear the cattle swish their tails, the wet crunch of their methodical jaws, but cannot see them yet. I lie still, my hands under my neck, letting the scene around me return. I see red berries, dried by the sun to puckered pellets on a wild currant bush, the embroidery of unfurling ferns at my side. A grasshopper, green and shaped like a peapod, makes a long leap from a fern and lands on my chest. He rocks up and down with my breathing, and when I blow on him he shoots away, drowned from sight in the tangle of the grass.

Now there appears the low-slung, munching head of a cow through a gap in the bushes. I hear others following after. Her loose, fawn-colored neck skin stops swaying under her chin when her glossy, dark eyes fall upon me. She wags one ear forward, then the other, her black, slime-wet nostrils sucking clues of scent from the air. When I do not move she steps closer, her lashes brushing down over mournful pupils, and the others behind her take an imitative step, bringing them into view. The herd of ten or a dozen gradually clusters into the clearing until they are standing in a respectful semicircle, all gazing at the motionless white object on the grass. None ventures an exploratory gesture until their leader gives the signal by moving first. The grass is juicy and lush here. I am probably lying in the delectable center of their cropping ground. Will they advance and threaten me, realizing their superiority in strength and number, or will my human status (naked, prone, and passive though I am) ward them off to look for other pasture?

I am too immersed in my conviction of belonging to be afraid of these slow-moving, tranquil-breathing creatures who hesitate above me; yet they do look large and heavy there, weaponed (are they aware of it?) with sharp horns and hooves. I see my little image reflected in each pair of stuporous, noncommittal pupils, but I decide to stay motionless. The leader takes two steps forward; the others imitate, keeping the semicircle intact. And two more steps. Their heads do not sink to sample the grass; the white object lying there is a fascination greater than food.

What can they want of me? A strange emotion, more awe than fear, keeps me lying rigid. Haven't they recognized me as human then? Without my clothes, do they sense me as some object they have never encountered, the meaning of which must be discovered? Yes, it must be so, for the leader takes another step, carefully, and lowers her head. With her gray, shoelike tongue she takes a lick at my toe.

Am I really becoming part of the woods, and is it recognition of my metamorphosis that attracts her? The others stand waiting for her judgment. She raises her head and looks round at them, running her tongue over the bridge between her nostrils as if sampling the taste of me, considering its quality. The herd is alert and waiting, but her communication must have been one of skepticism; they do not advance. White and green saliva slides from the corners of the lead cow's lips as she stares at me expectantly, wishfully.

It does not occur to me to say a word or make a gesture of self-identification. I find I am flattered by their interest, intrigued by speculation as to how I appear to them. The smell of the farmer in his sweaty overalls, pitchfork in hand, they know; the laconic command in his voice, his calloused, impersonal palms relieving their udders in the stalls at morning and nightfall, the unconscious contact of his forehead with their flanks as the two hard jets of milk cross each other squealing into the pail. They are accustomed to the vegetal and mineral smells of the forest, their summer domain, and all season nothing has disturbed their daylong green routine of aimless meandering, mindless munching, their eyes reflecting nothing but the sky's serenity, the stillness of their drinking pool. And today they come upon an ambiguous white object in the sun on the grass, with an undefinable smell and shape. Is it alive? Scarcely. And yet, is it not breathing? But it does not assert itself; it cannot be human. Vegetable, rock, beast? No. What then?

Or perhaps they have recognized me as human—the lick at my toe confirmed it—and awareness of my helplessness is dawning on them, being signaled this minute to the others by the enterprising leader as she lobs her thick, hair-frilled ears back and forth, and the sun glints wickedly on the white points of her horns. I feel all at once how it would be if their blunt, split hooves stamped on my belly. No, it cannot be. Their eyes are too wide and meek, they are too hesitant—no flicker of fury in their faces.

Maybe it is love, then, the cows all feel for me? Their leader has sensed my repentance of the human state, my retreat from the sin that was the first thought, my return to animal grace after the long betrayal, before the temptation to mentality seized a natural creature and raised him arrogantly on his hind legs. Maybe they are welcoming me back among them to the wisdom, the peace and beauty of existence outside the cage of thought, and maybe the lick on my toe was a tentative caress, a sign of recognition and forgiveness.

So, I still keep silent and motionless. And the fawn-colored leader steps closer, and this time licks my knee and goes on licking, confident now, absorbed. An eagerness like hunger has come over her. Her tongue at first is pleasant-feeling but soon rasps like a file; her forelegs with their knobby, grass-stained knees are planted solidly at my side. And her tongue moves up my leg, wide, hot, full of friction.

Oh, why have I let them get near me? I cannot hope to push her away with my puny legs and arms. And now the others have arrived, their heads lowered determinedly all around me. Three of them begin, with heavy, drooling tongues, to lick my feet. I will be licked from head to heel, slobbered over; I am their strange delicacy to be rolled over and over in the grass, pushed this way and that by their many avid tongues.

And now it comes to me what it is they believe me to be or what wishfully they would make of me: a slab of salt, discovered on this miraculous day in their hilly meadow. It was not here yesterday, but it is here today, a gift of mankind or of nature. Their warm, eager, snuffling breaths descend upon my sweating skin. My tardy panic is so intense that I am paralyzed. I want to draw up my knees, spring erect, and run. But all I can do is raise an arm and say a husky "Shoo!"

At my motion the old leader's head jerks up; she backs away as if stung in the forehead by a bullet. The other cows start, and fall back instantly. Brimming with their own panic now, they bound away, crashing through the brush, staggering into each other, and they stop only when their leader does, beyond the low bush wall. From there they fearfully look around at me over tremulous hindquarters and agitated tails.

I sit up with a thrill of power. They stumble down the hill. I stand up and begin to dress. At sight of my head and shoulders, they move together defensively into a clump on the path. They recognize me now. There is an injured, balky frown between the eyes of the leader. The rest are sullen and comatose. They look as if they expect me to pick a switch and herd them home.

I take an opposite direction, turning my back on them, forcing myself to a moderate pace, although my feet want to hurry. A complex of feelings tries to unsnarl in my head. The back of my neck is still cool with fear and my knees loose. Why? I wonder, since it has turned out that *I* am the power and the danger, not they. They have already forgotten their fright; they are back to munching; while I must settle this turmoil in my stomach before it will consider supper. At the same time, my chest is warm with a strong, brandy-like pride. Superior to them all: I, alone, with my thin skin and small bulk, because. . . . Because to them I am an apparition, a thing outside their ken, a being with hands that can seize and use objects, a stick, a rope, to dominate them; a thing that operates by thought. One lifts one's hand, and the brutes retreat as from something supernatural.

But, thinking so, I feel guilt. There is something wrong; there is something ugly about all the things that a hand can do. I think of the monkey, with his *four* hands all restless and sly, that he uses interchangeably to eat or scratch or grab with—and his tail almost like a fifth hand. The monkey's face and forehead, puckered with calculation: is there a new "first thought," beyond the human and more base, wriggling up the spine into that crafty little head?

Evening has moved in now over the ground, filling the spaces between the boulders and under all the bushes with thick, furry shadow. That tree with the bronze leaves ahead—is it a beech? I remember passing it on my way up, just after I left the road and entered these woods. As I get nearer to it, my footsteps unaccountably slow down. Everything looks peculiar in this light that hesitates so long on summer evenings. I am not lost. I think I know quite well where I am, and after that tree there will be the road down, where I will turn south to the farm where I am staying.

But aren't the leaves of the beech turning red and redder as I look? Its trunk, smooth and gray between the warts of bark—is it expanding? It seems, as I stare in the uncertain light, to be breathing. When I reach it, stand next to it, touch it with my hand, what if it should *do* something and I should then see what it really is?

I wish that it would. And I wish that that high boulder sitting in the ravine, mottled with moss so that it resembles the back of a giant toad—cold, mindless, lonely—would hear my footsteps, would relax its petrified pose and turn toward me, revealing its true form.

Before me the ground rippling with stripes of shadow and

above me the sky stirred into motion by feathers of pink in the west seem together to arch and stretch. As I pass the beech and the boulder, and walk down hill, it is as if earth and sky were shifting—as if a fold between them were smoothing out. I focus on that fold. Is it really only the sunset changing hues, or is there a cord, a sort of braid uncoiling from under the horizon—gray, then rosy, as it lengthens and thickens—passing between the earth and into . . . into the body of—? Some prone and immense shape filling all the distance . . . I feel that the events in a dream are about to clarify. If only this transparency of light will last a moment, if I can keep my eyes fixed: beyond, higher, farther still, there will appear (but the light is fading now) a great, serene profile which, when it is distinct, I will find I have always known.

From the Window

1

A carpet of shadow covers the triangular space where Waverly Place, Charles Street, and Seventh Avenue meet—the shadow of a somber apartment house with a weather-streaked awning between its entrance and the curb. Small shops on Charles Street (a grocery, a Chinese laundry, a cabinetmaker's) take up the building's ground floor. Waverly Place, an alleylike crevasse further narrowed by parked cars, runs to a point at Perry Street. The triangle's third side is carried south by Seventh Avenue, a broad rapid river of wheels.

The shadow (this is on a November morning between ten and twelve, before the sun passes behind the west facade of the Avenue) has a bare flat look. Out there at the juncture of the three streets the cobblestones, etched rough in sunlight, turn smooth under the shadow. An early broom of sunbeams has scoured them; now they feel the mop of shade. In the middle of the triangle, as if on a little stage, a flag writhes its colors at the top of a white pole, and two benches face the cement pedestal of the flagpole.

Around or across this stage go people, dogs, babies in carriages, bike riders, peddlers with their carts, long buses, high trucks, plump taxi cabs, low-bellied shining cars. Sometimes an old horse-drawn delivery wagon bumps by, or, from the station on Charles Street, the dragon-red fire engine ponderously turns

---

From May Swenson Papers, Washington University Libraries. Probably written in the early to mid-1950s, judging from the 23 Perry Street address on the manuscript and echoes of imagery found in poems in *A Cage of Spines* (1958).

the corner, a joint at a time, then shrieks and clangs down the Avenue. There comes a policeman on a brown horse, a navy-and-gold blanket under the saddle. There goes a postman with his back rounded under his scuffed, gaping pouch.

All these come and go like performers—a circus troupe assembling for a parade or scene changers crossing the stage between acts. When will the performance itself take place? It is like a hastening to rehearsal. Or is it a constant intermission? Is there a grand finale, to be held elsewhere, for which they are gathering here? They are always crossing, *going by* this stage—of which my third floor window on Perry Street is the proscenium—and they appear within it only as long as it takes them, on various feet and wheels, to pass beyond the frame.

2

There is a sky in the frame, sometimes having traveling clouds in horizontal motion or snakes of smoke, white or black, pulsing vertically from thick chimneys to the south. And this morning the thinner, daintier smoke of my cigarette spreads a scrim between my eyes and the stage, removing it to a romantic distance.

A beer supply truck stops before the grocery store on Charles Street. It is butter yellow, the name in blue hugely lettered upon its side in imitation of old German script. A girl and a man, bareheaded, he carrying a parcel, walk over the paved triangle where the flagpole stands and wait for the traffic light to change. As through a hole between pursed lips, pulling in its green tongue and darting out its red one, the light clicks and changes. They cross. The two isosceles spaces between their knees trade angles—right, left—his flat shoe stepping beside her hoof-heeled one. A corner of his coat is folded stiffly back as on a hinge; her hair, taken over her shoulders by the wind, is riffled to a shape just like the flag above them.

The front page of a newspaper with some heavy headline scrapes in the gutter down there; the yellow truck has gone. A bus, green with dirty buff top, snuffles along Seventh Avenue on fat dithering wheels. An open truck, full of raw wood boxes, new nails shining at their seams—the vehicle slumped and weather worn but its goods bright (a sunny sawmill color)—trundles boisterously downtown. A green and white taxi slinks around the corner of Charles, barely avoiding a boxer dog tugged back, rampant on his leash, by a short thumb-shaped man who holds a pipe upside down in his teeth. A lanky boy in a brown and tan blazer sprints between crawling-on cars, his hands slapping the flanks of his jeans that are silvered from many scrubbings; the cuffs are rolled slovenly above his socks, which have fallen into pleats; his shins are bare, his feet square and clumsy in oiled work shoes.

3

It is the third morning, at the same time, and the mat of shadow is almost the same shape—a little larger. Its northeastern corner reaches to the gasoline station on the uptown side of the Avenue, where the two pumps, one orange, one blue, stand like husband and wife on their white-washed platform, their hoses each hooked up at elbow height. At that corner, on the base of the lamp post (tall, attenuated, shaped like a wilting lily—foolish, ornate, endearing remnant of the past in this ancient part of the city—its dim globe a lugubrious, ripe, but never-falling tear), is a sign saying, in crimson: CARS WASHED.

A one-wheeled pushcart, with a cowbell on a string between two slats nailed to its front, is shoved up Waverly by a troll-like man in shoes with bent-up toes; a pointed wool cap sits on his ears. The bell tonks in rhythm with the iron-covered wheel bumping over cobble humps. The cart has two greenish-gray bundles in it (old clothes, I guess) and the man's hands are like cracked leather wrapped around the old slick wooden handles.

The flag at the top of its pole is limp today; there is no wind. Boys are chasing one another on the cement triangle below it, jumping on and off and over the two anchored benches. There are four boys, all the same height, wearing aviator helmets; their legs and torsos are springs; they run, fall, roll, bounce erect again like tumbling bears. One has his arm in a dirty cotton sling, his coat brought together with a safety pin; its empty sleeve flaps as he sails over the bench, falls, and rolls to his feet with the others. A perforated metal vent in the pavement gushes steam from the drains below, as if a crocodile down there were belching; and each of the cars, constantly littering the Avenue, lets out a bluish whiff from between its back wheels.

Garbage trucks, two of them, are directly across the street below my window now, on Perry Street, their sides shuddering with their inside grindings. Battered, clattering cylinders are hoisted in the gray-gloved hands of Negroes uniformed in gray, the cans, the trucks, themselves the color of dust. They dump the redolent fodder into the broad, unhinged hind maws (for these beasts eat with their rears); the stained, dripping iron tusks clash down, and the instant digestion is heard within: of tin cans and bottles, bones and rinds, peels and rags, old girdles, hats, bunion-split shoes, twisted clothes hangers, bent frying pans, hot water bags, headless dolls, busted toy wagons, worn brushes and combs matted with hair, and, no doubt, dead rats still in their traps, the bodies of cats, cagebirds, puppies trussed up in those parcels of burlap tied with string.

Now the barrels and corrugated cans are slammed empty onto the curb, their lids (which are chained to the railings in front of each house) are spanked down on them, and, the gray gurgling bellies having finished their munch at this end of the block, the Negroes push their visors back on bulbous, sweating skulls and climb into the heads of their beasts, who grumble on, to crouch further down the street, where I hear the grinding and slamming begin again.

4

Today there is no shadow over the intersection. The sky is a blotter of whitish gray. A ceiling has been lowered on the stage, the lighting withdrawn to a diffuse pallor without source. Colors are different; all the blinds in the windows of the big gray building at the base of the triangle, I notice, are a dim green; its facade is featureless without ledges of shade. The smaller rectangles of houses on Waverly Place, with their windowboxes and scrolled stoops that look so cozy in sunlight, are combined now into one long, bleak flat.

Running fast with head down goes the dirty snow-colored horse before the covered wagon of a vegetable dealer, whose bushel baskets dance on the planks inside. The horse wears blinkers; a yellow khaki blanket partly warms his back. His thick white breath boils from his nostrils. It is very cold today, with a north wind slicing over the roofs. It shakes the windows in their frames and seizes the ringlets from chimneys, scattering them instantly in the rough air. The flag is missing from its pole (stored away now for the winter, I suppose)—its naked brass ball at the top quivers rigidly in the wind. Ragged papers swoop in the street like stiff, angry birds. Two real birds, pigeons, mottled marble their bodies, climb the air laboriously and land on the roof of the gas station, walking in a jerky circle, their necks crimped in between huddled wings, the pink of their feet gone gray with cold.

Almost no one is on foot in the street. Well, here's a greatcoated man with a fur collar, carrying a black leather bag that must be a doctor's. He emerges from a doorway of one of the Waverly houses, dark as a mousehole in this grim light. But he merely stoops into his black car at the curb; a purplish smoke begins to putter from its behind.

5

Waverly Place is a canal of silver light. Sun is back this morning, a Sunday. But, as I write it, a cloud like a plump, white hand covers the sun, and the scene shifts. Waverly shrinks to a narrow dark slot. Then the hand moves aside in the cold blue up there, again uncovering the canal below with its ripples of cobbles pouring into the bay of the Avenue.

All the shadows, big and little, are deep blue. Every walker wears one—attached to his heels and pudgy, if he's coming toward me; if he's moving the other way, it unreels from his toes, skinny and long. The parked cars stand on ink-blue patches; their tops gleam fiercely. But a black hand now reaches for the sun, which slips through its fingers and arrows down, then is snatched in again.

The flag is up today, languidly licking around its pole. Newspapers grabbed from the wire trash baskets by the wind in the night are turned over in the gutter and indifferently paged by drafts from passing cars. There is the sun again throwing needles over everything: the water towers on the roof of the square gray building on Charles Street are silver vats, and the leaning plus-rods of television antennas are picked out slicingly against the sky like crossed foils.

Two mamas are wheeling perambulators side by side over the triangle. One of the babies toddles in front of her high equipage wheeling her own "baby" in a miniature carriage. Then there goes a third woman in the opposite direction, pushing a go-cart with, instead of a child, a bag of groceries seated in it. A red motorcycle spotted with oil and soot has paused, its engine muttering among the cars stopping abreast for the light. The driver flexes his legs, drops one toe and then the other to the ground, raises his goggles and blows his nose, and pulls down his goggles and steps on the gas pedal and spurts on at the flick of the green.

Will the black or the white hand win? They're still playing chess in the sky.

A quarter to twelve, and the church two blocks away on Eleventh Street has spilled its children. A clot of little girls, well buttoned up, capped and gloved but with knees bare, trots across the street, swinging their handbags importantly. Shrill boys gallop around them, mittens tied to wrists and flying; they shoot imaginary pistols, crying, "Bang-bang! Got one! She's dead." The girls ignore them, except that they consciously sway their hips under their flared coats. A man leading a Russian wolfhound with a long, smoky coat (body like a bear except for the comical up-scrolled tail and the thin muzzle that wears a supercilious grin) plods diagonally toward me, having crossed the street; and the dog is a bush of blond light that, as he gains the curb and the shadow, turns blue and opaque. The dog raises his hind leg against the hydrant on the corner of Perry, and, this being in the sun, he strikes it with a shining stick of silver.

6

I sit in my opera box (it is a December evening) as if in a yellow cave, for the lighting is reversed. Beyond the proscenium is darkness, and here the lamp is lit. It has begun raining. I can see three of those teardrop streetlights: on the west side of Charles and Seventh, on the east side, and to the left on Perry and

Seventh. Each of the wet cobbles of the Avenue is outlined as in an etching, with four slivers of light. A sash of green, and then of red, is laid down over the intersection by the black-visored traffice signal. A chain of square gems falls vertically down the front of the big ugly building across the triangle: the top window is blue (it must be a kitchen); beneath it is a lemon one; then an unlit square; then a dim orange one horizontally ruled by venetian blinds; and a dark window again; and in the lowest frame blooms a table lamp with a strawberry shade.

The arched entrance under the awning is lighted. The neon sign over the grocery drops a crumpled reflection, like pink cellophane, in a puddle on the pavement. The tiled gas station stands out whitely, its floodlight blessing the heads of the conjugal pumps on their platform.

A taxi, its lighted tiara on top signaling that it is empty, crawls out of the black crevasse of Waverly, and its headlamps are like an animal's stealthy round eyes. A bus goes by, lit inside, the heads of people in it all colors like bean candy in those long boxes whose contents can be seen through transparent sides. On the roof of a high building downtown on Christopher Street, a penthouse with one wall all glass has dark marionettes moving—to music, for they wiggle. Below the penthouse are the scattered rectangles of other windows, appearing to be apertures in the gunmetal sky; the frame of the building is not outlined at this distance.

Across the triangle, past the benches dripping rain, three striders under one umbrella cross beneath the street lamp, their shadows laid down as one thick bar with a domed top and several scrambled legs.

7

The little rain is falling straight down, seeming to make the air visible on this gray morning. A stippling of minute gray dots composes the scene like a photograph in a newspaper. In dips of the pavement the drops are bouncing. The cobbled Avenue has a greased texture; reminds me of the back of the rhinoceros in his tank at the zoo—exactly that dusky, gray-greenish heavy-overcoated color of wet rhinoceros—the cobbles shrug away the wet that cannot penetrate while they continue to gleam with it.

The taillights of the cars smear the hide of the street with red. Instead of shadows, vague reflections glide beside the cars. Walkers wear boots and carry umbrellas from which the pricking raindrops glance off like steam. But the rain is very gentle and steady in its overall falling, being unmolested by any wind. Dark surfaces are shined and made darker. The bulging tarpaulin over a moving van backing away from a stoop on Waverly, the slicker and helmet of a traffic officer (from behind he looks like a nun) who stands spread-legged on the intersection thumbing the traffic downtown, the feather-curly coats of two spaniels being yanked through the wet by an impatient hotel doorman—all these "darks" in the picture are polished and highlighted by the rain.

The flagpole is empty, its tarnished ball being doused like an upturned face by the rain. (I wonder who puts up the flag and takes it away, and when?) An umbrella like a red tomato, another blue and Persian domed, float along beneath the flagpole; now they are collapsed at the door of the grocery store and disappear inside.

8

Two days of it. Soggy, saturated with rain, are bricks and plaster, the concrete walks the color of mud. All yesterday the wind pushed at the heavy drapes of water, fringes of rain dragged over stone, rasped against the windows. Hunched shapes under umbrellas vibrated behind the blowing curtains of water, as did the bodies and wheels of cars wobbling and kicking up spray.

This morning is dusky and blurred, street sounds muffled in the heavy air beyond my window. The scene is empty under a clabbered ceiling of bumpy gray. The flag lets itself out like a horse's head stretching over its stall—a little tiredly; the blue corner is like a blinker—but draws back and hangs its head, dozes again. The ribs of a slain umbrella lie in the gutter.

The only bright patch I see is the window of the grocery store, where a hill of oranges, and another of lemons, makes a tiny, gay stage. Light gleams there, from behind, so that this becomes the show—like a peep show—a brilliant warm little square, far away. Without shadow the triangle down there seems especially empty and wide, monotonously stroked by passing wheels.

The oranges are a pile of suns; the lemons form a flatter pile. If you quartered one and hooked its webbed transparent shape onto a sky of summer over a dark lake, it would be a moon in profile. The lemons in the window are passive, quiescent, wax skinned, each an ellipse with the suggestion of a nipple. The oranges are all round and hot and whirling—whirling fast inside the aggressive borders of their pyramid; they spin from side to side and from front to back, an axial and a rotary motion in one, it seems to my eyes. Arrows of fire might be darting from the friction of their skins. I avidly drink this brightness that pricks the center of grayness: noon fruit and night fruit—miniature planets, warm and cool.

9

The mailman is at the green box on the lamp post at Perry and Seventh, unlocking it and gathering white envelopes there, like eggs from a coop.

There are five objects on the corner where the bus stops. Because of their grouping they look like people and also because each has its own character. There is the bus stop sign, black and white, short, with a round face, a peaked black hat on his head. These are a pair of short white poles (one stooped a bit) both wearing square red top hats—I guess they are markers of some sort. Then there is the fire hydrant, a round stubby silver-hatted person, seeming to be leading the conversation. He looks like a cross between Winston Churchill and a pot-bellied pygmy. Finally, there is the ample empty wire trash basket squatting in a dignified way a little apart from the others. She has the manner of trying to appear important, even elegant. Her criss-cross sides snare the sunlight, and her aluminum bottom flashes. There the five of them stand. Are they waiting for the bus? It comes, stops, but never takes them aboard. Beneath them, through the rusty pavement grill, they feel the shuddering of the subway and hear the rain water gargling down the gutter's drain. They are having some gossip together. Perhaps they are discussing the ruined umbrella, her snapped handle and tattered black skirt pulled inside out over her face, lying disgracefully in the gutter.

10

Everything I have for breakfast is yellow. The egg I open has a yellow globe set into white plush, like something in a curious treasure box. The rind of my grapefruit, just eaten, is yellow with green pores in its skin, and the little compartments inside are a paler, gauzy yellow. Butter—a small neat-cornered loaf on a long dish—is the sunny tint of dandelions and has their flat, yet silky, sheen. The honey jar draws strands of light from the window to its amber center as if it were a magnet, and when I dip into it the tawny slow-flowing stuff comes rounded like a horizon above the hollow of the spoon. The cut of cheese that forms a smooth ramp on its plate, and is pocked with marks like those on the moon, is orange-yellow and the narrow pipe-shaped fall of coffee into my cup is yellow-brown.

Beyond the window is a mist that covers "the stage" outside like a heavy cloth. I hear fog horns from the Hudson. And so the scene is a near one this morning—is on my table, where my fingers might be actors moving among their props: to the pulpit of the sugar bowl, over the two steps of toast, up the turret of the coffee pot.

All at once, before my eyes outside the blank window, two thick ropes stretch down, and I hear footsteps on the roof. I have to open the window to look up, and I see a big hook, from which the ropes depend, fastened to a projecting ledge of the roof. The ends of the ropes lie in snaky rings in front of the stoop below. Standing on the pavement in the fog is a mahogany upright piano with an old quilt thrown over it. Two men, one on the roof, the other below, are calling directions to each other. There is a block-and-tackle thing, I now notice, attached to one of the ropes. How strange the red-grained piano, with its white and black keys, looks down there in the street! Forlorn and nervous she looks and seems to be shivering or trying to hide under her blanket. Are they going to put the piano on the roof? I imagine that, when snow comes, it will fall on this piano standing upon the roof, the weight of the flakes perhaps sounding a chord, muffled, cacophonous and prolonged, like a medley of all the mooing notes now coming from the river.

A brown canvas belly-band has been buckled around the piano and tied to a rope. The man hollers from the roof, and the other man pulls on the free rope. She is being lifted, and I think I feel the piano's panic as her casters scrape the pavement then leave the ground. She is so large yet so helpless. If she should fall, the head of the man under her would be crushed as easily as I once saw a cabbage broken when stepped on by a zoo elephant, who in this way reduced it to bite size for his dinner.

Up she comes, level with the first story. And twirls a little in the air. And up to the second story, the rope whimpering in the metal groove of the tackle, a sound as if the piano, in her tight corset, were scared or weeping.

Well, they didn't put her on the roof. (If they had, when she rose past my window I could have stroked her keys and played a trill on her to make her feel better.) A man at the window of the second floor apartment, where the panes had been removed to make a wider entrance, pulled her in by the halter and lowered her to her new stall; and then the loosened ropes were dropped past my window, which I shut. I returned to my breakfast.

11

A pallid sun, and the carpet of shadow across the stage (narrow now, because the year has slipped a notch to the north) is tissue thin, a barely-to-be-traced rectangle over the cobbles. Tops of buildings in the downtown distance are bluish apparitions, without detail or thickness. Hoar frosted is the scene, colors muted in the gray breath of winter.

Someone has put a broken vacuum cleaner beside the wire trash basket: two old crones, one fat (filled with wadded newspapers), the other lean except for her goiterous bag of dirt, are getting acquainted there on the corner.

An ambulance goes by with a ting-ting-ting of its bell sounding frail and not alarming but forlorn. The white and brown cab is sealed like a secret, the slits of windows revealing nothing; a white-coated intern sits by the driver. A hallucinatory smell of ether comes to my nostrils as I watch it. Three cops on motorcycles ride by in the opposite direction, one after the other; they are rigid in their black coats on their rigid sputtering steeds, veering downtown bulletlike toward some target.

12

The Ginkgo tree in front of my window, like the skeleton of a tall fish, has all its curved thorny branches stuck out begging for snow to pad its nakedness. This morning a sparrow sat for a moment, exactly level with my eyes, rocking with his claws clasped upon a branch, inflating his feathers that were the same brown-gray as the bark. He wiped his beak, left and right, on his puffed chest and then stretched and whirred upward and away.

13

The dwarf-woman, who lives on Charles Street, is coming to the mailbox with her cat (a long pale albino with pink eyes) lying across her shoulder like a fur piece. The cat has a collar and leash, but he hates to put his paws to the icy pavement. Usually, when I see them, the dwarf-woman is scolding the cat as she tries to drag him on the leash; he holds up his feet, one after the other, and shakes them, meowing to be taken up.

Now she is reaching to the knob on the lid of the mailbox, managing to seize it by straining on toe and jumping up; after several bangs of the lid, she gets her letter into the slot, the cat's claws remaining secure in the nap of her coat. She pulls him loose and sets him down. His tail whips rapidly while he glares at her.

She is a sculptress, I have heard. In the ground floor window of her house I have sometimes seen her clay figures—humans and animals—and always they are modeled foreshortened in the same way as herself. She has a broad pretty face, large blue eyes, and wavy yellow hair that is rather coarse.

Puffs of hoary breath come out of the cat's pale pink mouth as he draws his spoke-whiskered lip back from his teeth and meows; he lifts and shakes his feet piteously above the rime on the pavement. Finally, she shovels him to her shoulder, turns, and makes her cumbersome way home.

14

What is it I am waiting for? What performance? The street is dull today. Scenes only repeat themselves.

The shadow over the triangle has swerved farther to the west with the sun's lower loll in the winter sky. The shadow, the clouds, the spine of the tree in front of my window—these are the only *live* characters in this passive, synthetic city play. Or, rather, this incessant rehearsal, ritualistic and hurried, this habitual crusade without visible destination. There is the monotonous march of traffic, the sun striking the panoplies of cars, the rub of their myriad wheels over the street, the clanking groan of subway cars below ground, the drill of airplane engines crossing overhead. Bricks and cobbles, the metal lamp poles and hydrants, manhole covers, pavement subway grills, ash cans, iron railings, fire escapes, television crosses that form whole forests of painfully gleaming steel upon the flat tops of buildings—all are part of this hectic yet static dance of the inanimate, which continues despite all weathers, despite seasons.

The scene is constantly moving—or, rather, being moved—for the city does not grow, change, and expand from *within,* as does natural life; it is inorganic, soulless. As seem the people in the street. And why is this? Is it simply from their association with their hard, bright vehicles and their hard, boxlike dwellings? Is it because their actual shapes, the sinuousness of their bodies, are camouflaged by clothes of chemical texture that imitate the stiffness, angularity, and shininess of their machines and furnishings?

The flag, when it is undulating in the wind—I will name it a fourth person, along with the shadow, the cloud, and the little tree. But the flag is not there today. Whoever raises it must go by the weather report instead of the weather. Cloth (if it is cotton from the growing boll or silk from the moving worm) still keeps the properties of life. Is this why the flag keeps its animal grace?

The clouds are torsos in the smoky blue above jagged roofs, their lower bodies obscured in haze from the chimneys. They expand and metamorphose; they are blessedly unpredictable. A jetplane, a rigid shuttlecock, is now thrusting between the clouds, and another and still another follows; the undeviating drill of their engines amplifies, is sustained on, a single megalomanic note. The sun's shafts cannot melt them. They fly on, straight into the Gorgon's eye. And this is frightening. Now, they are black streaks penetrating the clouds, contaminating them, like nails in whipped cream.

The old dull red of one of the narrow houses on Waverly Place, with its sooty stoop and the flower boxes on its sills that, in summer, drip the blue trumpets of morning glories, is darkening now as the shadow of the opposite building mounts the brick front. In their aging, those mottled bricks are achieving the patina of rubbed velvet. Almost, the little house—which must have sagging floors inside, which has a mossy hidden garden at its back—is coming alive. As the clouds, the ascetic Ginkgo tree, and the breathing shadows are alive. During its soft, unnoticed hundred-year inertia a soul has crept into it, the soul of natural decay.

The beer truck, yellow and grand as a circus wagon, stands as usual beside the grocery store. If only, when its back doors swing open, lions would leap out!

15

And here I am, still in my box over the bleak opera of the city, waiting for a drama that never begins. It is January already. Christmas is over. I remember how the windows, with their wreaths and baubles, their miniature Christmas trees stippled with colored electric teats, shone garishly and inappropriately above a drab, iron-floored stage by day, a black, wind-invaded stage by night. Then the trees were stripped and evicted from warm living rooms into the gutters, where they lay flinching under the wind's punishment until the children set fire to them, and, briefly, they were brilliant again in a wild banshee dance of cremation.

Now the square has returned to gray. The street is almost empty this morning. Sky, the flats of buildings, the cobbled stage, are alike—gray and bare. It is dirty and cold out there. There is nothing going on, except the frost cobwebbing the air.

16

Why have I expected a drama, a circus on this granite, this inorganic scene? The metal bodies of vehicles are hard to make into animals. I have made the street into rhinoceros hide, the flag into a horse's head, the little boys into tumbling bears, the traffic light into a mouth or an eye, the gas pumps, the lamp posts, the bus sign, the fire hydrant, the trash basket, the benches in the triangular square, into persons. Why? When there are real people constantly passing below my window? Perhaps because I do not know *them,* and I do know these objects, which stay in their places and which, for my eyes, have acquired the individuality of friends.

The Ginkgo tree, in his iron jacket, rooted in a square foot of earth below my window, betrayed me when he gave away his last leaf; like a carp's skeleton he now sticks upright there in the cold. The sparrows who used to cluster on his limbs like plums have been plucked away by winter. The dogs who choke against their leashes in the street are all captive toys of their slow owners. I look for life and movement that is not mechanical and wish for the sun to strike through its gray bandages, so that the shadow of the building, at least, will move, will deepen, flow, and shift. Meanwhile, the languid smoke of a chimney on a factory roof becomes my symbol of nature, of gracefulness and change.

17

Something astonishing has happened in the night!

I only wish I had got up earlier, to be in my seat when the act began—or, should I say, just as it finished? Had I been warned and awakened, I could have run down the stairs at dawn and, with *my* feet, made the first marks, before a single black wheel track could scar that fleecy floor. There would have been a crisp, browsing sound with every step as I moved across the first triangle on that wide, thick, unblemished rug. I would have been the first to smell the new air, the breath of clouds and mountain tops, brought at such a time to the city.

For the stage has been turned into a soft, opulent interior. Under a ceiling of dark slate the furnishings are padded, pillowed, and flounced with rich cashmere. The cars, huddled at the curb along Waverly and Charles, are fat white hassocks. The gas station looks grandly upholstered under its puffed roof, and the man-and-wife pumps in front of it are tall in high, pure-white top hats. The pate of the flagpole has been given a white toupee, its pedestal is piled with down, and no one yet has sat upon those perfect cushions that inflate the two benches there.

The sills and copings of all the buildings are lined with plush; the stoops, the steps of fire escapes, every roof and chimney edge, is coated with the same clean and frail yet thick, cozy material. Water towers on the roofs are peaked pavilions, and each hydrant, mailbox, lamp post wears a plump and tasseled cap of white. The awning at the entrance of the gray ugly building (backdrop to the stage) has a sleek fluffy hump, an elephant blanket glistening with sequins.

In every joint of the Ginkgo, in front of my window, is a tuft like lamb's hair, its branches weighted with luxurious wool, and the iron harness that it wears around its trunk is new, as if of white ribbons.

Oh, furry world, I take you back again! Your noise hushed by a vast softness and whiteness, your sooty stone hidden under this new growth that is like the blond grass of clouds! Your sharp metal, your cruel angles and fissures, your stern verticals now soothed and rounded, tenderly repaired and covered with the fresh and beautiful skin of winter!

Here come the children bouncing out of school at noon, throwing themselves onto the triangle as if it were a great deep bed. They tromp and roll in feathers there, seize handfuls from the cushions, sculpture "angels" with their bodies pressed into the soft hills of the benches and onto the piled table around the pole. Dogs, in their colored suits, are mad with excitement and make their masters slip and fall, as they surge in circles on their leashes. A spotted Dalmatian (I know him—he belongs to a neighbor and has one amber and one blue eye) has got free, and with his back doubled like a greyhound, is racing up the white corridor of Waverly, a dust of snow swirling behind him.

Then what will be the scene tomorrow? Surely this new world cannot last. By then this spaciousness will be divided, trampled, darkened, the one perfect performance over. Is this the Act, and the only one? Those I have watched, were they its confused rehearsals? And now, when the Hero—oh, handsome whiteness—appears at last, does he do so in order to melt, to die, before me?

No, all the stages are the acts, their properties the actors. The scene, the scene—whatever its costume—is the act. The Hero in white, is the Hero in gray, is the Actor.

II
On Poets and Poetry

A Poem Happens to Me

I do not know why I write poems or what makes me write them. Often, when I want *to write a poem,* I cannot—or, if I stubbornly sit down and write something anyway, I discover sooner or later that it is *not* a poem. I suspect this may be because, by concerning oneself with making a poem, one is so conscious of going through the correct motions of doing so, that the spirit of the creation refuses to enter the hard, premeditated clay, and, when it is finished, all the physical parts may have been admirably fashioned, but no passion is there to animate the figure.

It does not breathe.

It is like making a wonderful violin complete in every way, except that one can't get music from it.

On the other hand, it sometimes happens that I am unwilling to write the poem but that it forces itself from me without permission. A poem that happens in this way will often be inexplicable to myself, as to source, content, or significance. Months later, or years later, such a poem may "dawn on me," and I know for the first time what it is I have written. Sometimes I agree with my own observation, and sometimes I think it absurd.

These detached instances of creation seem not to be mystic, trancelike, or extrasensory—I think they are common to most artists in whatever medium.

In reviewing some of my past work, particularly my early work, I have been surprised to find that some juvenile bit of philosophy—sometimes venturing on the prophetic—some statement or observation that I, at the time, could not possibly have arrived at through experience, has turned out to be an

---

From May Swenson Papers, Washington University Libraries. This unpublished work was probably written in the mid-1950s.

apt commentary on events or states of mind that I am experiencing today or which have since been corroborated by first-hand knowledge.

For instance, one of my first poems, called "Plea for Delicacy in Love" dealt with the psychic play between man and woman in a coital embrace—being chiefly the attitude of the woman in contrast to that of the man. At that time I had had no sexual experience and was slightly, though probably erroneously posted on the literary information available on such a subject. But years later my personal experiences exactly bore out the philosophy of the poem—and I was quite aghast upon reading it the other day, wondering how the devil I knew all that then!

As I said, the full portent of a poem is not always evident to the writer himself, either while writing or after the poem is done. And it may be years, or never, before he arrives at an understanding of his own work.

Then, too, it is my frequent experience to start writing one poem and find, upon its completion, that I have written another—maybe entirely at variance or even diametrically opposite to what I set out to say. This always gives me a vague feeling of guilt—and I deplore such absence of integrity of purpose. Yet these inverted poems often turn out quite good, and, though the hens' eggs sometimes hatch goslings, perhaps one fowl is as good as another.

The act of creation itself (and I believe most artists will be obliged to admit this) is a special experience. By this I mean that it is unlike any other experience. How unlike? So far, no poets have been very adequate in clarifying that point. As for psychology, or any other *science,* attempting to fathom omniscience, the idea (and frequent experiments only too well prove this) is, of course, naive, to say the least.

Yes, even terms, nomenclature, words, for this experience are lacking, adding another difficulty to the attempt at describing the creative act. That is why I have fixed upon the unsatisfactory term *omniscience.*

When I am seized by a poem that demands to be given voice—I might say, when I am obsessed by some spirit ("daemon," I believe D. H. Lawrence once called it) that demands a body of me, if I am alone so that there is no outside source of distraction, I grope for a pencil and paper and sit down. I say "grope" because physical actions seem more or less "reflexive," and the mind leads the body, but as if from behind glass. That is, I am closeted within my mind, and my body moves about obediently on the other side of that transparent door, quite efficiently but beyond my notice.

Then I become perfectly still, my eyes turned in one fixed direction.

Sometimes it is many minutes before the first words of the dictation come. When it comes, my hand, with the pencil, rises. Rises and begins to write—lightly and fleetly, pausing now and then as if to listen. On many occasions I remember relaying to my hand a mental aside, namely: Do not be abrupt; be careful or you will frighten away the fish! In the first moments anxiety poises the mind at very pinpoint of concentration to catch the thought—for the balance between obscured reception and perfect articulation is extremely precarious.

I feel my hand writing as if it were not part of me but a tool held and directed by my mind.

The dictation continues, by this time, consecutively and swiftly—for, like the opening of neuron synapses to the brain after partaking of liquor or a drug, the cortical ducts and nerve centers seem to open and become unimpeded so that thought transference achieves a high efficiency.

Sometimes, however, the unreeling of the content occurs in reverse, the last portion or conclusion of the poem revealing itself first and working backward to the beginning. Another common phenomenon is the appearance first of the climax, or purposive element in the work, whereupon the introduction and denouement branch out from the nuclear center to either side, until the theme completes itself.

After the main kernel, the nucleus, the lifestuff, has been translated—given form or body—the automatic quality of the translation may wear off, gradually, like ether. And again I return to the familiar jacket of my flesh. I relax.

The rest of the poem may then be born quite consciously, simply through a logical, workmanlike persistence.

A work that owes its realization to more or less automatic, or internecine, creation tends, once the motivation ceases, to be inflexible for further molding or revision, at least for some time. The matter-of-fact mind refuses to deal with the child of an alien upstart conception, and it is very seldom that the identical machinery of omniscience that produced the particular work in question can be reinduced. This imposes an unfortunate inevitability on the "dictational poem," whereas, the poem that occurs "scientifically"—that is, as a result of ordinary conscious logic and motivation—has the advantage that it remains malleable and can be chiseled and polished and thereby improved to an unrestricted degree.

After completing an automatic poem, it is quite useless now to read the poem and expect to know what one has written. It may be days before it has *cooled* enough to reveal its permanent shape and color.

Likewise, the mind, through which the birth has passed, must serve the double function of appraising its offspring, of judging it—and for a while it will be so distorted by birth and labor as to be undependable as a critic.

What artist has not, upon ejecting some new raw creature of the brain, looked down at the thing, in consternation and horror, and asked: What is it? Where did it come from? And what had *I* to do with it?

Similarly, as the act of creation itself (whether consciously instigated or whether the poem be *visited on the creator*) is a special experience. The physical and mental elation upon successful completion of a poem or any work of art is a thing quite outside, and if I may say so, superior to almost any other satisfaction.

The emotion takes the form of a deep and abundant sense of well-being and a feeling of liberation—something akin to the release of hormonal and adrenal juices after sexual satisfaction—a feeling of complete satiation and relaxation.

I once wrote (and this too, incidentally, was an observation made during the adolescence of my art):

> The Poet
> when he has made a thing to his liking
> dips from the same deep-spiced bowl
> and knows the same full content
> as that of a Lover
> on the morrow after he has lain sweetly
> with his beloved.

The experience might also be likened to that succeeding confession or self-abnegation before some mild, astringent priest—the all-compassionate conscience—the Self, itself. I am reminded of the remark of a friend, a writer, who said: "Writing is to me a confession, not a profession."

The consciousness of self-revelation and abnegation that enters into the aftereffects of expression give it the aspect of a psychic purge and a mental and spiritual purificant.

"Writing is like dying and being born again," says my friend. Yes, it is death and birth being brought to within a desperate circumferential hair's breadth of each other—as if two stars of opposite poles swept together and *almost* grazed! And the innocent witness and unwitting perpetrator of this near-collision returns to the plane of the Matter-of-Fact, to look about him with new and blinking eyes at a somehow grayed world.

On Richard Wilbur's "Love Calls Us to the Things of This World"

The modern lyric is autonomous, a separate mobile, having its own private design and performance. It may be little on the page yet project a long and versatile dance in the mind. Its total form and gesture is not a relative; it is an absolute, an enclosed construct. Some readers, opening the volume of a lyric poet, are apt to approach the poems sequentially, comparatively, considering them as an independent row of things in the box of the book—when, in fact, each poem is a package individually wrapped. I like to see the poem first as a shut box or package to be opened, within which is an invention whose particular working I hope to discover. Something can be felt about it even before beginning to read: its profile on the page, its regular or irregular pattern of stanzas, length of lines, their symmetry, its wide or thin shape, its look of bulk or lightness. For instance, before reading, I see that Richard Wilbur's poem is a squarish vertical, built of six stanzas, five lines each, running to thirty lines. Each stanza is indented, and there are dropped-line indentations within some stanzas. The lines show a regular rhythm pattern with an occasional eccentricity. I now read the opening line of the first and last stanza and find a four-beat line; I see that the title announces this beat. (Later I discover that five as well as four-beat iambics are used.) Glancing down the end words of the lines, I find no outer rhymes. I suppress attention to the content and quickly read through the poem for its sound alone. I want to determine the mainsprings of its music before releasing its images into consciousness. There are no deliberate

---

Originally published in *Berkeley Review* 1 (1957).

internal rhymes either, yet the poem has evident harmonic values: there are numerous assonances, alliterations, consonant matings, recurrent *ing* endings. The meter seems not to be one obviously selected and imposed; it is consistent in the overall, elastic in its parts; it rises, flows, expands, sinks; it has a billow or a bump now and then. It comes to a noticeable halt in the very center of the poem, at the middle of the last line of the third stanza. The movement of the top half is fluid and swift, that of the lower half slower, more dense—this is felt not only in the leap or walk of the meter but also in the vowels and consonants predominating (*i, e,* and *l,* for the most part, in the first half, and principally *u* and *k* in the latter half).

So far, the box has been opened and the mobile examined as a *still;* its top surfaces have been handled coolly. Any number of other poems could show the above superficial features but give a different performance when "turned on" in the mind. For me it is the images and their expansion into metaphor that constitute the main motion of a poem—for these awaken concrete associational responses and, while the sound must augment, in fact be inevitably welded to, the image, by itself sound is the more abstract feature, for me.

With the flow of the image into the mind, I give myself up to the magicianship of the poem, postponing analysis until later. I let myself be caught up, uncritically, and ride within the poem, to experience as intuitively as I can *its* experience, which I hope will be a fresh one. Wilbur's "Love Calls Us to the Things of This World" proves to be that. My reactions after a first reading are these: (1.) I enjoyed it. (2.) It was an exciting ride. (3.) There was something unique about it; at the same time, it felt familiar. Up to the middle, to the conclusion "That nobody seems to be there," it felt as if I had seen and recognized the very simile he has found: clean clothes, blowing on a line, are disembodied souls or angels. This partly because the incident is so common that everyone has seen it and partly because the analogy is so fitting in each of its details: a shirt is white, it is empty of body, but floats or flies, therefore has life (an angel). Wilbur here has brought an unconscious association of my own into light; this is a joyful shock, and it seems magical. But, were this all, it would be a "little" poem, exquisite, playful, nothing more. It might be dismissed with the thought, "I could have done it; I've had the same experience." The unique, and more mysterious, part of the poem is the lower half, where *he* reacts to his own metaphor, as an individual and as a representative of modern man. The philosophical content adds unexpected solidity and durability—so that my impulse is to read it again and, several times, to find out "what he is really saying." And, doing so, I find that I cannot reach a point of final decision as to whether he is saying "only *this*" or "underneath this, also *that*" and perhaps "underneath *that,* etc." This is what keeps the poem from being too quickly "grounded"—to land in the box of no-longer-played-with-toys. Since it gives a somewhat different performance each time it is set going in the mind, it stays alive.

Attempting to lift the layers of meaning, I see several sets of clues, all having to do with physical sensations. There are at least six, pertaining to Sound, Relative Tension, Shape, Color, Motion, and Relative Weight. The poem begins with the "cry of pulleys" as a line of wash is hoisted into the morning air. This *Sound* (1) opens the poem (and the eyes of the sleeper). Later "The soul shrinks . . . and *cries*" and later, the soul *says* "in a *changed voice . . .* " Similarly, contrasts of *Tension* (2) may be followed throughout the poem. Consider these words and their placement: *pulleys* (with its extra association of being pulled), hangs, shrinks, gallows; and then: calm swells, impersonal breathing, yawns. There are these allusions to *Shape* (3) or its absence: bodiless, angels, bedsheets, blouses, smocks, white water, steam, dances, world's hunks and colors, waking body, man, nuns' habits. *Color* clues (4): *White* is indicated or suggested for: soul, dawn, angels, water, steam, linen, pure. *Red* is suggested in: rape, rosy, warm look, love, waking body, ruddy gallows, swoon, nobody seems to be there, shrinks, *punct*ual (with its extra association of punched holes). *Black* is suggested in: bitter love, gallows, thieves, undone (with its double meaning), heaviest, dark habits, difficult. *Motion* clues (5): *Angels:* rising, swells, breathing, flying, conveying, speed, moving and staying, swoon down, quiet, dances. *Soul:* hangs, shrinks, descends, accept. *Steam:* rising. *Man:* rises. *Nuns:* walk in a pure floating. *Relative Weight* (6): bodiless clothes / souls, heaviest nuns.

The whole poem (in its material, structure, and expression) is in fact an epitome of relative weight and equipoise. As noted in regard to its rhythm, the imagistic action is also brought to a point, a pause at the very center, with the words "that nobody seems to be there." The lower half of the poem is made into a ground, a base of thought (*re*action) for the emotion that is unfurled in the upper half. There is a descent, a hardening, a graveness (the result of gravity!) in the last three stanzas. But then, with the sense, the sound, the image of the final two lines, "And (let) the *heaviest* nuns walk in a pure *floating* / Of dark habits, keeping their difficult balance" the ethereal is joined to the earthy (soul to body, imagination to reality) and *balance,* the significant concluding word, is revealed as the synthesis of the whole poem, simultaneously giving the clue to its meaning *and* its form.

A single large metaphor emerges from a series of exact observations, its separate features closely corresponding to the mundane event that takes place, the hanging of the wash. The "soul *hangs*"—and one of the bodiless "persons" on the line is Richard Wilbur. By an act of possession (the obverse of being possessed but just as useful for the seizing of poetic power) he becomes a part of his subject. He then experiences in each of its particulars the dramatic life of the row of souls in the air: he is one of the angels. He is one of the "hunks and colors" acknowledged by the sun; he "descends in bitter love to accept the waking body" of the man.

Taken at face value, the poem is direct and transparent. It seems to project a mood of primary exuberance, freedom, playfulness; air, space, clean forms, spontaneous motion are its atmosphere—a poem to free the muscles and freshen the mind—for so skilled without stiffness, so lighthearted without gaucherie, is Wilbur able to be. But it has the added weight of its somber accents. It is anchored and steadied by a guy of thought, just as is the line of flying clothes, so that it is "moving and staying" at the same time. There are ominous, painful, even violent suggestions in this fair and buoyant poem. They are not noticed at first, but they are what furnish its intricacy and constitute enough ambiguity so that its analysis cannot be exhausted. With his very first image he warns himself (and us) with the innocent/ugly word *hangs* that is resounded later in *ruddy gallows.* Hidden in the whiteness, the cleanliness of the angelic crowd, a *hanged soul,* a *false dawn.* There is at one extreme "the terrible speed of their *omnipresence*" and at the other "a swooning down into so rapt a quiet that *nobody* seems to be there." That there are thieves among the nuns, that they are heavy in their "dark habits" (with the double meanings of these two words), and the wish for only "clean dances done in the sight of heaven" may indicate other levels of meaning having to do, perhaps, with the poet's conscience, with doubt about his own equilibrium, with a questioning of his self-faith, or with criticism of a larger Faith. If I look to the title to name a single intention for the poem, I can arrive at several possible equations. Does "Love" that "calls us" equal the "angels" that cry us awake in the squeak of the pulleys? Do "The Things of This World" equal "the heaviest nuns" who in "dark habits" must keep "their difficult balance"? Are the (pure) "things of *this* world" presented here as opposed to a false, a hypocritical, even cruel "heaven"? I would as soon be content with the unparadoxical first-thought meaning that, with the insights of love, we see deepest beauties and miracles in the simplest things "of this world"—our daily lives.

Something more—much more—could and should be said about Wilbur's sonic devices, which are integral to his imagery and magnify the charm of the poem. A full analysis would consume more space than I am allotted, but, if I now read the piece aloud, chief emphases seem to ring out, in the first half, from words containing the vowel sounds *i, e,* and *a.* If my count is correct, there are, respectively, seven, six, and seven such words. Alliteratively, as well as within words, the *l* sound occurs fourteen times. A delightful fusion of music, movement, image, and emotion is seen, for instance, in the lines: "Now they are rising together in calm swells / Of halcyon feeling, filling whatever they wear / With the deep joy of their impersonal breathing." In the second half of the poem *u* is the most emphatic vowel sound, occurring, as I count it, twelve times, and the *k* sound is the ruling consonant, beginning, or included in, sixteen words. Example: "Yet as the sun acknowledges / With a warm look the world's hunks and colors." The lower part of the poem takes on a darker, harder cast for me, partly because of this, while the upper poem is higher pitched, lighter, more fluid. The response to sound in a poem is so subjective that it has not as much value for analysis as does image. For instance, the *a* tone conveys mystery for me (probably from association with the word *awe*); the *u* sound repeated suggests bluntness, heaviness mixed with fear. Curiously, in stanza 3 the sequence of the words *place, conveying,* and *staying,* because of the vowel sound *a,* suggests intense whiteness, even apart from the image. While confirming my other theories about Wilbur's poem, these sonic impressions I believe to be too personal to carry any but secondary importance for the interpretation of content, although they sharpen my total appreciation.

A Matter of Diction

The last time I met Marianne Moore was the first time I really *met* her—met her sitting down, and face to face, I mean—with the privilege, it seemed, of asking any question and getting a personal answer.

It was at J. Laughlin's house in the Village in the spring of this, her seventy-seventh Birthday Year. She sat in a deep chair near the fireplace, wearing one of her famous black three-cornered hats—this one with a small brim. She had on a blue spring suit—primary blue, the blue of a zoo balloon—which matched her eyes and set off her buttermilk skin. Her long-boned hand, with a green ring, held the china cup in which a wheel of lemon rocked in orange pekoe. I had on a red suit and sat on the floor, by her knees.

On the other side of a small table to her right sat Vernon Watkins, lean, ruddy faced, blue-eyed too, with bright gray hair. (Miss Moore's hair, which used to be Irish red, is blanched like the fleece of a fall dandelion now.) The few other guests were silhouettes against the open-shuttered windows. The day was misty, but jonquils on the mantel and by the window suffused the wide-boarded, rather bare room with a yellow like strong sunlight.

Moore and Watkins were in conversation about mutual friends in England and Wales. I failed to keep track of what they said, I was so absorbed in comparing the differing inflections of their voices chiming and tangling together.

Marianne Moore enjoys talking. I am awkward at it and would rather listen. I sat down by her knees the better to overhear her but also to be close to her and satisfy my greed to look

---

Originally published in Tambimuttu, ed., *Festschrift for Marianne Moore's Seventy Seventh Birthday by Various Hands* (Tambimuttu and Mass, 1964).

at her. Perhaps the right question would occur to me. I was unprepared to answer any myself, and made a botch of that when, with curiosity, she turned to me. I did finally manage to ask her what she thought about the astronauts. I meant: What about the monstrous and marvelous prospect of man making it to the moon and maybe to other planets? But she interpreted me in another way and said: "Well, I like John Glenn. Isn't it terrible that he slipped in the bathtub?"

When I wanted to rise I found a garter had come undone on my stocking. Having got down like a cat, I had to get up like a heifer—while holding down my skirt-hem with one hand, I tried with the other to keep my cup from skidding off its saucer. I learned that the posture of idolatry may lead to dis-grace.

Marianne Moore's poetry is uniquely unself-conscious and unself-centered. Who of us is able to be such an acute instrument for the objectification of sensual perceptions and states of mind as she, without emphasizing *self* as a subject? There is neither self-pity nor self-aggrandizement in her poems. Where a capital *I* begins an observation, it is never to say, using the excuse of being a poet: "See how *I* have loved, or suffered. . . . See what *I* have discovered." It is rather to present, often in the plainest terms, a wisdom, a conviction, a piece of advice that has a general application. She dares to do this in the midst of language often as incredibly opulent—and this to a purpose—as the peacock's tail.

In "Voracities and Verities Sometimes Are Interacting" she says:

> I don't like diamonds;
> the emerald's "grass-lamp glow" is better;
> and unobtrusiveness is dazzling . . .

And in "Critics and Connoisseurs":

> There is a great amount of poetry in unconscious
> fastidiousness . . .

In "Armour's Undermining Modesty":

> Arise, for it is day.
> Even gifted scholars lose their way
> through faulty etymology.
> No wonder we hate poetry,

and stars and harps and the new moon. If tributes
cannot be implicit,
give me diatribes and the fragrance of iodine . . .

Here we see her underlying attitudes: modesty, matter-of-factness, but combined with an individual conviction that is monarchial. It is on such ribs that her extensive, audacious, hypnotic peacock display of language is supported. She continues to teach us that poetry is not constructed with ideas or sensations or revelations or passions, though these are its seductive spots and glitters, but that instead it depends on a strong, limber, complex, organic trellis of technique—in short, its is made with *language.* As she herself has said in one of her essays: "it is a matter of diction, of diction that is virile because galvanized against inertia."

Even such a poem as "What Are Years?"—a pure polemic, if you like, or moral precept—(it could be a psalm, and it is an exhortation; I would put it equal to anything in the Bible as a soul healer and a soul strengthener)—owes its power to operate upon our heart muscle and our brain stem to the concentrated and emphatic interplay of a few sounds—specifically to the use of the consonants, *s, t,* and *r.* Witness the final stanza:

	S	*T*	*R*	*Letters*
So he who *str*ongly feels,	3	1	1	20
behaves. *T*he ve*r*y bi*r*d,	1	1	2	18
g*r*own *t*aller a*s* he *s*ing*s*, *st*eels	5	2	2	26
his fo*r*m *str*aigh*t* up. *T*hough he is cap*t*ive,	3	4	2	34
his migh*t*y singing	2	1	—	16
says, sa*t*isfaction i*s* a lowly	5	2	—	24
*t*hing, how pu*r*e a *t*hing is joy.	1	2	1	23
*T*his is mo*rt*ali*t*y,	2	3	1	15
*t*his is e*t*erni*t*y.	2	3	1	14
	24	19	10	190

If we count the total occurrences of the letters *s, t,* and *r* in this one stanza, three letters account for 53 usages out of a total of 190. If we count the remainder of the letters used, we find that only in the case of the vowels *e* and *i* do we get a quantity comparable to that of the three consonants *s, t,* and *r.* Remembering that vowels are the liquid in the soup of language, while consonants, although proportionately more numerous in our alphabet, are generally scantier per word (or spoonful), then this proportion of three particular consonants thickening the mixture makes a concentrated dish indeed. A daring dish, an amazingly artful one, which yet tastes absolutely natural and is *nourishing.* We have little inkling of how much protein there's in it until we analyze the syntactical elements. Nor do we need to do so to get the good out of it palate wise as well as digestively. *What* it says feeds us—and, if we look to know *how,* that is an extra delectation. Not only the right words, sense wise, but their right composition, tongue-and-tooth-wise (sound and texture), is what we find when the recipe is analyzed.

In the whole poem, "What Are Years?" which comprises three short stanzas (nine lines each), the *connotative* words that employ the letters *s, t,* and *r,* total, amazingly, 49. All other words of the poem total 74, of which many are inherently inactive words or connectives such as *the, and, a, that, what,* etc. Going at it another, and simpler, way: in the whole poem there are 49 connotative words that employ *s, t,* or *r.* There are only 11 connotatives that do not. Eight of those significant active words contain all three consonants: r*esolu*t*e, mis*f*o*rt*une,* st*i*r*s,* str*ong, imp*r *is*o*nment,* str*uggling,* st*rongly* str*aight*—and four of them present the three sinewy predominants together in their order of magnitude. Indeed, S*he* "Digesteth Harde Yron."

I believe that here is a case of "unconscious fastidiousness." Certainly, Miss Moore did not concoct the recipe and then cook the soup. She went by taste. And, finding that the flavor improved with more and more of the same three herbs, she simply relied upon consistency. It is I who have extracted the formula *after* the invention. Nor could it be reapplied in writing another poem, even by Moore herself. The hypotheses follow the experiments in her case.

We've all been given courage by her beautiful daring, her abundance, her naturalness that is as cunning, various, and splendid as Nature's own. And her moral responsibility. She is a rascal and a revolutionary of form, of aesthetics. She is an uncompromising idealist as to content, to truth. Especially we *women poets,* as we are called, are grateful and lucky in possessing the grand and indelible example of her work and of her life. She is inimitable because she devises her own contests, makes her own rules, and, at the point least expected, disconcertingly reverses them, so as to demonstrate that "it is not the acquisition of any one thing that is able to adorn." As for "women poets," our deviation into creative rather than procreative tracks is grudgingly sanctioned these days but on a carefully segregated basis. Our poetry is "credited" with "special feminine sensibilities," etc., and critical comparisons are made with the "equal (perhaps) but separate" assumption as a base. Is there a distinction as fixed as pigmentation between the intellect and the imagination of male and female poets? Does each depend upon some different Hormonal Muse? Perhaps this is what I wanted to ask Miss Moore's opinion on. But then her poetry itself annihilates the debate. Note her oblique allusion to the issue in "Sojourn in the Whale," in which the reference is to a male England and a female Ireland:

> Trying to open locked doors with a sword, threading
> the points of needles, planting shade trees
> upside down; swallowed by the opaqueness of one
> whom the seas
> love better than they love you, Ireland—
>
> you have lived and lived on every kind of shortage.
> You have been compelled by hags to spin
> gold thread from straw and have heard men say:
> "There is a feminine
> temperament in direct contrast to
>
> ours which makes her do these things. Circumscribed by a
> heritage of blindness and native
> incompetence, she will become wise and will be forced
> to give
> in. Compelled by experience, she
>
> will turn back; water seeks its own level": and you
> have smiled. "Water in motion is far
> from level." You have seen it, when obstacles happened
> to bar
> the path, rise automatically.

Imbedded here, by the way, is Marianne Moore's inner self-portrait. We are provided, besides, with a precise example, metaphorically and technically, of "diction that is virile because galvanized against inertia."

The Poet as Antispecialist

What is the experience of poetry? Choosing to analyze this experience for myself after an engrossment of many years, I see it based in a craving to get through the curtains of things as they *appear* to things as they *are* and then into the larger, wilder space of things as they *are becoming*. This ambition involves a paradox: an instinctive belief in the senses as exquisite tools for this investigation and, at the same time, a suspicion about their crudeness. They may furnish easy deceptions or partial distortions:

> Hold a dandelion and look at the sun.
> Two spheres are side by side.
> Each has a yellow ruff.
>
> Eye, you tell a lie,
> that Near is Large, that Far is small.
> There must be other deceits . . .

W. B. Yeats called poetry "the thinking of the body" and said: "It bids us touch and taste and hear and see the world, and shrinks from . . . every abstract thing, from all that is of the brain only—from all that is not a fountain jetting from the entire hopes, memories, and sensations of the body." But sometimes one gets the inkling that there are extra senses as yet nameless, within the apperceptive system, if one could only differentiate them and identify their organs.

Not to be fully aroused to the potentialities of one's senses means to walk the flat ground of appearances, to take given designations for granted, to accept without a second look the name or category of a thing for the thing itself. On that ground

Originally published in *Saturday Review,* January 30, 1965.

all feelings and notions are borrowed, are secondhand. The poetic experience, by contrast, is one of constant curiosity, skepticism, and testing—astonishment, disillusionment, renewed discovery, reillumination. It amounts to a virtual compulsion to probe with the senses into the complex actuality of all things, outside and inside the self, and to determine relationships between them.

Aroused to the potentialities and delights of the senses and the evaluating intellect, and using them daily, the poet, however, comes eventually to their limits and notices that their findings are not enough—that they often fall short of yielding the total, all-comprehensive pattern that he seeks. A complete and firm apprehension of the Whole tantalizingly eludes him—although he receives mirages of it now and then that he projects into his work. He is not so separate from every man as not to be fooled by tricks of perspective, seduced by the obvious, or bogged down in old and comfortable myths.

The limitations of our minds and sensory equipment partly stem from the brevity of our physical lives. Stendhal somewhere says that man is like a fly born in the summer morning and dead by afternoon. How can he understand the word *night?* If he were allowed five more hours, he would see and understand what night is. But, unlike the fly, man is sorely conscious of the vastness of the unknown beyond his consciousness. The poet, tracing the edge of a great shadow whose outline shifts and varies, proving there is an invisible moving source of light behind, hopes (naively, in view of his ephemerality) to reach and touch the foot of that solid what-ever-it-is that casts the shadow. If sometimes it seems he does touch it, it is only to be faced with a more distant, even less accessible mystery. Because all is movement—expansion or contraction, rotation or revolution—all is breathing change.

The experience of poetry is to suppose that there is a moon of the psyche, let us say, whose illuminated half is familiar to our ordinary eye but which has another hemisphere that is dark. And that poetry can discover this other side, its thrust can take us toward it. Poetry is used to make maps of that globe, which to the "naked eye" appears disclike and one-dimensional, seems to "rise" and "set" rather than to orbit; which remains distant and merely a "dead" object until, in the vehicle of poetry and with the speed of poetic light, we approach it. It then enlarges and reveals its surprising topography, becomes a world. And passing around it, our senses undergo dilation; there is a transformation of perception by means of this realization of the round.

Miniature as we are in the gigantic body of the cosmos, we have somehow an inbuilt craving to get our pincers of perception around the whole of it, to incorporate infinitude and set up comprehensible models of it within our little minds. Poetry tries to do this in its fashion. Science tries it, and more demonstrably. The impulses of the scientist and the poet, it seems to me, are parallel, although their instruments, methods, and effects are quite divergent. Contrasts between science and poetry are easily illustrated by such apparent opposites as: objective/subjective, reason/intuition, fact/essence—or let me boldly say: material/spiritual. A point of contiguity between them, however, is that poet and scientist both use language to communicate their findings.

As a rule, the scientific investigator works as one of a team. He works with formulas or with objective facts that are classified and reported as nakedly as possible so as to convey, in each instance, a single, specific, unambiguous meaning. The poet works alone, handling concrete sensual particulars, as well as their invisible and intangible essences, with the tools of intuitive perception; he then presents his discoveries wrapped in metaphor, metrical patterns, and, often, multifarious symbols. The scientist has an actual moon under observation—one he soon hopes to have under manipulation—although no robot or human explorer has yet succeeded in getting to it. "Until one does," I read not long ago, "scientists cannot tell whether the lunar surface is packed hard, porous, or buried deep in dust." And, "because of fuel limitations of the rockets that will orbit the moon and lower a ferryboat to the lunar surface, moon landings must be held within five degrees north and south of the moon's equator and within forty-five degrees east and west of the moon's central meridian. Within this narrow zone of safety, flat lands must be found to receive the spaceships from earth."

My moon is not in the sky but within my psyche. More or less subliminal, it orbits within the psyche of every man, a symbol both of the always-known and the never-to-be-known. I do not try to land on that moon. To do so would be to choose lunacy.

But in 1958 I wrote a poem called "Landing on the Moon," which outlines, in its first three stanzas, a capsule history of the moon's psychic pull on man since primitive times to the present. The two concluding stanzas speculate about whether it is well for man to succumb, literally, to that hypnotism and let himself be drawn up onto the moon:

> When in the mask of night there shone that cut,
> we were riddled. A probe reached down
> and stroked some nerve in us,
> the glint of a wizard's eye, of silver,
> slanted out of the mask of the unknown—
> pit of riddles, the scratch-marked sky.
>
> When, albino bowl on cloth of jet,
> it spilled its virile rays,
> our eyes enlarged, our blood reared with the waves.
> We craved its secret, but unreachable
> it held away from us, chilly and frail.
> Distance kept it magnate. Enigma made it white.
>
> When we learned to read it with our rod,
> reflected light revealed
> a lead mirror, a bruised shield
> seamed with scars and shadow-soiled.
> A half-faced sycophant, its glitter borrowed,
> rode around our throne.
>
> On the moon there shines earth light
> as moonlight shines upon the earth . . .
> If on its obsidian we set our weightless foot,
> and sniff no wind, and lick no rain
> and feel no gauze between us and the Fire,
> will we trot its grassless skull, sick for the homelike shade?
>
> Naked to the earth-beam we will be,
> who have arrived to map an apparition,
> who walk upon the forehead of a myth.
> Can flesh rub with symbol? If our ball
> be iron, and not light, our earliest wish
> eclipses. Dare we land upon a dream?

Psychologically, then physically, what will happen to man made to mount the moon? The moon being his first wobbling step in a march to the stars? Either extinction or mutation? In an eon or two will he have become a rocket and a robot combined? Maybe. Yet, whether it is well for him or not, I think man will probably colonize the moon, eventually infiltrate the solar system, and go beyond. It may be his destiny. But he may have to pay for it with a transformation amounting to an evolutionary replacement of his species by some other creature-thing, *Homo mechanicus.*

I confess to being envious, in a way, of the astronaut. Though only in my imagination, where I can make him hero and lone adventurer. What an array of absolutely new sensations is handed him, like a Christmas paintbox; what an incomparable toy, his capsule with its console of magic dials, gauges, buttons, and signal lights; and what a knight in shining plastic he is in his silver suit. To escape the earth-ball, its tug, and one's own heaviness! To dare the great vacuum and, weightless, be tossed—a moon oneself—around the great roulette wheel with the planets! But, in actuality, could I bear that claustrophobia in a steel womb, attached to that formidable placenta by a synthetic umbilical, dependent on a mechanical nipple for my breath of air?

In space there is so little space. And who but a preconditioned, tranquilized, de-nerved, desensualized, automatically responding "test subject" could stand for long that swaddling as in a rigid iron lung? Not only freedom of movement and of action but freedom to think an aberrant thought or do an individual impulsive deed must be forfeited, it seems to me. Hooked to the indispensable members of his team by the paraphernalia of intercommunication, the astronaut, I imagine, must learn to forget what solitude, what privacy, tastes like. His very heartbeat becomes public, his body and brain an encephalograph, a fluoroscope, a radio, a video screen. First trained to become a piece of equipment; next, perhaps, born so. (Sometimes I long to remember my life as a cephalopod under the sea and cannot.)

But let me go back to a consideration of the poetic method and its effects, compared to the scientific.

For the poet self is a universe, and he is embarked on a conquest of inner space. From the outside, in this accelerated age, our consciousness is being bombarded with the effects of rapid change and upheaval. It's as if we could see the earth shift and change while we walk on it. Familiar space and time have hooked together, and we have spacetime. Matter has split into uncountable explosive bits and become energy. On the one hand—and virtually with the same engine—man prepares to fly to the stars, while on the other he seems intent on annihilating himself along with his sole perch in the universe. There is the temptation sometimes to stuff up the "doors of perception" and regress to that long-ago world that was flat—that was static and secure, since it rested immovably on the back of a turtle! Because the poet's pre-creative condition must be an emptiness, a solitude, a stillness close to inertia. It is a condition of alert passivity, with blankness behind and before him, while he is centered within the present moment, expectant only of the vividness to come, slowly or suddenly, with the combustion of sensations and impressions gathered and stored beforehand from his active life.

The method is the opposite of analytic industry spurred by communal effort (teamwork) proceeding according to prearranged outline, operating upon the material from the outside. Rather than grasping it a piece at a time, construction wise, the poet seats himself within his subject, at its axis, so that, equidistant from all points of its circumference, he can apprehend its potential form as an immediate whole. This is the organic technique, allowing the growth from within, from the initial seeds of attention, until, as Rilke puts it, "All space becomes a fruit around those kernels." I speak here of poetry in its conception; obviously, there is an industrious and conscious work of building to be done before the body of a poem is complete.

Science and poetry are alike, or allied, it seems to me, in their largest and main target—to investigate any and all phenomena of existence beyond the flat surface of appearances. The products as well as the methods of these two processes are very different—not in their relative value but in the particular uses that they have for their "consumers." Each has a separate role and concern toward the expansion of human consciousness and experience. Poetry has a psychic use. Along with the other arts it is a depository for, and a dispenser of, such psychic realizations as wonder, beauty, surprise, joy, awe, revelation—and, as well, fear, disgust, perplexity, anxiety, pain, despair. It provides an input and an outlet for all the complex, powerful, fleeting grains and rays of sensation in the human organism. It is a quickener of experience, and it renews the archetypes and icons necessary to the human spirit, by means of which personality is nurtured and formed.

"The world is poetical intrinsically," Aldous Huxley has written, "and what it means is simply itself. Its significance is the enormous mystery of its existence and of our awareness of its existence." Who or what are we? Why are we? And what are we becoming? What is the relationship between man and the universe? Those are questions that ached in the mind of the first poet. They can be said to have created the first poet and to be the first source of the art of poetry. Does the fact of our consciousness, unique and seemingly miraculous among all of nature's creatures, a priori indicate a superconsciousness shaping and manipulating the cosmos?

How is it that with our minds we can explore our own minds? And can we develop a technique to explore Mind—that aspect of the universe we might postulate exists in addition to its mere structural organization? Maybe such a Mind is not yet in existence but in process; maybe our nervous systems and cortexes are early evidence of its future evolution. As Huxley reports in *Literature and Science,* psychologists know a great deal, but as yet they "have no recognized hypothesis to account for the apparent interaction of mind and matter in a simple act of consciousness." Nor is there even a firm hypothesis to explain the operation of memory. But atomic physics (the most exact of the sciences) is uncovering a factual foundation for many intuitions of existentialist poets and philosophers. According to a statement by physicist Werner Heisenberg, cited by Huxley, for the first time in the history of the planet man approaches a willingness to admit that he is alone with himself "without a partner and without an adversary." This I believe to be an intuitive hunch, not only of the poet or philosopher but of every thinking man when in moments of extremity he is forced face to face with his own soul. Huxley puts it that "man is in process of becoming his own Providence, his own Cataclysm, his own Saviour and his own invading horde of Martians." And he adds: "In the realm of pure science the same discovery—that he is alone with himself—awaits him as he progressively refines his analysis of matter." Modern science, according to Heisenberg,

> shows us that we can no longer regard the building blocks of matter, which were considered originally to be the ultimate objective reality, as being things-in-themselves. . . . Knowledge of atoms and their movements in themselves—that is to say, *independent of our observation*—is no longer the aim of research; rather we now find ourselves from the very start in the midst of a dialogue between nature and man, a dialogue of which science is only one part, so much so that the conventional division of the world into subject and object, into inner world and outer world, into body and soul, is no longer applicable and raises difficulties, For the sciences of nature, the subject matter of research is no longer nature in itself, but nature subjected to human questioning, and to this extent man, once again, meets only with himself.

From reflection on a statement such as this one can almost reach the spooky conclusion that all we conceive as objective, and under examination by our sensorial and intellectual equipment, is really subjective and a projection of our own heads!

In 1665, or thereabouts, the American poet Edward Taylor wrote a remarkable poem trying to penetrate into the origin of the universe. A portion of it reads as follows:

> Infinity, when all things it beheld,
> In Nothing, and of Nothing all did build,
> Upon what Base was fixt the Lath, wherein
> He turn'd this Globe, and riggalld it so trim?
> Who blew the Bellows of his Furnace Vast?
> Or held the Mould wherein the world was Cast?
> Who laid its Corner Stone? Or whose Command?
> Where stand the Pillars upon which it stands?
> Who Lac'de and Fillitted the earth so fine,
> With Rivers like Green Ribbons Smaragdine?
> Who made the Sea's its selvedge, and it locks
> Like a Quilt Ball within a Silver Box?
> Who Spread its Canopy? Or Curtains Spun?
> Who in this Bowling Alley bowld the Sun?
>
> Who? who did this? or who is he? Why, know
> It's Onely Might Almighty this did doe.

It's interesting that Edward Taylor should have made Infinity, that great abstraction, the protagonist of his poem, even though he refers to it as "he," and his expression, "It's Onely Might

Almighty this did doe,"—*i.e.,* Energy—sounds like an intuition prefiguring a finding of modern science rather than reflecting (as he no doubt consciously intended) a God-centered metaphysics of the seventeenth century.

The poet's universe had better be centered within the present; it had better not install itself (and stall itself) in anachronisms either conceptual or expressionistic. Because the poet, I believe, should be in the vanguard of his time. He can, in his unique way, be a synthesizer and synchronizer of the many components and elements of a great new pattern emergent in the investigations of biologists, psychologists, anthropologists, astronomers, physicists, et al. The poet's material has always been nature—human and otherwise—all objects and aspects of our outer environment as well as the "climate of the soul" and the "theater of the emotions." The poet is the great antispecialist. Still possible in our overorganized, compartmentalized culture, and still needed, is the work and the play of the artist. As a free-floating agent, medium and conduit, a kind of "divining rod"—he may pass anywhere—over, into, around, or through the multifold fabric of experience and present the results of his singular discoveries and delights to fellow searchers, fellow beholders.

The play of the artist is psychologically very important. As the philosopher Huizinga has written in *Homo Ludens:* "in acknowledging play you acknowledge mind, for whatever else play is, it is not matter. Even in the animal world it bursts the bounds of the physically existent. From the point of view of a world wholly determined by the operation of blind forces, play would be altogether superfluous. Play only becomes possible, thinkable and understandable when an influx of mind breaks down the absolute determinism of the cosmos."

I said earlier that a point of contiguity between the poet and the scientist is that both employ language to communicate what they find. At this point there is also a crucial departure, for language is not only a tool in poetry; it is its very being. In a poem, Subject is not presented by means of language, but Language is the thing presented with the aid of subject. Being merely instrumental, a scientific exposition can be restated in various ways without a loss of end effect; when new facts render its message obsolete, such expositions are replaced and forgotten. But tamper with, or reconstruct, the tissue of a poem and you deal death to its cells and molecules. The poet reaches for a vision of reality that is whole, seamless, and undivided; if he succeeds in that, his product need not suffer obsolescence. True art combines the properties of change and endurance.

What is it in poetry, beyond subject, beyond what is being said, that is given? The management of language for the poem must be such as to capture and fix the essence of the immediate experience—the sensation, illumination, extra dimension—that the poet felt when the impulse for the poem (the emotion or psychic mental discovery that engendered it) fell upon him. It must be such that the receiver of the poem recapitulates, as it were physically, the same illumination because it relates to or fuses with a vision within himself, dormant and dark until the moment the beam of the poem strikes into him. In the handling of his material, which is language, metaphor is to the poet what the equation is to the mathematician.

In one of his essays on art, published as long ago as 1919, Ezra Pound said:

> We might come to believe that the thing that matters in art is a sort of energy, something more or less like electricity or radioactivity, a force transfusing, welding, and unifying. . . . The thing that counts is Good Writing. And good writing is perfect control. It is quite easy to control a thing that has in it no energy—provided that it be not too heavy and that you do not wish to make it *move*. . . .

Discussing the origins of language, Pound said:

> The whole thing is an evolution. In the beginning simple words were enough: Food; water; fire. Both prose and poetry are but an extension of language. Man desires to communicate with his fellows. And he desires an ever increasingly complicated communication. Gesture serves up to a point. Symbols may serve. But when you desire something not present to the eye or when you desire to communicate ideas, you must have recourse to speech. Gradually you wish to communicate something less bare and ambiguous than *ideas*. You wish to communicate an idea *and* its modifications, an idea *and* a crowd of its effects, atmospheres, contradictions . . .

> Words and their sense must be such as fit the emotion. Or, from the other side, ideas, or fragments of ideas, the emotion *and* concomitant emotions, must be in harmony, they must form an organism . . .
>
> Poetry is a centaur. The thinking, word-arranging, clarifying faculty must move and leap with the energizing, sentient, musical faculties.

At one time, wishing to clarify to myself the distinction between poetry and other modes of expression, I put down these notes:

> Poetry doesn't tell; it shows. Prose tells.
> Poetry is not philosophy; poetry makes things be, right now.
> Not an idea, but a happening.
> It is not music, but it sounds while showing.
> It is mobile; it is a thing taking place—active, interactive, in a place.
> It is not thought; it has to do with senses and muscles.
> It is not dancing, but it moves while it remains.

. . . And it is not science. But the experience of poetry is animated with the insatiable curiosity of science. The universe, inside and out, is properly its laboratory. More plain than ever before is the potent fact that we are human particles in a culture of living change. We must either master the Great Whirl or become victims of it. Science is unavoidably reshaping our environment and in the future will influence prominently the next development of individual man and his species. Art, more intimately, deals with, and forms, the emotional and spiritual climate of our experience. Poetry can help man stay human.

A Note about *Iconographs*

To have material and mold evolve together and become a symbiotic world. To cause an instant object-to-eye encounter with each poem even before it is read word after word. To have simultaneity as well as sequence. To make an existence in space, as well as in time, for the poem. These have been, I suppose, the impulses behind the typed shapes and frames invented for this collection.

I call the poems *Iconographs* with such dictionary derivations in mind as these:

icon	"a symbol hardly distinguished from the object symbolized"
icono-	from the Greek *eikonos,* meaning "image" or "likeness"
graph	"diagram" or "system of connections or interrelations"
-graph	from the Greek *graphē,* meaning "carve," . . . "indicating the instrument as well as the written product of the instrument"

Also, this comment on "The Art of the Middle Ages" (Columbia Encyclopedia, 3d ed.) helped me choose the title:

> [It] was governed by a kind of sacred mathematics, in which position, grouping, symmetry, and number were of extraordinary importance and were themselves an integral part of the iconography. From earliest times it has likewise been a symbolic code, showing men one thing and inviting them to see in it the figure of another.

Originally placed at the end of Swenson's *Iconographs* (New York: Scribner, 1970).

I suppose that these were my aims. But I come to definition and direction only *afterward.* It has always been my tendency to let each poem "make itself"—to develop, in process of becoming, its own individual physique. Maybe this is why, once the texts were fixed, I have wanted to give for each an individual arrangement in the space of the page.

I have not meant the poems to depend upon, or depend from, their shapes or their frames; these were thought of only after the whole language structure and behavior was complete in each instance. What the poems say or show, their way of doing it with *language,* is the main thing.

Poetry is made with words of a language. And we say, "But, of course." It is just this "matter of course" that poetry holds to the nostrils, sticks into the ears, puts on the tongue, flashes into the eyes, of anyone who comes to meet it. It is done with words; with their combination—sometimes with their unstringing. If so, it is in order to make the mind re-member (by dismemberment) the elements, the smallest particles, ventricles, radicals, down to, or into, the Grain—the buried grain of language on which depends the transfer and expansion of consciousness—of Sense. And no grain, of sense, without sensation. To *sense* then becomes to *make sense.*

With the physical senses we meet the world and one another—a world of objects, human and otherwise, in which words on a page are objects, too. The first instrument to make contact, it seems to me, and the quickest to report it, is the eye. The poems in *Iconographs,* with their profiles, or space patterns, or other graphic emphases, signal that they are to be seen as well as read and heard, I suppose.

An Interview with Cornelia Draves and Mary Jane Fortunato

So many musicians start earlier than poets, in knowing what they want to do. When did you begin writing poetry?

I think I was about thirteen. My father had a typewriter, an old-fashioned Underwood. I had been keeping a diary. I had been writing down my thoughts. And then I'd been doing school papers. That was what you were supposed to do in school. I remember my dad left the Underwood on the dining room table. I didn't know how to type, but with two fingers I copied something that I had written on this typewriter, and it came out in a form on the page that looked like a poem. The lines were short. And I think I said: "This is a poem." I think it happened that way.

Do you do most of your writing on the typewriter?

No, I do it in longhand first.

Did anybody in particular influence you to write poetry?

No, not in the early days. One thing that made me write was that I was never a social person, and I didn't have a terribly jolly childhood. I had a lot of brothers and sisters. I was the oldest one. It would seem that there would be a social atmosphere, but I was always escaping from the family, from taking care of the

---

Originally published in *New York Quarterly,* no. 19 (1977). Copyright *New York Quarterly*. Reprinted with permission.

kids, and going off to be alone. Then I guess I got a little too lonely, and I began to create things to amuse myself.

Being an innovator and an independent stylist, have you ever tried the traditional forms, the sonnet and the villanelle?

No, I never have. I develop my own forms, but I don't begin by saying: "I'm going to invent a form in this poem, and it's going to have so many lines and perhaps such and such a rhythm." It doesn't happen that way. I mean I don't predetermine.

You've written two books called Poems to Solve *and* More Poems to Solve, *containing what many call "Riddle Poems." Could you tell us something about the Riddle Poem?*

Well, those two books are really selections from my other books. They were issued by Scribner's as books for young readers. I chose these poems from my other collections, thinking that young people would be interested in this particular device.

They happen in this way: if I am observing something, I don't think about its name or its label to begin with. I think of how it is affecting me. Take this ashtray, for instance. I think I look at it the way a painter would. Unless I were going to diagram an ashtray or make a picture for a Sears Roebuck catalog.

But for a painter the thing that interests is its form and its particularity, its characteristics, what it does to him—his eye, the way he sees it. And the very last thing he would write at the bottom of his painting is: "Painting of an Ashtray." The label is the least important thing. In my way of perceiving things, I think I approach it that way, that I don't give it a name. So, the Riddle Poem is called that because the name of the thing that's being talked about is not in the text and not in the title. But it is hinted at so particularly in the poem that, for whoever is reading it, it will become defined for him without his having been told its name. That's what makes it a Riddle Poem.

And these are compilations of these poems that have happened from time to time? It's not that you worked into that particular direction—they happened and they still happen, is that it?

Yes, although they haven't happened for quite some time. I think the last one that happened was a few years ago, a poem called "Speed" that the *New Yorker* published. What it is, is about insects and butterflies being smashed on the windshield of a car that's moving very fast through meadowland. This kind of painting, as I call it, gets splattered on the windshield. When the car stops you can see all these butterflies and things that have died in this way. As you read the poem, I think you gradually find out what it's talking about.

The first Riddle Poem I published is called, "By Morning." It's about snow falling. That happened to be the first poem that the *New Yorker* ever bought. But the *New Yorker* insisted on calling it "Snow by Morning," which made me mad. That gave it away.

Did you know that Emily Dickinson wrote Riddle Poems? She has one about snow:

> It sifts from leaden sieves —
> It powders all the wood —

The curious thing is that I hadn't read hers at the time I wrote mine. And I saw it later and was so amused and interested that she had one like that.

In "Seven Natural Songs" (which was the earliest one I made) I put the answers at the bottom, in tiny print. After that I didn't put any answers. There are seven different things of nature in it.

Would you like to read one of your Riddle Poems? Here's one: "Living Tenderly."

> My body a rounded stone
> with a pattern of smooth seams;
> my head a short snake,
> retractive, projective;
> my legs come out of their sleeves
> or shrink within
> and so does my chin.
> My eyelids are quick clamps.
> My back is my roof;
> I am always
> at home.
> I travel where my house walks;
> it is a smooth stone.

It floats within the lake
or rests in the dust.
My flesh lives tenderly
inside its bone.

That's a turtle.

Yes, a turtle. And also I guess it's me. I realized afterward that I had described myself.

In your poems do you make a conscious effort to use poetic devices?

When I notice something of that kind happening, if I like it, I let it happen, and then I make it more emphatic when I do my revisions.

In that poem "Of Rounds" there is a use of repetition, isn't there?

I got that one just from going to the Hayden Planetarium and watching the model of the solar system that they have there. The little sun and the planets around the sun relate to one another the way they actually do in the sky. That's what started that poem.

You say that all your stimuli come from the environment. Do you ever use anything from dreams?

Yes, I do. I think dreams are a part of your environment. Things can be very vivid in your dreams. Dreams have this aspect of mystery and not quite understanding what is happening. But it's very significant. And you don't know quite why it's significant. And dreams come from your subconscious. Art comes a lot from your subconscious.

What about notebooks? Do you keep a notebook by your bed?

Most of the time when I'm working on a poem I'll have a copy of it wherever I am, if I'm walking or riding. And, of course, it will come to bed with me—on my night table—so that if I'm able to solve something before I go to sleep I'll do it.

How do you feel about rhyme?

I use rhyme occasionally. I usually don't use it with absolute regularity.

In "The Wave, The Flame, The Cloud, and the Leopard" it is used. This is one of your most regular poems. There is an a-a-a-a—

That is probably the most regular poem I have ever published. It's very incantatory.

And then in "The Engagement" you use an a-b-c-b *rhyme. But you are not conscious when you read your poems of the rhyme, which makes it all the more clever—to incorporate the rhyme and not be conscious of it.*

Yes. It's very boring to have a rhythm at the end of each line, especially if you have regular rhythm within the rhyme—unless you have a good reason for it.

Some of your rhymes are most unusual. For instance, you have burlap *and* dapple*—rhymes like that.*

I do internal rhymes a lot.

Yes, and random rhyme and assonance. You use them all very effectively, but they're concealed. In one of your notes somewhere you mention using sound symbolism, verbal texture, allegory, and organic metaphor. Just what is organic metaphor?

Where the metaphor moves all the way through the work, and it builds with just one metaphor.

Do you use punctuation very much?

Well, strangely, I started out with none. My early work doesn't have conventional punctuation but, rather, a substitute for it. There might be spaces or the lines so arranged that you have to read it with pauses. I would begin with a capital but would not use the period. Then later on I began to use punctuation, and more and more I used it, until I use it entirely now. Isn't that odd, because it's sort of upside down? I am discovering there is a reason why punctuation was invented. And it can be clarifying, and there's no real reason for leaving it out.

Some of your uses of spacing are very interesting. In your poem "A Wish" you have between each word a space, which makes you read the poem in a very deliberate manner:

> *Out of an hour I built a hut*
> *and like a Hindu sat*
> *immune in the wind of time*

That's exactly what I wanted. To slow down your eye, which will slow down your thought, which causes a rhythm and causes you to think in a sort of—it's that sort of a philosophical-mystical poem that you would want to do this with.

Your poems do have a great deal of detail and precision, sometimes as if you were writing right on the spot. Do you actually do that—write on the spot?

In a lot of my work the impulse has come right out of what I would be doing or where I would be, what I would be looking at or what I'd be feeling. And I would stay with it, right on that spot, until I had a first draft.

You use a great many cloud images; you have "Swollen-Breasted Clouds," "Skins of Clouds On Torn Blue," "The Cloud-Shell."

Now that you point them out to me, I realize I do have many cloud images. I didn't know that. It's true that one is not conscious of one's own consciousness. You don't know what your mind is tending to do. You are at least two people. There's your mind, and then there's your mind following your mind. It gets very schizophrenic. The things that the mind does are unconscious. And yet it has a kind of logic, somehow.

How far does the original impulse carry you before you begin to rewrite work?

If you can get a first draft done while you're still in that fresh immediacy or being struck by something, it's right. There have been times when I've been trying to finish a poem and have been distracted, and not only does the intensity of it fade in your mind and in your emotions, but also your mood about it all fades away. You let an hour go by and go back, and you say: "Well, this isn't so hot. Why did I bother with that?" You might give up. So I've learned to try very hard to stick to the first draft until the poem is brought round to an end.

Do you keep notes, in order to get your original impulse back?

Yes, I get it from the first draft and from reading it and from notes. And from research. I have a long poem called "First Walk on the Moon." I wrote that secondhand. I got it from the TV; I got it from reading—and from imagination.

But not many of your poems are that type that you have to do a lot of research. What about revision? Do you revise extensively? Do you have an average number of times?

Yes. One always has to revise—with rare exceptions. There's a poem that's been anthologized a lot; a line from it is in *Bartlett's Quotations*—it's called "Question"—and that came as it stands, almost, in its entirety.

Do you like being called a nature poet?

I certainly don't mind being called a nature poet. I think that's one of my things. But I have other things.

Do you write on the subway?

Yes. "Riding the A" was one of those. I think I finished it up at the Cloisters on the lawn.

Do you have a special time that you set for yourself every day when you work on your poetry, or does it just happen sometimes?

It's an up and down thing. It's either something that comes very, very easily and with great enthusiasm so that ideas for poems are proliferating in my mind and I can't wait to get them down. Or else nothing's happening.

That reminds me of this poem called "How Everything Happens," which is about how creativity happens. "When nothing is happening / something is stacking up to happen." That's the way it is with the tide. When there's space between the breakers it's because it's pushing up to make a bigger breaker. So I tell myself that. You're going to get on the pinnacle of a breaker.

Do you have a strategy to get yourself going again?

Sometimes I'll just sit down and empty my mind. Everything comes out. Even if it's just: "Nothing's coming out, nothing's coming out, nothing's coming out," I just type that. I just keep typing and whatever enters my mind I will type that down. Two sheets single-spaced of that. And then I'll read that over, and there will be something there that will attach itself to something else. It will lead to something that happened yesterday. A kind of concretion will take place. I'll be reminded of something that I wanted to write about and that I never quite got to. It will sometimes start something.

When you say the environment influences your poetry, the city environment and the country environment and the sea and all, then you're exposed to other environments?

Well, I find that traveling is good. I always write a poem if I take an airplane trip. Very often a poem will start in the airplane. I'm having a new experience. I'm seeing something new, or I'm just generally excited. Or—it's long ago, now. It's over ten years ago that I went to Europe. On the ship going over I was writing like crazy. Travel seems to do it.

You give poetry readings. Do they stimulate or slow down your writing? Does it help you as a poet to give the readings?

It helps my ego. To that extent I suppose it's useful. But anything of that sort interrupts my writing—like teaching, too—I find that I can't teach and write successfully. I become so absorbed in my students' work that it tends to take the place of my own, which makes me jealous.

What do you think about poetry workshops?

I've conducted them on occasion.

Did you ever attend one?

No, I never attended a poetry class or workshop. But I think that's the way poets are being developed these days. I think there are several different ways of being creative. I wouldn't say that one way is better than the other. My need is to find my own way and quite alone. To be in a workshop trying to do my thing while exposed to other people's things would not suit me.

How do you conduct a workshop? You said that you seek originality and that you don't model. Do you suggest that your students model?

I suggest that they do what works for them. I attempt to discourage them from imitating, because I think that imitation and creation do not get along together. You can do imitation, I suppose, as an exercise.

Do you assign exercise poems?

No, I never do that when I am teaching. What I do is give them assignments that exercise their senses and their ability to be attentive, to become more observant and particular and precise.

Do you think there's enough discipline in craft today for young poets?

I think there's an awful lot of bad poetry being published, in fact an awful lot of nonpoetry. I think that discipline is a part of art. I think the artist learns how to discipline himself and how to discipline his work. And yet it seems that the tendency is to be free. Anything goes. Let's spill it all out. But I hesitate to criticize because it might mean that I just don't understand what's happening these days. And that I want it to happen like it happened with me.

But aren't there some kind of craft principles?

I think that there is an order. I think that the work of art finds an order. I don't think it needs to have an order imposed from the beginning. I don't think it has to fit into an order, but I do think the order has to be found in the process. It's almost synonymous with the word *art.* I just can't see it any other way.

What about your students? How do you transmit this idea to them, that there has to be an order?

Well, I do it by considering their individual work. When the poem is before us I will say something like, "I don't understand what connection this line has with the rest of the work," or "I don't understand why you can't leave this line out, why it has to be this way." In other words, everything in the poem has to be inevitable, so that if anything is changed it's going to ruin it.

Of modern poets, are there several whom you would suggest?

Poets that I find healthy to read: one of them is Theodore Roethke. Some of the older poets like Whitman, Hopkins, James Stephens, Emily Dickinson. Among living poets some that come to mind that I have strong respect for are James Merrill, Elizabeth Bishop, Bill Meredith, W. D. Snodgrass, Anne Sexton, Dick Wilbur, Tony Hecht. There are others. When I was starting to write, Cummings interesting me a lot. His playfulness. Marianne Moore interested me. I have to say that I don't read other poetry in order to be stimulated to write my own. When I'm stimulated by literature it's generally not by poetry. Science, or the news of the day—new discoveries. Reading other poetry doesn't generally bring out mine.

What is the significance of that centaur image that has been talked about so much? There was something that led up to the poem that you call "The Centaur," which appeared first in A Cage of Spines.

"The Centaur," you know, is a childhood memory. The girl in this poem (who is myself) feels herself to be the horse. So that's how the centaur image comes into that. Then there is a poem called

"Another Animal," and it starts out with the centaur. The centaur is part human and part beast. I think the significance of it relates to my feeling for animals, my love for horses, which I always had. Monsters are mythical beasts. You know, I do have a lot of animal poems. I've always felt myself to be an animal, so to speak. I can really accept the idea of having evolved from the animals.

Then it's an image for you that's in your life experience?

Well, the poem "The Centaur," which is a remembrance of a childhood experience with a hobby horse, was really experienced. I think this is what makes a person an artist: to live yourself into something so thoroughly that you become this thing. When I was ten and I was riding this switch that I cut from a willow tree, it was really true that I felt I was riding a horse, to the extent that I became this, that I was experiencing it so vividly that it was as though I became it. I think this happens with the artist. What you are making, you really live at the time. That is expressing the experience.

You may speak about yourself in certain images, but you don't speak about yourself directly. There are other themes that have interested you besides nature in your poetry.

Science comes into my poetry quite a bit. The space program, the astronauts' experiences fascinate me. Many of my poems are from the sciences. There's a recent poem called "Teleology"—it's many things at the same time. It says:

> The eyes look front in humans.
> Horse or dog could not shoot,
>
> seeing two sides to everything.
> Fish, who never shut their eyes,
>
> can swim on their sides, and see
> two worlds: blunt dark below;
>
> above, the daggering light.
> Round as a burr, the eye.
>
> its whole head, the housefly
> sees in a whizzing circle.

Human double-barreled eyes,
in their narrow blind trained

forward, hope to shoot and hit
—if they can find it—

the backward-speeding eye
in the Cyclops head of the future.

I think that's a poem that when you get to the end, you'd read it over again to find out what it really says. What is the Cyclops head of the future? Why is it called teleology? Teleology refers to the end result of something, the target of the future, the prediction for it. So that's an *-ology*. The various *-ologies*—they interest me.

I'm not religious. I was brought up very religious; I was brought up as a Mormon. They are very religious; they call themselves the Latter Day Saints. They think they are the Chosen People. My parents came to this country as the result of their conversion to the Mormon Church from the Lutheran. I was brought up very strictly in a religious way, which made me turn away.

If there is any hope for understanding the world or understanding the universe, I think that the closest thing we have to it is the discoveries of science. I don't know how close that is, but I also think the artist is on a little search. I think that is one of the impulses of the artist—that you have to unravel the mysteries. Something is going to be revealed to you, and, if you keep your senses very sharp, you're going to have a vision. The whole pattern is going to be somehow magically seen.

Do you think that, in addition to science, the artist holds the interpretation to all this?

That's it. The artist and the scientist are our two hopes.

What would you say are the most important attributes of a poem?

A number of attributes have to work together, and it's the combination—a poem is a complex. What makes it poetry instead of prose is simply the way the language is handled, as far as its sound, its image, its texture, its motion or muscularity (not even to mention *what* is being said), is woven together naturally—all these are important. The way every word is joined with every other word. The complex of it. And then concision, having it tight. The other nice thing about a poem is its small size along with great weight.

In the old days you could hear its rhyme and its rhythm. Of course, what's happened today, instead of poetry we have the modern troubadors, the singers with their guitars. What's committed to memory is the tune and the lyric of it. But originally poetry was like that. The language used to be in your head, in your ear, and you'd quote it.

What poetic devices do you use, for instance, in your poem "The Lightning"?

That's one of my iconographic poems, and the first thing you notice about it is the way it looks on the page, with the lightning streak of space running through it. So that it has a visual metaphor before you begin reading it, and it says:

> The lightning waked me / it slid under / my eyelid a black book
> flipped open / to an illuminated page then instantly / shut /
> words of destiny were being ut- / tered in the distance. /
> Next day as I lay / in the sun a symbol for conceiving the /
> universe was scratched on my eyeball / but quickly its point
> eclipsed and / softened in the scabbard of my brain / my cat
> speaks one word . . . / he receives with the hairs of his body
> the whispers of the stars / he is held by a thread to the eye
> of the / sun and cannot fall into error. / Any flower is a
> perfect ear . . . / When will I grope my way clear of the
> entrails of intellect.

It's about trying to find a pattern, or have a vision, the power of the unconscious. It's sort of what the artist expects and wishes for—to be given some kind of extra knowledge because he's ready for it, always looking for it. Because really what do we know about the reasons for things and about the origins of things and about the ends of things? It's all very mysterious. Unless you can believe in a God with a long white beard in heaven sitting on a cloud. We really don't know. We really don't know anything. But it always seems that we are about to know something. We are going to get ready to know something.

How do you feel about poets interpreting their poems?

I think the poem should be autonomous and should explain itself. But the poem needs from the person who is reading it whatever he thinks it needs. Sometimes the poet can't explain everything that's in there.

There's always something in the poem that the reader gets, that is revealed to him, an interpretation of his own.

I think so. The reader has a right to interpret the poem in his own way. What it means to him is important. He shouldn't feel he has to be confined by what is told to him by the poet or anybody else. That's the whole thing.

Do you consider the revision as much a creative act as writing the poem itself?

If you were to transfer it to another art, let's say sculpture, the beginning thing in sculpture would be the figure modeled out of clay. As a whole, it would have the general shape that the artist intended. But, in refining it, you would have to do an awful lot more to it to bring in the details. Little attentions must be given to it, and that's what revision is. If you have a good general beginning, a draft, you want to make it more so. You want to make it more itself.

Some poets insist that they revise very little. Robert Lowell says that he revises over and over and over and over and over again.

Sure he does. And you know Auden would sometimes revise after his poems were published, so there are various published versions, and the latest version would be the only authentic one.

Have you ever revised after publication?

I've been tempted to, but I haven't done it. I don't think I would, even if something could be improved. I don't think I would want to impose my new self on my old self.

You wrote an essay in Poets on Poetry *about similarities between the poet and the scientist. And yet there are dissimilarities.*

They have dissimilar methods. But I feel that the artist and the scientist are after the same thing. They are after truth. The way things really are. And to make that actual to people.

Well, the scientist seems to get definite results, but the poet . . . do you think that poetry has really an influence?

On the scientists?

No, on the general public.

The only thing that has influence on the general public is advertising. Don't get me into that, or I'll rant and rave!

And now we must come to the shaped poem.

Except that I'm through making shaped poems. *Iconographs* was published in 1970, and that's already seven years old. Since then I've done two or three others, and that's the end. I took it as far as I could go. I had satisfied my eye enough. *Iconograph* is a made-up word of mine, which means image writing. After the poems were done—and I wouldn't even know they were going to be shape poems or anything—I would give them a typographical arrangement on the page. The shape that you would then see would have something to say about what was being said in the poem.

The poem came first? And the shape afterward?

Yes. Always. This is not really concrete poetry.

John Hollander has done a book of poems he calls Type Shapes. They're very interesting and clever. But he did it the opposite of the way I did it. He did the shape and then fit the text into the shape. "Out of the Sea Early" is a shape poem that appears in *Half Sun*. It's also a riddle poem, so it's several things in one.

The trouble with iconographs is that you can't usually get the printer to do what you want him to do. "Out of the Sea" is supposed to be round, because it's about a sunrise. It shouldn't be perfect on the edges, but it should be entirely round. The poem "Zero in the Cove" is supposed to remind you of a mirror. These poems are actually my manuscripts, which have been photo offset and reduced. This is the way I made it on the typewriter. If they were not typeset, there would be less room for error. That was the idea.

It's very interesting to pick up a book and have each page have a different shape.

I just thought it would be interesting to the eye. It is part of my playfulness with poetry. I designed this cover myself. It's supposed to suggest a giant typewriter ribbon. But it doesn't really matter if people don't understand that.

Shape poetry really combines the medium of sound and the use of the eye, whereas poetry originally was just to be heard and sung.

The shape poems are a combination of the two elements. I guess it's the centaur! But I think I go toward being simple rather than sophisticated.

You say you are going in other directions now. What are these directions?

I was afraid you'd ask me that. I won't know until I get there. I'm just halfway down that road, and until I get there I won't be able to define it for you. One thing that I am doing is something like prose poetry, but it's not really. I don't think it is. I'm working with some prose things, which just have the label "visions" on them. It's not patterned poetry. It's away from that. And yet it's not prose either. It's an in-between experiment, and it's just part of the search. It's part of the search and part of my insistence on invention. And not repeating myself and doing something different.

You spent time this fall watching the migration of the birds. Will that figure in your work?

Well, I've been trying to keep them out because I'm very bird-y. And, if I let myself, every poem would have a bird in it. I'm doing a poem right now; the first line is "A flicker with a broken neck. / We laid him on the lawn." Those are the first two lines.

Have you been influenced by your religious upbringing?

Yes, I think I would say so. I have a poem called "Gods: Children." I wrote this soon after my father died. It's really a poem about evolution, I guess. I have a poem that hasn't been published yet about my mother's death. My mother died last summer. The name of that poem is "Nature."

As a woman poet, has it affected the way you were received? Do you find any solidarity with other women poets?

I have a poem that anthologists keep asking for now. It's called "Women." But I haven't sat down to write any Women's Lib poetry, although I see myself a Women's Lib person. I always have. About being a woman and being an artist, I think that in a way it has been sort of lucky. Just as in a certain way to be Negro is a little luckier these days.

Do you feel you have been discriminated against as a writer and as a woman?

Well, there's general discrimination. Obviously, it happens. If you turn to any general anthology, you will find that the number of women poets is about one-fifth that of men. But not in a personal way. I think there are lots of women poets who are defending that area today and who are doing it more effectively than I. It doesn't always lead to art to be a polemicist. To be on the battlefield. It can take away. I do what comes to me. What asks to be done.

An Interview with Karla Hammond

Women writing from the 1930s and 1940s onward seem more preoccupied with nature, pastoral scenes, elegy, and praise (as common themes in their work); whereas today's women poets, in large part, view poetry as a means of psychological/confessional investigation, exploration of sexual identity and nationalistic consciousness, and as a vehicle of social commentary. Certainly, there are exceptions in either case, but is it a fair assessment, and, if so, do the culture, the media, and socialization alone determine what people will concern themselves with?

For me, nature includes everything: the entire universe, the city, the country, the human mind, human creatures, and the animal creatures. Nature is the big construct; so if I'm called a nature poet then I'm happy about that. It isn't simply the birds, the bees, and the butterflies.

If culture, the media, and socialization determine what people concern themselves with, it means that they are certainly overcivilized. Animals aren't human beings, but human beings are animals. They aren't only animals. They are human, but the human arises out of the animal nature. The animal is instinctive. It's the quality that makes it possible for us to live with the earth, with the universe, with nature. People should not lose their animal nature. I mean they will, but it's too bad. The media, socialization, and culture can turn people into artificial things.

Real poets don't follow the trend. They may be *with* the trend. They may be leading the trend, but they aren't hooked up to it. Psychological/confessional? Today some of the poetry

---

This interview took place on July 14, 1978, and was originally published in *Parnassus: Poetry in Review* 7, no. 1 (fall/winter 1978). Reprinted with permission.

within that vein will live and go on but not merely because it's psychological/confessional poetry. It will have to have some added *art* value.

How is poetry humanizing?

Not only poetry but all the arts. In the article in which I discuss this, I wondered what might happen as technology goes on. For, while I venerate science, I'm also afraid of it in its technological aspects. Cloning is talked about. What will be the next step in evolution? Will it be toward stereotypy, toward man and mechanism combined? It takes a person, a personality, to produce art. Conversely, art as an influence creates personhood. It humanizes—humanizes the one who makes it as well as all the others who enjoy it.

Elizabeth Bishop is one of the few poets mentioned in your work (your letter-poem for her). Do you think of her work as humanizing? And do you feel an influence from her?

Almost everything that E. B. has written stays with me. I will not say that she is a great *woman* poet. I'll say that she is a great poet. These days many people agree with that; so I'm not making a new discovery. Of course, she is humanizing.

Have I been influenced by her? Not necessarily, although neither of us writes confessional poetry. E. B. has always stayed with the objective, the large view, the impersonal, which contains the personal if you look into it deeply. I have this tendency but not because of any influence of hers. I think we share some of the same basic perceptive equipment.

Is it plausible to speak of influences?

My earliest poetry wasn't influenced by anyone because I didn't read poetry when I first began writing. When I discovered Marianne Moore's and Cummings's work, I was intrigued. I was interested in Marianne Moore's subject matter, her objectivity; she wasn't writing about her emotions. As to Cummings, I liked his playfulness. I was attracted by the way he made words actual on the page—pages of poetry that looked different from the ordinary. Language for the poet is what pigment is for the painter. Part of my pleasure in a painting is to notice just how the colors are applied, or placed, by brush or palette knife.

Your poems frequently emphasize "things" as opposed to people. Have you "felt" Rilke's, Williams's, or Ponge's influence in this regard?

That title of my latest book, *Things Taking Place,* is an old one. It's been in my mind for a couple of decades, and finally I'm using it. If I've been influenced by other poets, it's been subconscious. It's seldom that reading poetry stimulates me to write. Rather, I could say that I've felt affinities with the work of certain painters, for instance with Milton Avery, with Georgia O'Keeffe, with the constructions of Marcel Duchamp that he called "Ready-Mades." I once played a game of chess with Duchamp. It was a thrill. He was a guest at the MacDowell Colony for a week one summer that I was there. This was shortly before he died. We played billiards, too.

Writing in the latter half of the twentieth century, do you consider yourself a feminist?

I think I began to be a feminist at age three-and-a-half [laughs]. Certainly long before that word took on the meaning it has today. I don't actually like the word very much if it means to cut out the male. Male and female exist in every person. The world is made up of male, female, and combinations thereof. If the word means "I am Feminine and that's all I need," I disagree—that's extreme. It all depends on definition. I've always felt complete within myself as a person but sometimes felt that some of the rest of the world didn't find me as complete or capable as if I had been born male. This has annoyed me.

I raised the question because of your poem "Women," although I realize the comic irony intended.

"Women" wasn't written to be a feminist poem, but call it that, if you like. It was first published in *Iconographs,* and it's one of my shaped poems. Its shape might remind you of a rocking platform, which is a visual metaphor for what the poem is saying.

Were you to take it literally, you wouldn't realize that it really means the opposite of what it's saying. Why, it could be *anti*feminist [laughs] if you were to take it simply as a statement and you had no sense of humor.

Yes, but, see, I didn't read it that way.

You immediately knew somehow that it was a feminist poem? Because it was written by a woman?

No, no. Because I had a sense in reading it that if one said women should be pedestals (or on pedestals), by virtue of its construct . . .

Visual construct?

Yes, that it was contradicting itself.

Yes, but before it had that visual construct on the page it had an ordinary arrangement.

But the tone is ironic.

Yes.

"Dear, trusting, chafed"—the words and the sounds, too, create this impression.

Yes, it's an exaggeration of the male view of what a woman should be, or at least what a man used to think a woman should be. Men hesitate to voice such a feeling today, don't they? But many would still like her to be this way.

Yes. "An Old Field Jacket" suggests a certain feminist consciousness, doesn't it?

Are you fishing around for poems that could put me under that heading? There are a few, and "An Old Field Jacket" might be one. It was written at Purdue, where I was Poet-in-Residence a number of years ago. A friend and I went to an Army-Navy store, and I bought a jacket that had been worn by an army guy. I wore it for many years, when going camping, birdwatching, and whatnot. It was practical because it kept off the rain, and it had pockets. (I love pockets.) I imagined things about it—who had worn it—and I even copied and put into the poem the serial number on the tag sewn into the nape. Those details went into the poem and, I guess, gave it some spunk.

Your work reveals many interests—some in science and evolution. In an article several years ago you said, "Sometimes I long to remember my life as a cephalopod under the sea, and cannot." Are you suggesting a belief in reincarnation?

No. I can't believe in reincarnation because I have no evidence for it. As for "cephalopod," I'm just talking about evolution and that I'd like to know the origins of the human being and experience those origins. Do *you* believe in reincarnation? The people who do can't explain it, can't tell you *how* it happens, how it works.

Your saying "how it works" reminds me of your poem about the watch being taken apart and also that poem about taking your cat apart to see how it purrs.

I hadn't thought of that connection, that parallelism. You're right.

Some poems suggest that the astronaut might be a hero, and yet your treatment of the astronaut in "August 19, PAD 19" is ironic.

You felt that I gave him an ironic treatment? That poem came from watching a launching at Cape Canaveral. In fact, I have a note on it right in here, in the new book. Of course I watched it on TV. I keep saying that my poems are written on the spot [laughs]. Well, I couldn't go to the moon, even sit in a space capsule, although I would have loved to have done so; but some experiences have to be secondhand.

Did you have a scientific background in terms of schooling?

No. I went to Utah State University when it was called Utah State Agricultural College. This is in Logan, Utah, where I was born and where my Dad taught. But, at that time, it was a cow college. I received a degree in English and Art, but I'm not academic. The science courses there weren't very extensive. Perhaps I'm interested in science because I missed it in school.

But here's the note: "On August 19, 1965, the launch of Gemini V was scrubbed because of weather." The astronaut was in his capsule ready to go, and the count went all the way down to just before lift-off. Then it was aborted because of lightning. "Lightning's golden sneer" reflects my delight that the unpredictable weather could prevent the launch. Not that I didn't want to see the launch go off, but there is still an awareness that there are things mankind and technology cannot control. And I'm strangely glad about it, because mystery in itself is useful to us as human beings. If we ever got to where there were no mysteries left, we wouldn't be human. Have I illuminated anything for you?

The helplessness of the astronaut?

You're still referring to "August 19, PAD 19" and what is meant by "Never so impotent, so important." Yes, it is ironic. And the irony of there being so little space in space [laughs]. You know, the tiny capsule. At the Smithsonian you can go into the first Gemini capsule. It's round and barely big enough for a person to lie down on a little couch. Yet, they call it a space program [laughs]. There are other ironies:

Over my obsolete epiderm redundant with
hairs and pits of moisture
I wear my new, rich, inflatable skin,
the bicep patch a proud tattoo,
a galaxy of 50 States,
my telemetric skull, a glossy cupola
resembling the glans of an Aztec God.

This poem is simultaneously funny and serious. "Let them siphon my urine to the nearest star" and so on.

You have said: "Poetry doesn't tell; it shows. Prose tells." Is this because poetry deals with the inner landscape of the human being—the subcon-

scious and psyche, because it is an implicit and symbolic language as opposed to exposition, explanation, or description?

What I meant was that poetry doesn't talk *about* something. It presents the thing to your senses, so that it can be grasped whole. At least, this is what makes it poetry for me. My own feelings are that poetry doesn't talk about it; it doesn't tell about it. It isn't a story. There is narrative poetry, of course, but I want to *build* a poem with language as the material. My way of showing goes farther than even the presenting of images (which many poets do). I think of a poem as a mobile, almost a construct, something you can look around, that moves, that is concrete. You can almost hold it in your hand. I think of it as projecting to the reader something more actual, more graspable by his senses, than just words on the page. This has led me into the iconographic poem. I don't do this much anymore, but I did make a whole book of iconographs. That's a made-up word meaning picture writing.

Could you explain the difference between concrete poetry and your iconographics?

Apollinaire was one of the early concrete poets in France. Some good American concrete poets are Mary Ellen Solt and John Hollander. There are others who do nothing except show you one word, an abstract word, at that, taken apart on the page. That's just tricky and trivial. It doesn't give anything. Poetry has to give more than one aspect, more than one dimension. Less is not more when you get down to zero. (A Danish poet, Vagn Steen, published a book titled *Write It Yourself,* all the pages of which were blank.) But the main difference is this. The concretist starts out with his arrangement, and he fits the words into this arrangement. My iconographs are never designed until I have the poem absolutely finished and every word set. I never change a word in order to fit it into the frame. You see, it's the difference between the frame and the painting. Of course the painting must be major, not the frame. In fact, in the "Selected" section of *Things Taking Place* I've reprinted some iconographs without their "frames"—gone back to conventional arrangements.

Would you say that your earlier reference to the eye's primacy in poetry foreshadowed the visual achievement of Iconographs?

Oh yes. My eyes have been primal from the very beginning. It starts with my being nearsighted. It seems odd that a defect in one's eyes should make one visual, but being nearsighted, I look at everything more carefully close up and notice details. I think that this comes into my work. For me the eyes are the main sense, although all of the senses should come into play simultaneously, if possible.

What are some of the tools of your craft?

Everyone who writes has basically the same tools: a pencil, a pen, a notebook, paper, typewriter. Fortunately, it's simpler for a writer than for a sculptor, a painter, or even a choreographer, who at least requires a dance floor or an exercise bar. The writer's lucky in being able to work almost anywhere and with simple tools. (You see, I take your question very literally.)

More important, however, is one's attitude and posture. How to find and keep the mental posture that will let the poem through. It has to do with how empty you can make your mind, so that the new thing will come into it and be developed. It's necessary for me to rid myself of influences and forget other people's work. The new thing is what's going to be *mine.* It won't be suggested by other makings, either past or present. There is also the attitude of the ego. It's not good to think: "I am a poet and I'm now going to make a magnificent poem." Don't think of yourself as a poet. Don't label it a poem. What comes from some strong impulse or sharp experience, something that's almost knocked you down, or lifted you high—it might be beautiful or it might be crushing—this can start the poem. The posture of the poet should be to be alert, alive, awake. You can be physically relaxed, but your senses should be active all the time. You should be alive [laughs] and not asleep. It's so easy to be asleep or to be distracted—to eat too much and enjoy doing so, or any kind of self-indulgence. It's so easy to waste your life. But there's more satisfaction in using your life to make art. Although you can't be doing it all the time. At least I can't. You always hope that you can do more and more of it, oftener and oftener, and make it better and better. But our achievements somehow never duplicate our dreams. Still we keep on trying [laughs]. Or we try not to try too hard! To be ready, *when* it happens. And to seize it and use it *when* it happens, before it gets away. But, going back to your question: Tools. In *Things Taking Place* I have a poem called "The Wonderful Pen" in which I invent some magic tools. . . .

Have dreams ever amplified an experience?

I object to the word *amplified* because it suggests to me "made louder." (I take the literal first before anything else.) I have a poem called "The Pregnant Dream." It's about trying to tell a dream to someone who is too busy to listen. And *that's* part of the dream, so that's why it's a pregnant dream. Of course, this has caused funny little comments when occasionally I've read it. People who are imperceptive just grab words out of context. Someone will come up to me after a reading and say "I liked that poem you read about your pregnancy." Of course, it's not I, it's the dream that's pregnant, because there's something inside of something else [laughs]. A metaphor can be taken to be literal, and something literal can be assumed to be a metaphor, and, either way, a mistake is made. It's best if you can get the two together: the literal and the metaphoric—in the same word, the same image.

For me a poem does not begin with theory, with a preconceived notion of how to make it and what it should say. After the poem is done, I see what I have been doing and can make a theory out of it. That doesn't, however, help me to write the next poem.

You've said that poetry "is done with words; with their combination, sometimes with their unstringing." Do you regard revision as part of that "unstringing"?

In saying that, I might have been thinking of my poem about Robert Frost ("R. F. at Bread Loaf His Hand against a Tree"), in which the words are actually pulled apart to show words inside of themselves.

Why don't we just think of revision as what the word actually means: to re-view, to re-vise, have a vision again, to make it more exact. Revision means making the thing closer to what you first experienced, what prompted you to write the poem. It's important in that you want your first vision to still be there. It's not that you discard that vision and substitute something else, because the beginning impulse of a poem, the vision, for me, is primary. It contains the germ of what made me want to write in the first place. I want to keep that in, because, if I removed it, I'd get something else, probably something mechanical, rather than what I started out with.

Do you ever research material for a poem?

Yes. I try to be exact, and when I'm uncertain about something factual I look it up. When I was writing my space poems I researched material because I wanted to be factually accurate.

In "Things I Can Do in My Situation" you mention: "when I began / these notes. . . ." Does a poem generally begin with notes?

There's one other poem that actually has "Notes" in the title: "Notes Made in the Piazza San Marco." I was sitting at a cafe table in Venice in the Piazza when I began to set down my impressions. It really was notes in a notebook. In revision I let the poem stay rather rough like the notes. That's why I kept the title.

You don't keep a journal?

Yes I do. I don't keep one with the specific notion of using it for poetry, though things have come out of it for poetry. Sometimes I record a dream. My daybook generally begins with the weather. It has a lot of weather in it [laughs]. Weather, and how I feel inside that morning. It's a private record of my inner moods more than anything else—not really a poetic journal.

Do you find it difficult to write when you're traveling?

Usually not. I've often written poems in airplanes because I feel so relieved and free up there in the air. The pilot is taking care of everything. I've left one place behind, and I haven't gotten to the next place. It's an empty in-between state in which I have no responsibility except just to pay attention to my impressions and look out the window. I love those hours in the air. Several poems have happened there—at least their beginnings.

You have a poem about flying and Utah?

Yes. "Flying Home from Utah." When I'm in Utah seeing my folks, I'm asked to read that poem. They say "Oh, read your 'Flying Home to Utah' poem." But it's "Flying Home *from* . . ." [laughs].

I get back to my home town occasionally. Of course, they'd like me to stay. I've spent most of my life in the East; a great deal of my work has been done around New York City, some of it in Europe, some on travels all over the country.

In your New and Selected *book have you changed many of the poems from earlier books?*

I tried not to. I don't like to tamper with my earlier self very much. When I see poems that need to be improved extensively, I leave them out in making a selection. It isn't a good idea to impose your older self on your younger self because you've become a different person. What you produced when you were young had better stay in that form or else be discarded. Sometimes I'll make a small change, but I usually try not to do that.

The title, Things Taking Place*—is that because many poems deal with events?*

Yes, partly. And then it refers to their objectivity. I think of my poems as "things" rather than messages made of words. That title is a common phrase—my poems often use commonplace experiences—and, also, I like the idea of subject and object linked by the verb. Things (the poems) are taking their "places" on the pages. As actors do on a stage, for instance.

One of your more recent poems, "The Pure Suit of Happiness" in the following lines: "It has its own weather, / which is youth's breeze, /

equilibrated by the ideal / thermostat of maturity," reminds me of Stanley Kunitz's statement that youth is not a state of genius but a biological condition.

"The Pure Suit of Happiness" is a central poem for me because in addition to being about me, in a funny way, the imagery was derived from astronaut suits. Remember, I was fascinated by the space program.

"The pure suit of happiness, / not yet invented. . . ." Of course, it's a pun on the pursuit of happiness.

How I long
to climb into its legs,

fit into its sleeves, and zip
it up, pull the hood
over my head.

"Pull the hood / over my head" indicates that I'm really laughing at myself for wanting to hide.

It's got

a face mask, too, and gloves
and boots attached. It's
made for me. It's blue. It's

not too heavy, not too
light. It's my right.
It has its own weather,

which is youth's breeze,
equilibrated by the ideal
thermostat of maturity,

and, built-in to begin with,
fluoroscopic goggles of
age. I'd see through

everything, yet be happy.
I'd be suited for life. I'd
always look good to myself.

This is a typical poem of mine in that it's simultaneously serious and funny. It ties in with science and relates to an attitude about myself. Critics have pointed out, and it's true, that my poems are generally very objective and only more subtly subjective. Of course, you can't help talking about yourself if you're writing (unless you're under assignment from a publisher to write a trash book or something). If you're really writing, you're writing about yourself regardless of what you're saying in your writing. Art *is* confessional; it *is* autobiographical after all. Always has been.

Maxine Kumin said you're writing about yourself in that what you write is "invested with self."

That's a good way to put it. I like her pun there, too.

How do you respond to my analogy between your lines and Kunitz's statement? Would you agree?

Absolutely [laughs]. That's one of those aphorisms that's so very, very true and becomes truer as you get older. My attitude toward aging and my attitude toward having been young are in "The Pure Suit." My attitude toward happiness and attitude toward clothes are in the poem. Not that I'd *really* choose to be dressed in a suit with these strange attachments. On the other hand, there is a kind of literalness here about clothes. There's also the consciousness of Women's Lib. I've never thought of myself as an ordinary woman wanting flouncy clothes, makeup, or what-have-you. I just want what's practical. And I want what's magical! Because if I really had this pure suit of happiness, it would be as good to be old as to be young. I'd have youth and age at the same time. I'd "see through everything and yet be happy." I'd be suited not only for life but probably for eternity! So it's a comical, philosophical, serious, laughing-at-myself-but-really-meaning-it poem.

Would you talk about one or two of your other, newer poems?

I could say this about "October," a seven-part, quite long one. Each of its sections was written in one day in a given week in October, here in Sea Cliff, Long Island.

I was alone for that week, and I gave myself the assignment of writing the poem in that way. I wrote first thing every morning, before breakfast. I'd sit down at my desk and make a first draft. The revisions came later. It is, however, unusual for me to set myself projects. That hasn't been my habit in writing, but I did it for this particular poem.

Then you don't work on a schedule?

When I don't have too much else to attend to, like getting a book through the mill, or other business, I try to have certain hours for writing every day. But a poem doesn't often begin at my desk. The first line will come, say, when I'm riding on the train to New York or walking on the beach or maybe just because I wake up at night. A poem will begin that way, rather than by my deciding that today I'm going to write a poem. But "October" happened differently.

In "October" you speak of your "little desk of cherry wood" where you wrote your first poems. When did you start writing?

My Dad was a cabinetmaker. He taught mechanical engineering at the college I graduated from. *Mechanical engineering* is a fancy term for *woodworking*. He taught house building, wood carving, pattern making. He made most of the furniture in our house: the dining room table (mentioned in an early poem, "Lion"), a buffet in the dining room, and chairs. He was a wonderful craftsman and a great designer. In fact, I have a cellaret (for holding wine) left to me in his will. He designed it, constructed it, and carved the door on it, for which he won a prize in his youth.

As to your question, though, he made me a small desk of cherry wood that I mention in "October." That desk is lost, I'm sorry to say. I left it in Salt Lake City with a friend, who moved and left it with someone else. It was a beautiful little desk. The lid of it came down; I wrote in longhand on it. It had little cubbyholes and little drawers. Some of my first poems were made on that desk. I began writing at thirteen. I didn't know that I was writing poems. But when I'd type them out their arrangement was instinctive, and I'd say to myself: "This must be a poem. It doesn't look like a story."

Can you give me another recent example from Things Taking Place?

"Ending"—written perhaps a year ago—is about death. It's one of these funny/serious poems. In *Things Taking Place* there are a number of rather dark old-age and death poems in the first section; all newer poems are in the front. I've arranged the sequence backward, as I usually do my books, the opposite of chronological. "Ending" is at the end of the new poems section. The idea is one of those wishes: if only physical death were not the end. As far as any evidence I have, physical death is the end to human life. I wish that I could imagine how it could not be so. So here I'm taking this idea of the soul (which used to be thought of as inhabiting the body) being able to escape from the body and move into another environment [laughs]. I call this soul a "me." "Maybe there *is* a Me inside of me / and, when I lie dying, he / will crawl out. Through my toe. / Green on the green rug." This little soul, Me inside of me, is like a chameleon that changes color by what it walks on.

> Green on the green rug, and then
> white on the wall, and then
> over the windowsill, up the trunk
> of the apple tree, he
> will turn brown and rough and warty
> to match the bark. But you'll be
> able to see—(*who* will be
> able to see?)

See, I'm not there anymore. I'm dead. So that's amusing to contemplate. Or, I should say, *bemusing*. Well, the poem goes on, and it *is* ironic, imagining that I could escape death by having my soul become an "archaeopteryx"—early in evolution, a tiny lizard that had wings but didn't fly.

It's an interesting contrast to "On Its Way."

Yes, it is, in its tone and technique. "On Its Way" is an autumn lyric. Rhythmic. Elegiac. A nature poem!

As I said before, each poem is a thing in itself. After you've accumulated enough work, you can see threads that move through and connect, but my poems are separate constructs—

autonomous—which may explain why I have a gamut of treatments and styles.

You've spoken of the impulses of the scientist and poet being parallel. Are the impulses of the dancer or the choreographer and the poet parallel?

All the arts are like each other in what they attempt, I think. Many years ago, E. M. Forster, the British novelist (one of my pets), said that "Art for art's sake" is the right attitude. That was at a time when that attitude was questioned sharply. It's still questioned, I suppose. I believe that the poem, the dance, the painting, whatever, is valid enough to be made for its own sake. In fact, that's the best way to make it—not hitch it on to something else or require it carry something else, be a vehicle.

Has science given us a vernacular applicable to poetry?

If you look at poetry of the past, you find a different vernacular from poetry of the present. In the future you'll see more differences in the vernacular. We use the language that we read, we speak, we hear. Science is relatively late in the life of mankind. Science wasn't always there. It's language came into our lives, and, of course, it's been filtered down into art. This is to be expected. Scientists aren't actually giving us our vernacular. We just pick it up like we pick up slang or other language around us. It's just part of our lives. If there's a *glitch* in this interview when you've got it finished, it'll be your fault—O.K.?

[laughs] I remember in your analogy between the scientist and the poet, you spoke of the insatiable curiosity of both and the use of language as a medium.

Of course, there are differences between the artist and the scientist, but they're each on a search. In that comparison I was just talking about myself, because I'm on a search, although I didn't deliberately set out to make a search in poetry. I have a philosophical bent that harks back to a religious background that I abandoned. Other poets may not be on any search other than into their own selves. But I've been on a search into the universe and the human mind.

My intuition is the only launching pad I have, but scientists probably take off from intuition, too.

You're spoken of the poetic experience as one of "constant curiosity, skepticism, and testing—astonishment, disillusionment, renewed discovery, re-illumination." Would you add any other qualities to this list?

Yes, darkness, For every blazing galaxy, a black hole. I wrote the original list long ago. That's still the experience but add to that: darkness. When I say "for every blazing galaxy, a black hole," I'm usurping an astronomical image. Astronomers think they have discovered black holes in between the blazing galaxies. Similarly, there is a new psychological discovery that occurs as one ages.

The Term *Line* in Poetry

The term *line* in poetry has two meanings for me. The first is those words that come into my head at conception of a poem, that make me want to write it. I hear in my head a phrase, or a line, almost as if it were dictated, which—if it has significance—demands to be continued and become a poem. When the poem is finished, with all the words pretty much in order, I work out a specific arrangement of lines and line breaks and, sometimes, stanzas (or parts) I consider suitable for that particular poem. When that is complete, the "lines" become simply what is counted by an editor considering the poem for length.

I can best show what kinds of things I try to do with the division of lines by quoting and discussing a short poem: "September Things" (from *New & Selected things Taking Place,* Atlantic/Little, Brown, 1978).

Brutal sound of acorns
falling. Chokecherry-ink
beads have dried. On tile

bare feet still feel
stored warmth, eyes graze
a field of blue

water. A few lanquid
boats like flecks
of paint far out,

the lanyards tinkling.
Snag-nailed surf reaches,
drags back, over echoing

Originally published in *Epoch* 29 (winter 1980) as part of "A Symposium on the Theory and Practice of the Line in Contemporary Poetry."

pebbles. A lateborn
cardinal ticks and
whistles—too pale

and thin. Too vivid,
the last pink
petunia's indrawn mouth.

The line that came to me to begin with was the first sentence. The first draft of the whole text had the beginning lines set out in sentences, more or less, so that the arrangement arrived in one chunk of ten lines, with the period words coming at the ends of lines, for the most part. After a series of rearrangements, the pattern of six three-line stanzas, making eighteen short lines, was worked out.

Small objects are detailed in this poem: acorns, berries, boats tiny on distant water, pebbles, a bird, a petunia. Short crisp lines are right for it. They slow the eye and the voice. The rhythm is roughened and, to an extent, jerked out of the iambic. Vowel chimes and some alliteration occur, and this music is allowed emphasis by the pauses between stanzas—(space always indicates pause)—and by the slight hesitations that both eye and voice encounter at the ends of the lines. There are three wide-apart rhymes. They come at the ends of lines but at unexpected points: *-ink* in line 2, *tink*ling, line 10, and *pink,* line 17.

The appearance of the whole poem on the page is cared for: in print a narrow oblong. If the lines were longer, or if the stanza divisions were fewer, the whole would look awkward, the rhythm would sound conventional, attention would skim over the words too rapidly, and several little surprise components would remain unrealized. All of these elements are brought into play, not only by the words of the poem and their sequence but by how the lines and stanzas are divided.

The look of a poem on the page is important to me—what the eye sees before it begins to read. Certain poems of mine I call "iconographs" have shapes of print or other typographical features serving as visual extensions of metaphor. In that kind of poem the line lengths and breaks are chosen to accommodate the graphic effect. *The Watch,* for example, has line lengths and breaks based on the placement of pronouns of opposite gender at the ends of the lines: *I—He—him—her,* etc., resulting in long lines alternating with short ones and no division into stanzas. The pattern of "Stone Gullets," at first glance, seems to show five lines. When read, it turns out to have twenty lines, five in each section or column or stanza; the four sections are separated by line cuts dividing them visually, symbolizing the flow of water.

Each of my poems is given an individual setting, once the text is fixed. The number and length of lines, the line breaks, and the division into parts all *become* the final revision. In each case this is tied into the singular character and organization of the poem. So there is no overall formal metric or method that I attempt to apply to my work in general. All my arrangements, whether iconographic or not, are made after the entire wording of a poem is finished, not to be further revised as to content. What is done with language and what is said (the sense of the poem) are the major concerns with me. Any special effects are to be added afterward, and only if they enhance.

I do want the poem to be for the eye *and* the voice. It is made to be read silently, from the book. And reread. Or read aloud in the reader's voice. Or read from the platform by the poet. But when I am making the poem I hear it as an inner voice of my own, not as a voice projected to an audience.

I do want my poems to be distinct from prose. I want them also to be distinct from preimposed forms. I want them to be unpretentious, natural, accurate, while, at the same time, making organized use of the riches of language.

Foreword

To a student who wrote and asked for (1) my definition of poetry, (2) my notion of what purpose it serves, and (3) some pointers about technique, I recently replied: "Before there was the word *poetry* there was poetry. It came before any of its definitions. Definitions of course are made with words. So, how could poetry come before words when those are what *it's* made of? I'm talking about it here as a sudden realization or keen emotion in response to an experience. Poetry in the beginning, before language, was probably expressed with cries and groans, with whoops and chants. Pierced deeply by a mental discovery, strong feeling, or both at once, one wants to explain it—*explain it to oneself.* Words come then. To fix it in memory, to feel it over again, is the impulse. Language is the medium. Words are written, ordered as precisely as possible, to preserve in mind and senses the core of the original happening. Others, reading, can then feel these things."

And I continued: "When making a poem, don't be so worried about what form or system to use. Think less of technique and more of making it clear, accurate, complete. Go back again and again to your first vivid sensation or thought that made you want to write it. The poem should be something all yours, something that happened to *you,* so that only you can rightly reproduce its nuances and riches. It will tend to find its own form and fitting language. Be ready intuitively to recognize when that happens so you can emphasize it deliberately, help it along. You needn't worry at all about your readers or whether what you are doing is

---

From the foreword to *New Voices, 1979–1983,* ed. May Swenson (New York: The Academy of American Poets, 1984). Reprinted with permission.

poetry or what its purpose is. All of your consciousness (and conscience) will be spent on the work—and the play—of bringing the poem into being alive and kicking."

There was another point I wanted to make, but didn't—one hard for a young ego to accept: "Don't even label yourself a Poet. That self-view can overdetermine your work, can make it rhetorical or mechanistic or pretentious. When you have finished a substantial body of poems *they* may name *you* Poet."

"Big My Secret, but It's Bandaged"

The portrait of Emily Dickinson, familiar frontispiece in many books one opens about her, is from a daguerreotype taken in late 1847 or early 1848 at Mt. Holyoke, Massachusetts, where she went to school. She was about seventeen years old. This is the only authentic portrait existing as far as is known. Looking at it, I see—the face first:

> Little potato nose. Mouth rather wide, lips slightly parted. Eyes set quite far apart, dark irises with a tranquil but direct stare. Chin round, a little cleft in it, strong. Her right cheek might be dimpled, or it's the quirk of a beginning smile at the mouth corner. Brows almost straight, the right arched more than the left. The two strokes of the brows, like the eyes' directness, suggest an independent will. She is sitting up with a straight spine but with no stiffness in the pose, neck wide and proud, shoulders and torso still almost childish, her hands in the lap of her dark-patterned, high-waisted, full-skirted dress are loose and long, fingering a small bunch of short-stemmed flowers which might be violets. There is a narrow ribbon cross-tied in front around her bare neck. Her face is oval, forehead spacious, the two panels of her straight hair that is parted in the middle are drawn back symmetrically over the ears just showing the ear lobes. I wonder how her hair is fixed in the back.

Originally published in *Parnassus: Poetry in Review* 12, no. 2; 13, no. 1 (spring/summer/fall/winter 1985). Reprinted by permission. Essay on Emily Dickinson delivered April 15, 1984, at the Pierpont Morgan Library, New York City, auspices of the Academy of American Poets, in commemoration of one hundred years since the death of Emily Dickinson. The title is a line from Poem 1737 in *The Complete Poems of Emily Dickinson,* ed. Thomas H. Johnson (Boston and Toronto: Little, Brown, 1960).

Pleasing some readers and horrifying others was a false portrait of Emily first published in 1924 in *The Life and Letters of Emily Dickinson.* A photograph of the original daguerreotype was retouched. Her straight hair was replaced by soft curls brought low on her forehead and fluffed around her ears. A girlish white lace ruff was contrived around her neck. Eyelashes look drawn in; lips seem somehow altered to increase the smile. Emily's dark bodice is made white, the shoulders rounded. As reproduced in that book, the portrait was cropped to a bust, enlarged with only head and shoulders shown. Exactly who transformed the true likeness, uglifying it in this way, is not established. But it is said that, when the book was being prepared, Emily's sister Lavinia and her brother Austin agreed with the editor, Martha Dickinson Bianchi (who was Emily's niece), that the original daguerreotype was "too severe" for display as the poet's public image.

To this day, unfortunately, the concocted photograph of Emily Dickinson, making her look "cuter" than she was, is reproduced. I saw it just the other day on page 2115 of the latest *Random House Illustrated Encyclopedia.*

Here I want to look at a kind of portrait poem of Emily's. It is about the moon. She wrote several in which phases of the moon figured. In one, in which the crescent moon is "lying on its back" as we say, the first line is, "The moon was but a chin of gold." A face, you see, with only the chin showing. This one, however, is about the full moon:

> I watched the Moon around the House
> Until upon a Pane—
> She stopped—a Traveller's privilege—for Rest—
> And there upon
>
> I gazed—as at a stranger—
> The Lady in the Town
> Doth think no incivility
> To life her *Glass**—upon—

---

*glass—a wine glass? No.
—a looking glass? Seems to fit the context: a face—a portrait—But no.
—an opera glass, of course!

But never Stranger justified
The Curiosity
Like Mine—for not a Foot—nor Hand—
Nor Formula—had she—

But like a Head—a Guillotine
Slid carelessly away—
Did independent, Amber—
Sustain her in the sky—

Or like a Stemless Flower—
Upheld in rolling Air
By finer Gravitations—
Than bind Philosopher—

No Hunger—had she—nor an Inn—
Her Toilette—to suffice—
Nor Avocation—nor Concern
For little Mysteries

As harass us—like Life—and Death—
And Afterwards—or Nay—
But seemed engrossed to Absolute—
With shining—and the Sky—

The privilege to scrutinize
Was scarce upon my Eyes
When, with a Silver practise—
She vaulted out of Gaze—

And next—I met her on a Cloud—
Myself too far below
To follow her superior Road—
Or its advantage—Blue—

There are *pen* portraits, but not many, of Emily Dickinson as a physical person, a woman. Of course, there are *books* full of impressions and abstract evaluations of her as a *personage,* those boasting in a genteel way of connections with her, remembered associations, both firsthand and secondhand, rumors about her—a great and confused body of myth that collected and multiplied *after* Emily, the flesh-and-blood being, was beyond touch, invisible in her grave.

Since only a few letters written *to* E. D. survive, although so many that she sent to others have been collected, visualizations of her are fragmentary or obscure. A cousin who, being an orphan, lived in the household of Emily's brother, Austin, and his wife, Susan, as a child of six is quoted in a footnote, saying: "I never saw Emily Dickinson. In my remembrance she was a dearly loved cousin who wore white in winter as well as in summer, and who never would have her picture taken." (Notice that although the report is "I never saw her" Emily is remembered in white!) In a note for a biography by Millicent Todd Bingham (daughter of Mabel Loomis Todd, who assembled and edited the initial volumes of Emily's poems and letters) we read: "Though she saw no one grown"—(this after Emily's seclusion in her father's house), "a small child might sometimes step inside the doorway to receive a cookie fresh from the oven, or a flower from her hand. . . ."

The scarcity of physical descriptions is partly explained by the fact that *Emily hid herself.* "I have a cowardice of strangers," she confessed in a letter. And she hid her poems, even the fact that she was writing poems, from almost everyone. Near her thirty-seventh year she chose never to leave her father's house and grounds. However, in a "younger poem" (ca. 1862) Emily is seen striding out on a long hike to "visit the Sea," as she metaphorically puts it:

I started Early—Took my Dog—
And visited the Sea—
The Mermaids in the Basement
Came out to look at me

And Frigates—in the Upper Floor
Extended Hempen Hands—
Presuming Me to be a Mouse—
Aground—upon the Sands—

But no Man moved Me—till the Tide
Went past my simple Shoe—
And past my Apron—and my Belt
And past my Bodice—too—

And made as He would eat me up—
As wholly as a Dew
Upon a Dandelion's Sleeve—
And then—I started—too—

And He—He followed—close behind—
I felt his Silver Heel
Upon my Ankle—Then my Shoes
Would overflow with Pearl—

Until We met the Solid Town—
No One He seemed to know—
And bowing—with a Mighty look—
At me—The Sea withdrew—

"I started Early—Took my dog": Emily had a dog named Carlo, breed unknown but large and shaggy, as indicated in various letters of hers. "And visited the Sea—": so far the scene is literal. But then it goes deeper and deeper into a sort of surrealism, or Alice in Wonderland narrative, at the same time keeping the breathless feeling of the real sea, the real tide reaching onto the shore, following her, wanting to engulf her. It follows her almost home, to "the Solid Town" until "with a Mighty look . . . The Sea withdrew—." The sea is personified with male pronouns. This poem has the aura of a vivid dream (as a number of Emily's do—"In Winter in my Room" is another good instance). It may also be a disguised love poem. She has many of those, some very evidently in reference to men, others without question, because so addressed, were written to a girlhood friend, Susan, both before and after Susan became Emily's brother's wife. "The Mermaids in the Basement," third line of first stanza, "Came out to look at me"—how audacious that is, to refer to the lowest depth of the sea as a basement, which makes of the water a structure with an under-storey or sunken room.

In 1862, when she was thirty-one years old, Emily read an article in the *Atlantic Monthly* headed "Letters to a Young Contributor" by Thomas Wentworth Higginson, eminent and prolific man of letters. She wrote to him asking if he would say if her verse were "alive," and she enclosed four poems, thereby initiating a first shy correspondence with a published writer, which continued at intervals throughout her life. One of the enclosed poems was her famous "Safe in their alabaster chambers." But Higginson could not classify her poems. Who, in literature past or present, could you say she was *like* in some way? Her work was wildly different from the symmetrical and smooth prosody of the day. He found her verses "remarkable, though odd." He wrote her that her metric was "spasmodic." He advised her not to publish.

In her reply she thanked him "for the surgery," and in a later letter, after trying him with other poems, she wrote:

> I smile when you suggest that I delay to publish—that being foreign to my thought, as Firmament to Fin.
>
> If fame belonged to me, I could not escape her—if she did not, the longest day would pass me on the chase—and the approbation of my Dog would forsake me then. My Barefoot Rank is better. You think my gait "spasmodic." I am in danger, Sir. You think me "uncontrolled." I have no Tribunal.

Thomas H. Johnson, who edited the Harvard edition of the Dickinson letters in 1958 and *The Complete Poems* in 1960, suggests that, after a number of well-meaning but obtuse responses to her work, Emily finally accepted her destiny as an artist who in her lifetime would remain unknown.

Higginson sensed *something* valuable about her and about her strange poems, however. Unlike the verse of others who sought his opinion, hers he found impossible to forget, and he wrote asking for some facts about her and for a picture. Her letter of July 1862 supplied this sketch of herself:

> Could you believe me—without? I had no portrait, now, but am small, like the Wren, and my Hair is bold like the Chestnut Burr—and my eyes, like the Sherry in the Glass, that the Guest leaves. Would this do as well?

So we need to visualize auburn hair, perhaps hazel eyes, a small frame.

After eight years of baffling correspondence, Higginson in 1870 met the woman Emily Dickinson. He visited her at home in Amherst. She had repeatedly declined to meet him in Boston. Afterward he wrote to his wife: "I never was with anyone who drained my nerve power so much." (Without touching her, she drained the power from him.) "I am glad not to live near her," he wrote. He found her "enigmatic," "tense," likely to withdraw into her shell at the slightest cross-examination. "I could only sit still and watch, as one does in the woods," said he. Earlier, in a letter, he had written to Emily, "Perhaps if I could once take you by the hand . . . but . . . you only enshroud yourself in this fiery mist and I cannot reach you." Writing to his sister, Higginson once referred to Emily as "my partially cracked poet at Amherst." Which instantly reminds one of her poem (1862):

Much Madness is divinest Sense—
To a discerning Eye—
Much Sense—the starkest Madness—
'Tis the Majority
In this, as All, prevail—
Assent—and you are sane—
Demur—you're straightway dangerous—
And handled with a Chain—

In 1891, years after her death, when she at last had fame (or at least the rapt attention of the curious in the literary world of the time), T. W. Higginson published in the *Atlantic Monthly* an article about Emily Dickinson showing how well he had known her and stating that from the first he had had "the impression of a wholly new and original poetic genius" but one "elusive of criticism." Helen Hunt Jackson, who had a large reputation as a leading woman prose writer and occasional poet in America during the last half of the nineteenth century, was the single qualified contemporary who, while Emily was alive, did unequivocally believe her to be an authentic poet. There was scarcely the opportunity for other poets to know about her or to read her work. Ralph Waldo Emerson lectured several times in Amherst between 1857 and 1879 and stayed overnight in the Austin Dickinson house. He no doubt knew of Emily but knew nothing of her poetry. Thoreau, a private person himself, did not know of her. Walt Whitman did not know of Emily Dickinson. When she was asked her opinion of *Leaves of Grass* she replied: "I never read his book, but was told he was disgraceful."

Emily was in her forties when Helen Hunt Jackson, who had been shown her work by Thomas Higginson, urged her to let some of her poems be included in a projected anthology in which authors would remain anonymous. "You are a great poet," she wrote to Emily, "and it is wrong . . . that you will not sing aloud," meaning appear in print. Emily at first refused. After decades of being anonymous, and her poems invisible, she did not want them "discovered." Two years later, however, in 1878, at the persuasion of Helen and Higginson, as well as Thomas Niles of Roberts Brothers, publishers, in Boston, she allowed her poem "Success is counted sweetest" to appear in *A Masque of Poets,* edited by Niles. All poems in it were unsigned, and readers trying to guess who wrote "Success" could think of no one but Emerson as a possible author.

Finally, Emily gave permission and let a poem go out to the world. But with its printing the poem was tampered with by the editor, Niles, who attempted to "improve" it here and there. All of the "improvements" somewhat weakened the poem. Thankfully, Emily's original is restored to us. Earlier, without E. D.'s prior knowledge, the *Daily Springfield Republican* had printed poems of hers, and anonymously. Samuel Bowles, the editor, and his wife were among her correspondents, and she had sometimes enclosed copies of her writings as parts of letters. "I taste a liquor never brewed—" appeared May 4, 1861, in that newspaper, having been foolishly labeled "May Wine." Her later-so-famous "Because I could not stop for Death" was furnished with the printed title "The Chariot." The *Springfield Republican* of February 14, 1866, without Emily's knowledge, published the poem "A narrow Fellow in the Grass," giving it the title "Snake." She complained to Higginson in a letter:

> Lest you meet my Snake and suppose I deceive, it was robbed of me—defeated, too, of the third line by the punctuation, The third and fourth were one—I had told you I did not print.

She hated it that editors not only raided her poems and changed them but also gave them labels. They needed no names. When experiencing the full reality of something alive, one does not, to begin with, say its name:

A narrow Fellow in the Grass
Occasionally rides—
You may have met Him—did you not
His notice sudden is—

The Grass divides as with a Comb—
A spotted shaft is seen—
And then it closes at your feet
And opens further on—

He likes a Boggy Acre
A Floor too cool for Corn—
Yet when a Boy, and Barefoot—
I more than once at Noon

Have passed, I thought, a Whip lash
Unbraiding in the Sun
When stopping to secure it
It wrinkled, and was gone—

Several of Nature's People
I know, and they know me—
I feel for them a transport
Of cordiality—

But never met this Fellow
Attended, or alone
Without a tighter breathing
And Zero at the Bone—

Let's see how, without a title, we easily identify what is described and what's going on in this little Emily poem:

She sights a Bird—she chuckles—
She flattens—then she crawls—
She runs without the look of feet—
Her eyes increase to Balls—

Her Jaws stir—twitching—hungry
Her Teeth can hardly stand—
She leaps, but Robin leaped the first—
Ah, Pussy, of the Sand,

The Hopes so juicy ripening—
You almost bathed your Tongue—
When Bliss disclosed a hundred Toes—
And fled with every one—

This is *kinetic poetry*. Every movement and the *kind* of movement of the cat is reproduced by short, quick phrases, until the climactic line, in which Robin gets away. Reading aloud, your voice almost automatically imitates the suddenness of the cat: *She-sights-a-Bird—she-chuckles—she flattens—then she crawls*—etc.

Emily's sister, Lavinia, loved cats and had many. Emily saw them too frequently stalking her beloved birds. I recall few poems of hers with cats, whereas birds, particularly the robin, figure in so many. One of her most famous bird poems is:

A Bird came down the Walk—
He did not know I saw—
He bit an Angleworm in halves
And ate the fellow, raw,

And then he drank a Dew
From a convenient Grass—
And then hopped sidewise to the Wall
to let a Beetle pass—

He glanced with rapid eyes
That hurried all around—
They looked like frightened Beads, I thought—
He stirred his Velvet Head

Like one in danger, Cautious,
I offered him a Crumb
And he unrolled his feathers
and rowed him softer home—

Than Oars divide the Ocean,
Too silver for a seam—
Or Butterflies, off Banks of Noon
Leap, plashless as they swim.

Emily's subjects are what she saw daily, often from her window or in her conservatory, where she grew and kept blooming even in winter many kinds of flowers, some of them exotic. It was here, perhaps, that she met so many bees. Bees waft and hum through an extraordinary number of poems. Many are bumblebees. About 1877 she wrote:

Bees are Black, with Gilt Surcingles—
Buccaneers of Buzz,
Ride abroad in ostentation
And subsist on Fuzz.

Fuzz ordained—not Fuzz contingent—
Marrows of the Hill.
Jugs—a Universe's fracture
Co*ul*d not jar or spill.*

*Italics mine. —M. S.

What is a "surcingle"? In Webster: "a girth for a horse or other large animal." Her tiny subjects turn out to be large. Witness the philosophy in the second stanza. Her mixture of solemnity and humor is characteristic in many poems.

Here I will dare to offer a parody, a spoof, on Emily's poetic mannerisms, which is about one of her favorite miniscule subjects, the bee. It's clever, and it is not mean. In fact it's lovable, I think. John Frederick Nims, who wrote it, a fine contemporary poet, respects and adores Dickinson. Of course, he has scattered throughout the text that favorite punctuation mark, the dash, and has capitalized certain nouns, and he overemphasizes the singsong rhythm:

I never plucked—a Bumblebee—
Without I marvelled—"Ouch!"
Wise Nature—hath such ways to show—
Her children—"Mustn't touch!"

I never chewed—a Beetle up—
Sans pouting—"Icky-poo!"
Did Beetle taste—like "Choc-o-late"—
He were extinctive now.

I never did me—this or that—
Without—I something said.
I put a Pumpkin—on my neck—
And used to call it—"Head"—

Till Robin—cocked his dapper eye—
Impeachment—sir—of me?
As one who—off his rocker flip—
Or fruitcake—nutty be?

There's one assessment in John Nims's spoof we almost have to agree with: "I never did me this or that, without I something said." Emily recorded in her poems (as if in a secret diary to which, during her prolific years, she added every day) so much that she perceived and experienced, enjoyed or suffered, and philosophized about. She had an explorer's mind, and she was a skeptic—she could not be content with simply following and trusting the customs, beliefs, manners, morals, social conduct, assigned to well-born New England daughters a century and a half ago. And she possessed intense emotional urges, her senses always sharp and at full pitch. She needed to give vent to her great rushes of feeling and thought. Most of her poems are short, small in size, but they are thick. Thick in the same sense as a one-inch cube of precious metal may weigh more than a pillowful of feathers. Her best are multifaceted in both their form and content. They often have the simplest of surfaces and the most complex depths.

Astonishing is the quantity that she produced. To the year 1862, marked by the greatest flow, according to the poems so dated through the research of reliable editors, are assigned 366 poems, meaning she wrote an average of a poem a day that year. A number of them, even the most excellent, began as parts of letters she wrote to many friends and relations. For instance, she wrote:

> I send Two Sunsets—
> Day and I—in competition ran—
> I finished Two—and several Stars—
> While He—was making One—
>
> His own was ampler—but as I
> Was saying to a friend—
> Mine—is the more convenient
> To carry in the Hand—

In the Dickinson Homestead and earlier, in the House on Pleasant Street, writing poetry was not all that Emily had to do. There was one house servant, Maggie, who stayed as part of the family throughout her life, but Emily and Lavinia kept house for father and brother, tended mother, who was often ill, and saw to it that frequent visitors were properly entertained. Millicent Todd Bingham, in her book *Emily Dickinson's Home* (Harper, 1955), points out that:

> Toil (especially for the women) was the order of the day. Bear in mind that their duties were performed in layers of skirts which swept the floor, often measuring as much as ten yards around the bottom. . . . There was no central heating. . . . A woodbox in the kitchen was filled by the men, but the women kept the fires burning. . . . There was no running water. Water pitchers for every bedroom were filled each day from the kitchen pump. All cooking was done at home. Much was also produced at home . . . barrels of

flour and sugar under the pantry shelves . . . green vegetables and berries in the garden and fruit in the orchard in summer.

The task of baking was allotted to Emily: "she was also an expert and imaginative cook." Among her private papers found after her death were "poems jotted down on the backs of recipes or on grocers' brown paper bags while she was rolling out dough." In October 1856 Emily's rye and Indian bread won the second-place prize at the annual Cattle Show in Amherst. The cash award was seventy-five cents. She was also good with the needle. Clothes were homemade and by hand before 1851, when the Singer sewing machine was patented. There is a poem of Emily's that proves her acquaintance with thread and needle while making the endless task a metaphor for life itself. With so much real weariness in it, and yet a wry touch of humor (the line in the third stanza, "Like a dotted Dot—"), this poem, amazingly, looks past death to a dawn of resurrection, when, renewed, body and mind will be "strong."

Don't put up my Thread and Needle—
I'll begin to Sew
When the Birds begin to whistle → (Resurrection Morning)
Better Stitches—so—

These were bent—my sight got crooked—
When my mind—is plain
I'll do seams—a Queen's endeavor
Would not blush to own—

Hems—too fine for Lady's tracing
to the sightless Knot—
Tucks—of dainty interspersion—
Like a dotted Dot—

Leave my Needle in the furrow → (the furrowy cloth—but image of the plough is behind the needle)
Where I put it down—
I can make the zigzag stitches
Straight—when I am strong—

Till then—dreaming I am sewing
Fetch the seam I missed—
Closer—so I—at my sleeping → (sleep of death)
Still surmise I stitch—

As her letters indicate, much of her writing was done in her room at night while the others slept, all of it carried on in secret. Sundays were welcomed as writing days, since housework was curtailed and, because she did not go to church with the rest of the family, she had the quiet house to herself. One Sunday (as told to Mabel Todd by Lavinia) Father Dickinson, assembling the family for church, could not find young Emily anywhere. She had disappeared. "Late in the afternoon Vinnie discovered her rocking away peacefully in the cellar bulkhead, reading a book." With no sense of dereliction. Later she stated her attitude in this verse:

Some keep the Sabbath going to Church—
I keep it, staying at Home—
With a Bobolink for a Chorister—
And an Orchard, for a Dome—

Some keep the Sabbath in Surplice—
I just wear my Wings—
And instead of tolling the Bell, for Church,
Our little Sexton—sings.

God preaches, a noted Clergyman—
And the sermon is never long,
So, instead of getting to Heaven, at last—
I'm going, all along.

Emily did not like church, but she loved God. In the latter part of her life it was probably the social aspect of church she wished to avoid. She had intimate quarrels with God in some poems and was not above humorous blasphemy, for instance a remark in a letter to Susan, in 1854, who was by then her sister-in-law: "I was foolish enough to be vexed at a little thing, and I hope God will forgive me, as he'll have to many times, *if he lives long enough!*" Or this quatrain:

God is indeed a jealous God—
He cannot bear to see
That we had rather not with Him
But with each other play.

Another:

Papa above!
Regard a Mouse
O'erpowered by the Cat!
Reserve within thy kingdom
A "Mansion" for the Rat!

And:

"Faith" is a fine invention
When Gentlemen can *see*—
But *Microscopes* are prudent
In an Emergency.

Immortality was one of Emily Dickinson's "flood subjects"—a designation she herself made. Love was another. Two short poems from the decade of the 1860s:

The Soul's distinct connection
With immortality
Is best disclosed by Danger
Or quick Calamity—

As Lightning on a Landscape
Exhibits Sheets of Place—
Not yet suspected—but for Flash—
And Click—and Suddenness.

And:

Death is a Dialogue between
The Spirit and the Dust.
"Dissolve" says Death—The Spirit "Sir
I have another Trust"—

Death doubts it—Argues from the Ground—
The Spirit turns away
Just laying off for evidence
An Overcoat of Clay.

About three years before her death, which occurred in 1886, she wrote this meditative analysis. It sounds to my ear less confident, more questioning and skeptical than in her youth.

The Spirit lasts—but in what mode—
Below, the Body speaks,
But as the Spirit furnishes—
Apart, it never talks—
The Music in the Violin
Does not emerge alone
But Arm in Arm with Touch, yet Touch
Alone—is not a Tune—
The Spirit lurks within the Flesh
Like Tides within the Sea
That make the Water live, estranged
What would the Either be?
Does that know—now—or does it cease—
That which to this is done,
Resuming at a mutual date
With every future one?
Instinct pursues the Adamant,
Exacting this Reply—
Adversity if it may be, or
Wild Prosperity,
The Rumor's Gate was shut so tight
Before my Mind was sown,
Not even a Prognostic's Push
Could make a Dent thereon—

An ambiguous word in the line, "What would the Either be?" makes one pause. It is capitalized and is spelled *E-i-t-h-e-r.* It might be a typo, and she meant *Ether* or *air,* which would fit the context. But I think she meant both words: *Either* suggests that life after death may be true or not; there's no way of knowing before you get there (or before you don't get there). The last eight lines project the painful realization of the impossibility, while mortal, of seeing beyond the Gate *before* it opens to let the Spirit through:

Instinct pursues the Adamant,
Exacting this Reply—
Adversity if it may be, or
Wild Prosperity,
The Rumor's Gate was shut so tight
Before my Mind was sown,
Not even a Prognostic's Push
Could make a Dent thereon—

Neither of the two Dickinson sisters, Emily and Lavinia, married. Their brother, Austin, married Emily's schoolgirl friend, Susan Gilbert, actually with Emily's encouragement. She loved them both intensely, as letters preserved by Austin showed, and her intimacy with Sue grew with her friend's closer ties to her brother. It seems she felt herself a part of her brother's courtship. As the date of the wedding approached, Emily felt panic and wrote to Sue, who was away on spring holiday: "Oh Susie, that you should come to this! So when he takes you from me, to live in his new house, I may have *some* of you? I am sincere."

Emily was capable of more than one kind of passionate love, as many letters and many of her strongest poems attest. Since the conjectured dates of her poems are based on dates of the letters, when known, or otherwise on comparisons of her changing styles of handwriting, there are some clues to the persons who were the probable subjects of her love poems. Of the two lyrics I will quote, the first could have been written to Judge Otis Philip Lord of Salem, with whom she fell in love late in her life. Beginning about 1862, he visited Amherst and on several occasions, stayed at the Evergreens, Austin's and Sue's house "just through the hedges" on the Dickinson property. Perhaps addressed to Lord, this short lyric:

We met as Sparks—Diverging Flints
Sent various—scattered ways—
We parted as the Central Flint
Were cloven with an Adze
Subsisting on the Light We bore
Before we felt the Dark—
A Flint unto this Day—perhaps—
But for that single Spark.

A second love lyric:

Wild Nights—Wild Nights!
Were I with thee
Wild Nights should be
Our luxury!

Futile—the Winds
To a Heart in port—

Done with the Compass—
Done with the Chart!

Rowing in Eden—
Ah, the Sea!
Might I but moor—Tonight—
In Thee!

"Wild Nights" was addressed to Susan, according to some biographers. I think so, too. But prominent critics would rather not point to Emily Dickinson in this way. They prefer to think of her as a New England spinster with an unrequited longing for a suitable male lover and mate. Her sister Vinnie (as Emily called her) remarked on the subject after Emily's death, saying simply: "Emily was always on the lookout for the rewarding person." Early letters to young friends about to marry indicate that Emily felt the same fear of matrimony for herself as of succumbing to the established church. Yet she was ravenous for love and wrote: "Is there not a sweet wolf within us that demands its food?" A poem ascribed to the year 1860 reiterates the theme. In *The Poems of Emily Dickinson,* 1955, edited by Thomas H. Johnson, it is listed as "to an unidentified recipient":

What shall I do—it whimpers so—
This little Hound within the Heart
All day and night with bark and start—
And yet, it will not go—
Would you *untie* it, were you me—
Would it stop whining—if to Thee—
I sent it—even now?

It should not tease you—
By your chair—or on the mat—
Or if it dare—to climb your dizzy knee—
Or sometimes at your side to run—
When you were willing—
Shall it come?
Tell Carlo—
He'll tell *me!*

In their teens Emily and Susan called each other "Daisy" and "Dollie," and the nicknames reappear now and then even in late letters and poems by Emily. Sue was "Dollie," and a poem beginning "I tend my flowers for thee— / Bright Absentee!" ends, "Thy Daisy—Draped for thee!"

When Austin and Susan's first child, Ned, was born, June 19, 1861, Emily sent this poem "across the hedges" to Sue:

> Is it true, dear Sue?
> Are there *two?*
> I shouldn't like to come
> For fear of joggling Him!
> If I could shut him up
> In a Coffee Cup,
> Or tie him to a pin
> Till I got in—
> Or make him fast
> To Toby's fist—
> Hist! Whist! I'd come![1]

(Toby was the cat.)

A serious rift occurred between the two women beginning about 1868 so that personal visits ceased for fifteen years. Austin's wife became socially ambitious, haughty, and dominating. Emily withdrew from social life in Amherst but increased her writing of letters, and some still traversed the few hundred feet between the Homestead and the Evergreens. Richard B. Sewall, Dickinson's chief biographer, reported that some 276 poems and 128 letters are supposed to have been written by Emily to Sue up to 1885, a year before Emily's death. "One suspects," he adds, "that many letters" that came into Austin's possession addressed to his wife were destroyed "as too intimate" by him, or by Sue, who survived him by many years. And numbers of letters, whose originals are in the archives of Harvard College, that Austin received from Emily before his marriage but while he was courting Sue, have Sue's name or references to her partially erased or struck out. No one knows who the censor was. Sue's mercurial temper, even cruelty, was felt early by Emily, who, in an 1851 letter to her brother, wrote: "the world is hollow, and

---

1. From *Life and Letters of Emily Dickinson* by Martha Dickinson Bianchi, published by Houghton Mifflin Company, Boston. Copyright 1924 by Martha Dickinson Bianchi, copyright renewed 1952 by Alfred Leete Hampson. Reprinted by permission.

Dollie is stuffed with sawdust." Still, as late as 1877 (if the assigned date of the poem is correct), less than a decade before her death, Emily wrote this quatrain, with its little pun in the first line:

> To own a Susan of my own
> Is of itself a Bliss—
> Whatever Realm I forfeit, Lord
> Continue me in this![2]

Then, Emily's note dated June of the following year, in stark contrast, reads:

> Susan knows she is a Siren—and that at a word from her, Emily would forfeit Righteousness. . . . I was for a moment disarmed—This is the World that opens and shuts, like the Eye of the Wax Doll—

A terrifying and paralyzing image, this late slant reference to "Dollie"—but their bond (because Daisy would not let it) was never entirely broken. One can't help remembering the beginning of a letter Emily wrote over thirty years earlier: "Sue—you can go or stay—There is but one alternative—We differ often lately, and this must be the last." (After which there are known to have followed well over one hundred letters of notes over the years.)

Among Emily's papers found after her death were letters and drafts and fragments that have been ascribed to the late 1870s that were addressed to Judge Otis P. Lord of the Massachusetts bar, a friend of her father and eighteen years her senior. They were dramatic love letters. One rough draft was found on a discarded envelope addressed in Lord's hand. There is other evidence of the intimacy of their relationship and of its continuance until Judge Lord's death in 1884. Emily wrote letters and presumed poems to at least two other prominent men besides Lord and Thomas Higginson. (Beneath a formal style with Hig-

---

2. From *Emily Dickinson Face to Face* by Martha Dickinson Bianchi, published by Houghton Mifflin Company, Boston. Copyright 1932 by Martha Dickinson Bianchi, copyright renewed 1960 by Alfred Leete Hampson. Reprinted by permission.

ginson she was sometimes coquettish.) The correspondence shows evidence of a romantic attachment to both Samuel Bowles, son of the founder of the *Springfield Republican,* and to Charles Wadsworth, pastor of the Presbyterian Church in Philadelphia, whom Emily met there in 1855. Communication was almost entirely by mail. There is the mystery of the three long "Dear Master" letters she wrote presumably between 1858 and 1862, her handwriting, however, being the only clue to dates. She referred to herself as "Daisy" in one of them. The "Dear Master" letters are passionate and confessional, their drafts found among her papers with no identity of the person addressed, and it is not certain whether they were ever actually mailed to anyone. Some of her love poems were fairly certainly written with men friends she knew in mind. Most significant and containing one of her most stunning metaphors is the following:

My Life had stood—a Loaded Gun—
In Corners—till a Day
The Owner passed—identified—
And carried Me away.

And now We roam in Sovereign Woods—
And now We hunt the Doe—
And every time I speak for Him—
The Mountains straight reply—

And do I smile, such cordial light
Upon the Valley glow—
It is as a Vesuvian face
Had let its pleasure through—

And when at Night—Our good Day done—
I guard My master's Head—
'Tis better than the Eider-Duck's
Deep Pillow—to have shared—

To foe of His—I'm deadly foe—
None stir the second time—
On whom I lay a Yellow Eye—
Or an emphatic Thumb—

Though I than He—may longer live
He longer must—than I—
For I have but the power to kill,
Without—the power to die—

A loaded gun, an inanimate object, is capable of killing but does not die, as must its human master. Emily, in this poem, offers herself as a passive yet potent companion, hunter and defender who, even at the sacrifice of not sharing his pillow (sleeping with) her love, will stay awake to guard his head and keep him safe.

Emily's poem with the line that reads, "Big my Secret but it's *bandaged*"—is among those for which no evidence of date of composition exists. The word *bandaged* she italicized, using it in the sense of "bound up" or "wrapped," suggesting a psychic wound kept covered but obliquely pointed to in some of her poems. Nearly a hundred years after Dickinson's death the wound remains hidden, still throbbing, alive to speculation.

It is too bad that Emily Dickinson and Walt Whitman did not know each other, giants of poetry that they were, both unrecognized as such during their fertile years but firm in self-recognition. Thomas Higginson, with his high critical repute and who was believed a crusader for liberal causes, was as blind to Whitman's worth as he was to Dickinson's. In an essay in the *Atlantic,* October 1871, he wrote that "eccentricity (in art) though promising as a mere trait of youth, is only a disfigurement to maturer years." He said that the "discredit to Walt Whitman" was not that "he wrote *Leaves of Grass,* but that he did not burn (those leaves) afterwards and reserve himself for something better."

Could two geniuses make good bedfellows? Donald Hall, fine contemporary poet, had a poem in the *Atlantic* (July 1983). (How good that that distinguished monthly continues after more than a hundred years.) The poem in a witty way puts Emily and Walt together. It's called:

The Difficult Marriage

> The bride disappears. After twenty minutes of searching
> we discover her in the cellar, vanishing against a pillar
> in her white gown and her skin's original pallor.
> When we guide her back to the altar, we find the groom
> in his slouch hat, open shirt, and untended beard
> withdrawn to the belltower with the healthy young sexton
> from whose comradeship we detach him with difficulty.
> Oh, never in all the cathedrals and academies

of compulsory Democracy and free-thinking Calvinism
will these poets marry!—O pale, passionate
anchoret of Amherst! O reticent kosmos of Brooklyn!

But a significant way in which Walt and Emily resembled each other was in the great quantity of poetry they each produced. In each case there was a spate, a flood, an irrepressible avalanche, not all of it first rate but a large amount that, we now know, was, is, and continues as the fruit of genius. Dickinson's most prolific, creative years, from 1858 to 1865, were also years of intense emotional crisis as well as a physical crisis involving an eye affliction. Her mounting cognizance of her poetic powers came at the same time as the possibility of fame, as she correctly felt, was to be forbidden in her lifetime. Certain letters and certain poems of the period show she felt the threat of madness. First lines: "I felt a Funeral in my Brain," "The Brain within its Groove," "Pain has an Element of Blank." Let me quote the whole of:

The first Day's Night had come—
And grateful that a thing
So terrible—had been endured—
I told my Soul to sing—

She said her Strings were snapt—
Her Bow—to Atoms blown—
And so to mend her—gave me work
Until another Morn—

And then—a Day as huge
As Yesterdays in pairs,
Unrolled its horror in my face—
Until it blocked my eyes—

My Brain—begun to laugh—
I mumbled—like a fool—
And tho' tis Years ago—that Day—
My Brain keeps giggling—still.

And Something's odd—within—
That person that I was—
And this One—do not feel the same—
Could it be Madness—this?

Two famous poems beginning "I heard a Fly buzz—when I died" and "Because I could not stop for Death—" were written in 1862 and 1863 (evidence for these dates being well accepted). This was over twenty years before her actual death. There are other instances of prophetic poems. Emily instinctively knew everything about her Self—her outer and inner atmospheres and impulses. By intuition she knew everything about the World—about Process. And she apprehended the Unseen. She wrote:

I never saw a Moor—
I never saw the Sea—
Yet know I how the Heather looks
And what a Billow be.

I never spoke with God
Nor visited in Heaven—
Yet certain am I of the spot
As if the Checks were given—

One that I think of as "her Window Poem" so aptly gives us an image of Emily, self-confined to her room, as she was in later years, but superconscious of everything inside and outside of that private space. It's a morning poem—a repetition of many mornings:

The Angle of a Landscape—
That every time I wake—
Between my Curtain and the Wall
Upon an ample Crack—

Like a Venetian—waiting—
Accosts my open eye—
Is just a Bough of Apples—
Held slanting, in the Sky—

The Pattern of a Chimney—
The Forehead of a Hill—
Sometimes—a Vane's Forefinger—
But that's—Occasional—

The Seasons—shift—my Picture—
Upon my Emerald Bough,
I wake—to find no—Emeralds—
But—Diamonds—which the Snow

From Polar Caskets—fetched me—
The Chimney—and the Hill—
And just the Steeple's finger
These—never stir at all—

Serving as her vow of final retirement, on May 11, 1869, in a letter refusing Higginson's invitation to Boston, Emily declared, "I do not cross my Father's ground to any House or town."

She began to collect and arrange her extensive number of poems, making "fair copies" in pen and ink, grouping four to six folded sheets at a time and, with needle and twine, fastening or binding the spines into slim booklets. After her death in 1886 her sister Lavinia discovered in Emily's room a box containing about nine hundred poems, which she had collated in some sixty little "volumes" secretly *self-published;* so to speak. Other groupings, not threaded, but seeming intended for binding in such a way, were later found—and further poems and fragments turned up, some of them as parts of letters signed by Emily. Beginning with 1890, selections from the large cache of poems were edited and published piecemeal in several editions, initially by Mabel Loomis Todd, together with Thomas Higginson. Millicent Todd Bingham, Mabel Todd's daughter, and Martha Dickinson Bianchi, Susan and Austin's daughter, became later editors of letters and poems.

Eventually, but not until the middle of the twentieth century, collection and publication of her work culminated with a grand total of *1,775 poems* and fragments in the variorum text of *The Poems of Emily Dickinson,* issued by the Belknap Press of Harvard University (1955).

In her handwritten collections Dickinson gave no dates, nor titles, nor did she number her poems. Thus, scholars have had to try to locate them in a probable sequence by studying her letters (most of which she didn't date, either) and by comparing the various penmanships she employed throughout her writing life. The true chronology of *The Complete Poems* may never be conclusively known. The power of her greatest work (and it is a large portion) is not lessened by this fact, for each supernova in her universe of poems is autonomous.

In Emily's final decade, after the deaths of her father and of her mother eight years later, as well as of others close to her, her poems on the topic of death multiplied. "The overtakelessness of those / Who have accomplished Death" begins one; another, conjectured for the same year in which Judge Otis Lord died, 1884, reads:

> Each that we lose takes part of us;
> A crescent still abides,
> Which like the moon, some turbid night,
> Is summoned by the tides.

To Susan she sent an elegy addressed to the soul of eight-year-old Gilbert, Sue's child, the nephew Emily had especially loved:

> Pass to thy Rendezvous of Light,
> Pangless except for us—
> Who slowly ford the Mystery
> Which thou hast leaped across!

In her last years she discovered and incredulously wrote down that:

> Your thoughts don't have words every day
> They come a single time
> Like signal esoteric sips
> Of the communion Wine
> Which while you taste so native seems
> So easy so to be
> You cannot comprehend its price
> Nor its infrequency

Her production of poems declined, while the letters multiplied; often to her many correspondents she imbedded short aphoristic verses of greeting or condolence accompanied by a pressed flower or other token. Her empathy is expressed in this quatrain written as late as 1877:

> They might not need me—yet they might—
> I'll let my Heart be just in sight—
> A smile so small as mine might be
> Precisely their necessity—

Helen Hunt Jackson visited Emily at Amherst in October 1876, ten years before her death. Emily was far from well, having experienced her father's death and her mother's paralysis within the past two years. She had had a mysterious eye trouble, and psychologically she was dormant. The following quotation from Helen Jackson's apologetic letter sent after seeing Emily constitutes a late portrait of Dickinson:

> I feel as if I had been very impertinent that day in speaking to you as I did—accusing you of living away from the sunlight—and telling you that you looked ill. . . . but really you looked so white and mothlike! Your hand felt like such a wisp in mine that you frightened me. I felt like a great ox talking to a white moth and begging it to come and eat grass with me to see if it could turn itself into beef! How stupid.

Unexpectedly, though, Helen Hunt Jackson died a year *before* Emily—in 1885.

Emily kept herself unnoticed, nearly anonymous. It is her poems that project themselves; they are out front—are bold and strong. They were much too forward and innovative, both for *what* they said and *how* they said it, to be penetrated and appreciated by editors, publishers, or critics of her day. Emily knew what poetry was. Its definition grew in her along with the practice. Early on she wrote:

This was a Poet—It is That
Distills amazing sense
From ordinary Meanings—
And Attar so immense

From the familiar species
That perished by the Door—
We wonder it was not Ourselves
Arrested it—before—. . . .

And late in her life, this:

To pile like Thunder to its close
Then crumble grand away
While Everything created hid
This would be Poetry—

Or Love—the two coeval come—
We both and neither prove—

Experience either and consume—
For None see God and live—

She was talking about her talent, when during the flood time of her most creative year, 1862, Emily wrote:

It was given to me by the Gods—
When I was a little Girl—
They give us Presents most—you know—
When we are new—and small.
I kept it in my Hand—
I never put it down—
I did not dare to eat—or sleep—
For fear it would be gone—
I heard such words as "Rich"—
When hurrying to school—
From lips at Corners of the Streets—
And wrestled with a smile.
Rich! 'Twas Myself—was rich—
To take the name of Gold—
And Gold to own—in solid Bars—
The Difference—made me bold—

From the beginning she knew and unflinchingly declared: "The Poets light but Lamps— / Themselves—go out—" and Emily Elizabeth Dickinson, born December 10, 1830, died May 15, 1886, at the age of fifty-five.

From a description of her funeral, furnished years later by a cousin, Clara Newman, I briefly quote:

> They folded her in a little white wrap I had sewed for her myself the last Christmas . . . and she lay in her white casket in the hall of her father's house . . . bees and butterflies . . . buzzed a Requiem without the open door. A knot of field blue violets lay at her throat. . . . The service was very simple . . . (and when) concluded, six stalwart men whose faces she knew . . . (they had worked on the Homestead grounds) lifted her on their shoulders and bore her—into the street? Ah, no! That would have been a way strange for her. . . . The cemetery lay three fields away and, the bars being lowered, the light little burden led the way through meadows filled with buttercups and daisies.

And so the wish in one of her poems—whether made early or late in her life we do not know, it bears no date—was granted to Emily. She wrote:

Beauty crowds me till I die
Beauty mercy have on me
But if I expire today
Let it be in sight of thee—

She, whose craving for and insistence on immortality germinated in so many of her poems, was buried nearly one hundred years ago. What has not aged, and cannot die, is the body of her best work—at least as long as language lasts and human eyes and ears and tongues remain to feast upon it.

Sylvia Plath
A Recollection

I met Sylvia Plath just once, at Yaddo, in the late fall of 1959. My second book, *A Cage of Spines,* had been published the year before; her first, *The Colossus,* would appear in the following year, 1960. She was much younger than I, but, as no one knew at that time, she had only about three more years to live. Nor did I know, at that time, scarcely who she was, let alone who she *would* be, or what wide impact her poetry would make in both America and England. She and Ted Hughes had been at Yaddo almost two months by November when I arrived for a month's stay, and they were soon to leave, so no acquaintance to speak of really occurred. Their bedroom was on the ground floor of West House. Ted had a studio in the woods, while Sylvia's workroom, high and sunny with a balcony overlooking pines and part of a field, was on the top floor of West House. This had been my studio on an earlier visit. But it was only much later that I learned Sylvia Plath had been assembling her first collection, and had in fact written some of the poems to be in it, there at Yaddo.

My studio/bedroom was an apartment in East House, and one evening before dinner Polly Hanson[1] brought me to meet the Hugheses. Sylvia was in bed with a bad sinus cold and was also pregnant, Polly told me. She was not up to coming to the

---

This piece was sent to Peter Davison in 1987 at his request, and part of it was included in a book he was editing, *Bitter Fame: A Life of Sylvia Plath,* by Anne Stevenson (Boston: Houghton Mifflin, 1989).

1. A poet and the secretary of Elizabeth Ames, executive director of Yaddo.

dining room, and Ted was bringing her food on a tray. We found her sitting up in bed among pillows in the shadowy room under the hooded yellow light of a floorlamp, with pine boughs outside the window turning the twilight a vivid rainy green. Books and notepads, papers, pens, magazines, a box of tissues, a bowl of apples and grapes, nestled among the blankets. Sylvia, in a flannel bed jacket, blond hair to her shoulders, long limbed— I remember thinking her well paired with Ted, tall and big-boned. But he was ruddy. A remark about her own appearance, which I later found in Sylvia's published *Journals,* comes to mind: ". . . my podgy and doughcolored face." She was definitely unwell. They both sounded very British as we were introduced. A handshake and the flash of a smile, then Sylvia's head drooped, her dark eyes lidded, and she looked down into her lap.

III

The Floor

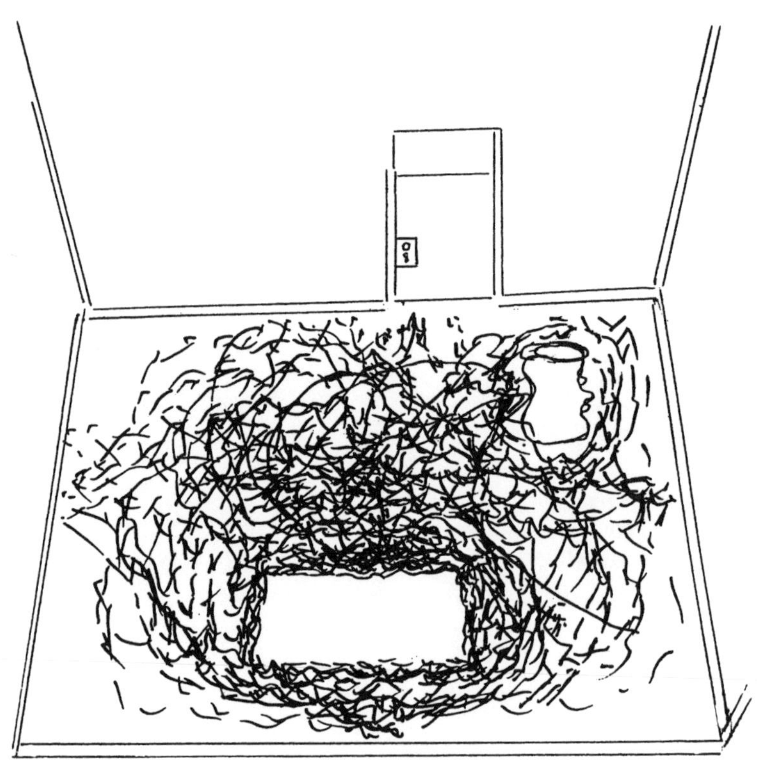

Fig. 1. Hobob's marks on the floor by the end of scene 3, in *The Floor*. Author's sketch, May Swenson Papers, Washington University Libraries.

The Floor

A Play in One Act

The Setting: a space. The Time: for the time being. The Players: LANLOR *and* HOBOB, *two "clowns."*

A scaffolding, probably of raw wood planks, forms a large open cube indicating the dimensions of a "room." The four "walls" as well as the "ceiling" are thus outlined. In the back "wall" is a "door" and, attached to the inside of its left frame, a block of wood painted to look like a metal lock with keyhole. Also attached is a doorknob in the usual place. But there is actually no door. The "floor" is the floor of a raised stage, situated at audience eye level, or in any case so as to provide an unimpeded view of the whole floor space. The floor is black and seems to be of a material like slate, since HOBOB'S *footsteps upon it leave white tracks.* HOBOB'S *footsteps can be seen to leave their marks on the floor as would chalk on a blackboard, and the marks remain.*

Scene 1

[LANLOR *and* HOBOB *outside the cube at the back.* LANLOR *is showing* HOBOB *around the cube. The two "clowns" are quite young and appear to be opposites as well as replicas of each other. In feature and body build they look alike. In temperament* HOBOB *is lively,* LANLOR *impassive.* LANLOR *is "taller" because he walks on stilts (raw wood planks about a foot high).* LANLOR *wears black pants, black shoes, a white collarless shirt with black suspenders, a high black hat with flat top on his bald head.* HOBOB *has thick black hair. He wears white pants, white shoes, black shirt, white suspenders, and a black squat rounded hat.* HOBOB

The Floor was staged at the American Place Theatre during its 1965–66 season and published in *First Stage* 6, no. 2 (summer 1967).

carries a bulging white duffle over his shoulder. LANLOR *and* HOBOB *proceed along upper stage left behind the structure, down across front stage, up right stage, and toward "door" in back "wall."*]

LANLOR: Here we are. Here's your room for the time being.

HOBOB: My room. That's good.

LANLOR: Always is fully furnished. Here's your key. [LANLOR *hangs a long chain with a big key around* HOBOB'S *neck. It falls to below his knees.*]

HOBOB: My key! [*He takes up the key and examines it with curiosity, then delight, as if it were something long coveted, unique.*] My key! My room!

LANLOR: For the time being.

HOBOB: For the time being?

LANLOR: The time being. . . . [*He takes a thick snap-lid watch on a chain from his pocket, opens it, and holds it to his ear.*] The time being 3 point, 3 point, point, point Q meters to apogee—9 minus P point 6 monometers to perogee. [LANLOR *holds the open watch at* HOBOB'S *ear. It can be heard going "ping-ping-ping* (pause) *ping-ping-ping* (pause)*." He closes the watch and returns it to his pocket.*]

HOBOB: Oh. So. . . . So I can move right in?

LANLOR: Move right in. Always is fully furnished. Always is open from the outside, closes from the inside. [HOBOB *about to fit the key in the lock,* LANLOR *stops him.*] Always is *open* on the outside. Always is closed on the *inside.*

HOBOB: Oh? [*He puts his hand on the doorknob, but* LANLOR *removes it, puts his hand on the knob, while with his other hand he adroitly pushes* HOBOB *and his duffle through the "door" into the "room."*] Oh. Thank you. [HOBOB *jostles the duffle to upstage left, the bag and his feet leaving white tracks on the floor. Meanwhile,* LANLOR *enters by stepping through the right "wall." His stilts leave no marks on the floor.* HOBOB *bends over the duffle, undoing it. The key on the chain around his neck, swinging and tangling, interferes with all his motions.*] Got with me all I need. Brought all I need, I guess, for the time being.

LANLOR: [*He takes out and snaps open the watch.*] The time being . . . at the fifth square of spiral acceleration bisecting the solar equator at an angle of 1,500 degrees. [*He holds the watch to* HOBOB'S *ear. It is heard going ping-ping-ping* (pause), *etc., until* LANLOR *puts the watch away.*]

HOBOB: [*After listening to the watch.*] Thank you. Good. Now. First, let's see. Got everything. All I need right here. If I can get my hands on it. I'm getting it. Almost got it . . . Here it is. [*He's found what he's been looking for in the duffle and straightens up, comes forward, holding two clean folded bedsheets. He untangles the key and chain from them. He looks all around the empty "room," puzzled.*] There's no bed.

LANLOR: Use the floor.

HOBOB: The floor? [*He looks around the floor. He notices the chalklike marks, takes some steps, and sees them traced on the floor. He speculates, shrugs, finally decides to accept the fact, and hide his surprise.*] The floor, huh?

LANLOR: Always is fully furnished. Use the floor.

HOBOB: [*Decides to comply. He spreads out the clean sheets, making a white rectangle on the floor near center stage. There is the constant business of the key and chain getting in his way. He walks all around arranging the "bed." Business of leaving tracks wherever the floor is touched. The bed made,* HOBOB *contemplates it with satisfaction.*] First thing is. . . . A good night's sleep. [*He takes down his suspenders, unbuttons his shirt, and takes it off, automatically looks around for some hook to hang the shirt on.*] No closet?

LANLOR: Use the floor.

HOBOB: The floor? Oh yeah. The floor. [*He lays the shirt on the bed, then takes off his trousers. After an automatic look around for a chairback or something, he drops them on the bed.*]

LANLOR: Use the floor. Use the floor.

HOBOB: The floor. Just the floor? [*He picks up the clothes and conscientiously pantomimes placing each on a "hanger" and hanging it in a "closet." Actually, he lays the clothes side by side spread out on the floor to the right of the bed.*] I'm getting it. I'm beginning to get the *hang* of it. See? [*He winks at* LANLOR. *He sits down on the edge of the "bed" facing front, removes shoes and socks. Looks up at* LANLOR *significantly.*] Use the floor? We've *been* using the floor, haven't we, Shoe-Shoe? [*He makes the shoes make some extra shoe marks on the floor. He picks up a shoe and, with the key, pretends to write something on the sole, then presses the sole to the floor to see if it will record a new mark. It does. He tests the floor with his finger to see if the mark is wet—smells his finger.*]

LANLOR: [*sternly*] *Use* the floor!

HOBOB: [*Startled, not knowing what is required, puts his shoes back on hurriedly and laces them. He gets up, jumps across the bed, and sets the shoes on the floor under the clothes in the "closet." He's undressed now except for his jockstrap, his shoes, and his hat, and the key on its cord. He fools around upstage, doing various leaps, iceskating, skips, etc., to see the marks on the floor made by his bare feet. Does handsprings, etc. Business with key getting in the way and clanking on the floor. Finally,* HOBOB *takes off his hat, extends it toward* LANLOR, *making a mock bow.*] Home is where you *hang* it, hey? Quite a floor you got here. Plenty of *room* for . . . for . . . Uh . . . Where do I hang my . . . ?

LANLOR: [*sharply*] Use the floor!

HOBOB: [*He is reluctant to put the hat on the floor. He regards it solicitously, brushes it, blows on it. He touches fingers to the floor testing for dust. He looks around, has an inspiration, and sneaks upstage to hang the hat on the doorknob.*]

LANLOR: [*warningly*] Use the floor! Use the floor! Don't touch! [*He strides after* HOBOB *and blocks the doorknob before* HOBOB *can touch it.*]

HOBOB: But couldn't I . . . ? For the time being?

LANLOR: [*Jerks out his watch, which begins its ping-ping-ping.*] Always is fully furnished! Always is always *closed* from the inside. Always is always open *only* from the outside. Don't touch! Always is . . . for the time being!

HOBOB: [*a bit frightened by the outburst*] O.K. I get it. I get it. So put that damned doo-dad away. [*After making* HOBOB *listen with the watch to his ear,* LANLOR *pockets it.* HOBOB *makes motions of brushing the floor above the clothes in the "closet" and puts the hat carefully there. He steps back, pleased with the orderly arrangement of his "closet" and of his "bed." He gets between the sheets, lies down, turns over to find best position, entangles himself with the key, sits up, untangles, handles the key reverently, caresses it.*] Nice to have a whole room to myself. At least for the—Wait! Let's see. I'll need the— [*He jumps out of bed and goes to duffle, searches, and extracts an alarm clock with a bell on top, proceeds to wind it.*] What's the time, by the way? For the time being, that is?

LANLOR: Always is fully furnished. The time . . . being . . . [*He takes out and listens to his watch.*] Two thousand four hundred and fifty-two grams under optimum pressure at 15 knots latitude, centripetal attitude, minus 411 inches.

HOBOB: Is that it? Good. Thank you. [*He listens to* LANLOR'S *watch, sets the hands on his clock, and sets the alarm. He gets back into bed, stands the alarm clock on the floor beside his head. Arranges key on cord symmetrically over his body on the outside of the sheet. Stage lights go gradually down to twilit.*] Nice to have a room . . . and a bed . . . and a key. Always is fully furnished. Always is always fully . . . Always is . . . [*His eyes close.*]

LANLOR: [*Pockets the watch, so that the sound stops, and, just before the lights black out, is seen stepping on his stilts through the right frame of the cube into darkness.*]

Scene 2

[*Full blackout for just an instant. Then alarm clock rings loudly. Lights full up suddenly.* HOBOB *jerks awake, sits up, stops alarm. Lies back down, hands behind his head, looking up at the "ceiling."*]

HOBOB: Sun's up. Coming up. Strong. Gonna be a fair day. How do we feel, Head, Hip, Heel? Fair? Fair, but Belly could use a meal. [*His eyes start to follow some movement overhead through the top of the cube.*] Those big plump soft deep clean white clouds up there floating. Feel fine. As if been sleeping on one of those. Fine. Do we all feel fine this morning? Eyes and Ears, any gripes, any tears? How are yuh, Hair? Are yuh all still there? Good. Good. Fine and Fair. . . . Good morning, Ceiling. How are you feeling? Blue? Good for you. Hey! What's that? Looks like birds flying over. Hey! Say! There seems to be no ceiling! [*He jumps out of bed, paces about, stares upward from various places in the "room."*] Looks like sky. Or could it be the ceiling's high and painted like that? Well . . . anyway . . . a fair day. Guess it'll be O.K.—for the time being.

LANLOR: [*He steps through right wall, taking out his watch.*] Good—Always is fully furnished—Morning! The time being: five-six-seven-eight and a little bit half-past fast.

HOBOB: Hello. Oh. Fine. Thanks. Now put away that thing, with its dang ding-ping. [*aside*] I won't mention the ceiling. He's liable to say "Use the floor"—and how would I know what for, what for? I'll find out what for. Give me time. [*in natural voice*] First things first. One thing at a time. Plenty of time. For the—No, not that! Time enough. Time, time, time. Some other time. When there's more. When I know the score. When everything's in order. For the—I mean, for *now,* I'll just go along with whatever comes next. When the right time comes I'll figure out what it's all about. [*He has taken his shirt from the "closet," put it on, and buttoned it. He takes up his pants to put them on, which reminds him.*] Say, where's the toilet?

LANLOR: Use the floor.

HOBOB: No!

LANLOR: Use—the—floor.

HOBOB: Well, O.K. . . . But. Well, O.K. . . . But just for the time being, I hope. [*He goes up behind the duffle and stands, back turned, to urinate, with* LANLOR *hurrying after him with the pinging watch, which he holds to* HOBOB'S *ear all the while he's urinating. Then* LANLOR *closes and pockets the watch, signifying operation done.* LANLOR *follows* HOBOB *downstage with* HOBOB *wiping and polishing the key on his shirttail.*]

HOBOB and LANLOR: [*in unison*] Always—is—fully—furnished!

HOBOB: [*He yawns, rubs his head, feels his jowls, looks around.*] No bath? [LANLOR *shakes his head.*] Use the floor?

LANLOR: Use the floor.

HOBOB: [*He goes to the duffle, gets out soap, shaving things, brush, comb, wash cloth, towel. Comes to center stage and places the things on the floor. Sits down on edge of "bed," crosses legs yogi fashion, arranges the things meticulously in front of him, putting all in readiness for washing, shaving, etc. He contemplates how to do it, mumbling:*] Use the *floor.* Use the *floor! Use* the floor. Use *the* floor? [*He rubs the soap vigorously between his hands, spits on the soap, tries motions of washing.*]

LANLOR: Use the *floor!*

HOBOB: [*He gets the idea. He rubs soap on the washcloth, gets on his knees, and "washes" a section of the floor in front of the "bed," the key on chain around his neck constantly getting in the way and banging on the floor. He then strops his old-fashioned razor and "shaves" the floor.*] How's that? Am I getting the *hang* of it? [*Looks up at* LANLOR, *who nods approvingly. Pleased with this success,* HOBOB *gets up, makes a bow to* LANLOR, *runs over to him, seizes his hand, and tries to kiss it.*]

LANLOR: Use the floor.

HOBOB: [*Drops to his knees over the "clean" space on floor and kisses it. Receives approval from* LANLOR. *He gets up, rapidly puts on his pants and sox while humming and whistling.*] Fine morning. Fine day. Sure glad I got a place to stay. . . . Let me see now. . . . What next? [*He goes to the duffle, rummages, and pulls out some white curtains. He looks around and is quite hurt and disappointed.*] No window!

LANLOR: Use the floor.

HOBOB: Use the *floor?* For a *window?*

LANLOR: The floor, the floor. Use the floor.

HOBOB: But I can't *see* through the floor. [*As* LANLOR *strides toward him menacingly,* HOBOB *claps his hands over his mouth, mortified at what he's said.*] Oh, I'm sorry, I'm sorry, I'm sorry. I'll use the floor. I'll use the floor. Only the floor. [*Optimistic again, he stuffs the curtains back in the duffle, searches around in it, and brings out a cup and plate, knife, fork, spoon, all of tin. Looks swiftly around.*] No cupboard, of course, No table, no chair. Never mind, I'll use the. . . . Shall I use the . . . ? *You* say it. *I'm* sick of it. . . . Aren't you going to say it? [LANLOR *remains silent.*] *Why* don't you tell me to use the . . . [*sarcastically*] Don't you *want* me to use the . . . [LANLOR *icily and silently exits through left wall on his stilts.*] Floor! Floor! Floor! I *will* use the floor. I'll *use* the floor. I'll use nothing but the floor, nothing but the floor. Look, look! I'm using the floor! [*He throws the tableware violently on the floor.*] I'm using the floor! I'm using the floor! [*He stamps around in a fit of contrition, whipping himself with the key on the chain.*] The floor, the floor, the floor! I am—using—the *floor!* For the time being. Do you hear? For the time being!

LANLOR: [*Enters and stands there on his stilts.*]

HOBOB: [*Runs to* LANLOR, *kneels, and kisses the floor in front of him many times.*] *This* for the time being. And *this* for the time being. And this and this and this. [LANLOR *finally shows approval by taking out his watch, opening it, and letting it ping.*]

LANLOR: The time being a negative and neutral charge detected on stellar radiographs seventy, fifty-six, and thirty-five with a rotation rate of minus three. [*Exhausted,* HOBOB *gets up, facing* LANLOR. *They stare at each other. There is a long immobile pause while the watch sounds.*]

LANLOR: [*portentously*] Always—is—fully—furnished.

HOBOB: [*compliantly*] Yes. Yes. Of course, of course. [*then brightening*] And for the time being! The time being . . . [*He grabs up the alarm clock, looks at it, listens to* LANLOR'S *watch, twirls the hands on the clock, indicating his eagerness to conform, singing with the rhythm of the pinging watch.*] The time being . . . the time being . . . being . . . being . . . being. . . . Always is. . . . Always is *always* fully furnished. . . . Never is ever empty. I'll get the *hang* of it. The ding and the dong and the dang of it. The sing and the song, the short and the long. The sling and the slang and the bang of it. [*in natural voice*] And lots of things, lots of things left to do. Like . . . Like pictures! What about pictures? [HOBOB *runs to the duffle, rummages in it enthusiastically, and brings out four picture frames. He stacks them against the duffle, then picks one up, examines it as if looking at a painting, comes forward and looks around, considering where to hang it. He decides on the "wall" at stage left, boosts the frame up into center of that space, and shudders as he discovers.*] *No wall!* [*Frightened, but compelled to test the other "walls" as well, he goes round with the "picture" to the other three sides of the open cube, lifting it into the center of each space, whispering hoarsely.*] No wall! No wall! No wall! No walls, even! Not even walls? What kind of a room do you call this? It's appalling! What'll I do?

LANLOR: Use the floor.

HOBOB: Sure. I knew you'd say that. O.K. What else is there? To do? So. O.K. We'll have to see. Have to see what? *Have to see how we can hang them on the floor.* So, then what? Just have to see. See what? See what's next. Try to figure it. Out. Some way. Some how. Some day. But just for the—For *now.* O.K. [*While talking, he mechanically, as in a trance, carries each of the "pictures" to a "wall" and sets them down flat on the floor, symmetrically arranging each one, balancing it, and making motions as if "hanging" it, knocking in a "nail"—(he uses the key for this)—and straightening each frame, on the floor. Stepping back, he views each "picture" critically until he is satisfied that all four are "hung" perfectly. Finished with the job, he comes to front stage, dusting off his hands, adjusting his clothes, mopping his brow with pocket handkerchief, etc.*] Whew! That took some doing. But I managed to get the *hang* of it, huh? [*winks at* LANLOR, *who remains impassive*] Come on, Sourpuss, crack your face. Smile, can't you? Place looks nice now, doesn't it? Beginning to look like home. It'll do, for the time. . . . Uh-uh! Watch out! I mean, No! *No* watch out! [LANLOR, *who has begun a gesture toward taking out his watch, stops.*] Got to think the whole thing through. Got to take an inventory. Let's see. This key. . . . Only thing I seem to have left with a natural function, so to speak. Gotta *use* it, somehow. . . .

LANLOR: Use the floor.

HOBOB: Ah, shad-ap! (I'm only joking, see?) But why don't you come sit down and help me figure this thing out? Don't you ever get down off those sticks of yours? Come on. Use the floor. Let's *both use it.* The only real thing around here, huh? Come on, take the load off your stilts. Might as well be comfortable for the time be . . . Oh-oh. I'm beginning to see how maybe it's me . . . myself . . . bringing on this whole mess. Is that it, Sourpuss? Use the floor with me, huh? [LANLOR *does not respond.*] Is it you don't want to sit and get your pants all chalked up? I don't blame you.

But I don't think it rubs off on a person. See? [*He turns his back to* LANLOR *and bends from the waist.*] My ass is clean. 'Course maybe it's just I have white pants on . . . Ah, come on. Take a chance. [*coaxingly*] For the time being?

LANLOR: [*He takes out his watch, striding toward* HOBOB, *who quickly removes the key cord from his neck, slings it along the floor so that it tangles around one of* LANLOR'S *stilts, which falls off.* LANLOR *tumbles down, the other stilt falling off. He rolls over and lands in a seated position. Meanwhile, he is listening to the pinging watch and saying.*] The time being two and a half kilometers deep, seven lightyears wide, expanding in its initial dimensions at the rate of four layers per century.

HOBOB: That's better. That makes more sense. [*He bends down and listens to* LANLOR'S *watch, which causes him to close it and put it away. Then* HOBOB *sits down facing* LANLOR, *who, with legs and arms akimbo, stares out over the audience, his profile to* HOBOB. HOBOB *puts the key-on-chain back around his neck, fingers it thoughtfully, and begins to use it like a rosary as he thinks aloud.*] The floor. The floor. The main thing is the floor. At least there's *this.* At least there's *here.* Where? Here. How long? Long and how wide? What? High long and Low wide? No. Yes . . . Deep? Yes. No/Yes? Know! So. So-so . . . Oh. Here! Hear? Hear? Hear-hear! [*laughs*] No . . . Now, Here is . . . Is? Is *Is?* Always is. All ways. Always is fully furnished. Room? No room. Know room! Then key? Keyhole. *The* hole? No. Not. No knot yet . . . O.K. O.K., key. And now. Now what? *Know* what? Now is . . . what? *What* what? And what then? And when then? And then why? Now is. Always is. Fully. Fully furnished. Why? Why *why?* Why, when when is! Now? Now! Now-now! [*laughs*] But *how* now? Oh-oh. No, no. For the time be . . . [*He breaks off, looking at* LANLOR, *who, listening for the last syllable, has made a gesture toward taking out his watch.*] I see. I think I see. I see . . . the key. This key. A key. *A* key. O.K. Oh, key. *My* key! *He.* He gave it to me. What for? What for the? For the. For the time. Being-as-it's-not-the-time. [*Says last phrase very fast, watching* LANLOR, *who is listening attentively but who does not take out watch.*] Not the time! Not the time! Being as, being as, and for the time but not the. Time. [*He looks at* LANLOR, *who still does not remove the watch.* HOBOB'S *monologue has been slow and halting. He now repeats it from: "The floor. The floor. The main thing is the floor" up to "For the time be . . ." quickly, as if by rote, while "telling his beads." Each time the word* time *is said,* LANLOR *makes a jerky gesture toward his watch pocket. After the repeat,* HOBOB *continues in slow thought-voice, with pauses.*] Being. Time. The. For. Aha! So. Use the floor. But the key? Me? My? I? He? Key? . . . he-me? This key? That watch? Ding? Me. Dong? He. Can it be? Be? Ing? Ping? Being-ping. Thing. Bing-bing-ping-thing. Bring. Brrring-Brrrrring-ging-ging-ging. Ring. Ring on a string. This? The main thing. The main . . . Floor! [*He gets up and stomps on the floor, jumps and stomps, then tiptoes in a circle around the "bed," paying close attention to the marks made on the floor by his movements. He gets down on his knees and crawls around the bed, watching the marks made behind him. He tries to erase a mark by rubbing with the side of his fist on the floor. His fist merely leaves new marks of the fist on the floor. He sits up yogi fashion and twirls the key on its cord.*] Ring on a string. Thing on a string. Use the O.K. Key. Oh, Key! Belongs to me. The floor, the floor, the floor belongs to Lanlor. He brought me here. I brought with me all I need. All I need. . . . I don't need it here. Don't need it no more. No ceiling, no walls, no door. Just the floor . . . and Lanlor. And Hobob. O-rob. Oh-oh. Ho-ho. So-so. . . . My key. His watch. His stilts. My duffle. My hat. His hat. And he? he-he! Dong-ding. Ding-dong. Ho-ho. Hobob. Oh-rob. Door knob! Door key. Key hole. *The* hole. Key *hole?* Hol-ee, Holee! Holy key! O.K., Key. [*He gets up and, watching* LANLOR, *fearfully, slowly, soundlessly, sneaks upstage to "door" to try to insert key into keyhole. Whirls around, shouting.*] No keyhole!

LANLOR: [*laconically*] Use the floor. [HOBOB *makes a collapsing hopeless gesture, and there is blackout.*]

Scene 3

[*A one-minute pause. Then lights up on same scene.* LANLOR *is seated cross-legged in the same place. His stilts are lying crossed on the floor in front of him.* HOBOB, *in a rage at last, is slamming around the "room."*]

HOBOB: What do you mean renting me a place like this? This is *no* place. What good is a key doesn't open anything? Doesn't lock anything? Can't come in by myself! Can't go out by myself! Can't come, can't go, *period!* You call this a room? The inside is more like an outside. Absolutely empty and not even solid, not even real, and a *prison* at the same time. Fully furnished, hell! What if it rains, what if it snows? Not even a roof over my head. Nothing here but a floor, and it *crazy*. Look at this mess! Can't even *move* without making a mess—and *permanent!* A permanent mess! [*He throws himself into a slide across the floor, leaving a wide white track.*]

LANLOR: [*approvingly*] Use the floor. Use the floor. For the time being.

HOBOB: Whad-a-yuh mean, "for the time being"?

LANLOR: [*jerking out his watch*] The time being: *A* squared to the fourth power, that is to say the fifth side being equal to the first thousand tons of thrust by means of the minimum reactor. [*The watch is sounding ping-ping-ping louder than usual.*]

HOBOB: Damn it! Will you stop that stupid stuff? [LANLOR *is calmly holding the watch up and out for* HOBOB *to listen to it.*] Gimme that! [HOBOB *intends to grab the watch, but his hand stops. He's still afraid.*]

LANLOR: [*mechanically*] And now the time being minus 201 degrees centigrade at the lower hypotenuse, and a 4-ply ultraviolet band seen at point 366 on the oscilloscope. [*He holds up the watch again, which continues to ping, now more piercingly.*]

HOBOB: [*his hands over his ears*] Oh, all *right!* [*He ducks his ear to the watch, fuming.* LANLOR *closes it and puts it away.*] I *have* to go along with it—for the time being. *NO!* Strike that! Oh, God! Too late! [LANLOR *pulls out the pinging watch again.*]

LANLOR: The time being emitted as an energy wave forcing a 98-point shift in the lower quadrant equal to 1,100 cubic epicycles. [HOBOB *immediately puts his ear to it.*]

HOBOB: O.K. I'll listen, I'm listening, I've listened. Put it away! [LANLOR *does so.*] What am I gonna do? How will it end? How will it ever end? What's the *use* of anything? What's it all *for?*

LANLOR: Use the *floor.*

HOBOB: The floor! Use it for what? This messed up place! Getting worse with every step I take. How am I ever gonna get it clean, even? And *keep* it clean? And suppose I *made* it clean, somehow—then what? What for?

LANLOR and HOBOB: [*shouting in unison*] USE THE FLOOR!

HOBOB: I notice *you* haven't left any marks. Why? What are those phony feet of yours made of anyhow? [*He lunges to pick up one of the stilts.*]

LANLOR: [*warningly*] Always is fully furnished. *Don't touch!* [*With a quick motion he attaches the stilts, but, just before he leaps to his feet,* HOBOB *snatches* LANLOR'S *hat off his head.* LANLOR *is seen to have a bald head, white, as if painted that way.* LANLOR, *in a menacing fury, clomps after* HOBOB, *yelling.*] Don't touch! Don't touch. Use the floor! Use the floor!

HOBOB: [*evading him, trying to calm his hysteria*] O.K. Keep your white shirt on, Egghead. Hey, don't get so mad. Just a joke, you know.

LANLOR: [*He can't catch* HOBOB *and comes to a stop, mechanically screaming.*] Use the floor! Use the floor!

HOBOB: [*taunts him, jokingly*] Want me to use the floor? [*He puts* LANLOR'S *hat down on the floor and makes as if to flatten it with his foot.*]

LANLOR: [*agonized*] DON'T TOUCH!

HOBOB: Here, Egghead. Don't get into a lather. Put the lid on. [*Instead of* LANLOR'S *tall hat,* HOBOB *snatches his own bowler from the "closet" and tosses it to land on* LANLOR'S *head.* LANLOR *settles it on straight, satisfied, not reacting to the exchange.*] There now. A wonderful fit. [*He kicks* LANLOR'S *hat out of sight behind him.*] Let's resume our mutual equilibrium, shall we? What time is it, by the way? I mean, for the time being? Time for me to go to bed, I believe.

LANLOR: Yes, yes, yes, yes. Use the floor. Use the floor. [*indicating "bed" on floor, calming down, relieved*] Always is fully furnished. [*In his usual style he removes his watch, clicks it open, and holds it to* HOBOB'S *ear.*] The time being retroactively fading on the dial to a point before point Zero where Always is always—Good—fully furnished—Night. [HOBOB *listens, nods, takes up alarm clock, and sets it.*]

HOBOB: Thank you. [*He straightens the bed, yawns, pretends to begin undressing. Lights are gradually dimming.* LANLOR *puts watch away and steps out through right wall, disappearing in darkness. Alone,* HOBOB *stretches out, still clothed, on his back on the bed, hands clasped under his neck. A white diffuse light comes slowly on above, shines through the "ceiling."* HOBOB *fiddles with the key lying on his chest, picked out glintingly by the light.*] Big moon coming up. Strong. [*He suddenly sits up.*] Gotta go. Gotta get out of here! How, I don't know. But I gotta go! [*Leaps up, pulls the key and chain over his head, throws it to the floor. He gathers up all his belongings around the room and packs them in the duffle—all except the two bedsheets. This is done hurriedly, sloppily, and without fussing about keeping anything neat or doing it right. However, when collecting the "pictures" he tests each "wall" as if it were solid, by pressing his shoulder against it. He lifts the duffle and "slams" it against the "door," finding it "solid." Looking apprehensively to the right, where* LANLOR *went out, he takes hold of the door knob, which doesn't turn. Shakes his head.*] Fake doorknob. And no keyhole! "Always is open from the *outside,*" he said. How do you *get* outside? [*Comes to center, looks up through "ceiling."*] Imagine. The moon can look in here. I can look out at the moon. But can't get out, can't *go.* [*He hunches down and then jumps up to "slam" his fist against the "ceiling" to prove it.*] "Use the floor," he says. That's all there *is.* So use it, O.K. But how? What for? [*He sees* LANLOR'S *high hat on the floor in the moonlight, picks it up, and puts it on.*] Fits, by god? That's odd. Or does it make us even? Funny we wear the same size. He even *looks* like me—except I still got hair. [*He begins to take up and fold the sheets. Puts the top sheet in the duffle. Taking up the second sheet, he finds the floor unmarked on the spot underneath the sheet.*] One clean spot left in this room! Well, well. [*Looks around at the white-scribbled black floor, with the one unmarked oblong in the middle, very black and shiny in the "moonlight." Experimentally, he lifts his foot over it, hesitates, then puts his foot down. Lifts it. There is no print.*] Well, well! [*He takes* LANLOR'S *hat off to scratch his head. Puts his other foot down, lifts it. There is a white footprint.*] Hey! What? Crazy! What does it mean? [*He dusts the print with the crown of* LANLOR'S *hat. The mark disappears. He gets the connection, puts the hat on, jumps on the black rectangle, finding that no marks appear while he has the hat on. Experimenting still, he takes up the key lying on the floor and, on hands and knees, moving around the clean patch, he outlines the oblong by pressing with the key.*] I'm gonna *use* it. I'm *using* it! [*As he does this, a crack appears all around the oblong as when a glasscutter is used, and the section of floor sags, finally dropping away below, silently, leaving a hole in the floor into which the "moonlight" falls.*] Look at that! And a hook! Here's a hook! *Now* I've got the hang of it! [HOBOB *examines a hefty metal hook fastened to the floor under the upstage edge of the hole. He takes the hat off, leans over, peering below.*] Black down there. Whew, worse than here! *That* room has got a ceiling all right. It's got no floor. . . . Always is fully furnished. . . . *This* floor is the ceiling of. . . . What about that? . . . Never is ever empty. [*Gets to his feet. Takes up the key. Stands with* LANLOR'S *hat on.*] This damned holy key. Done nothing but snarl me up and make an idiot out of me. But now I think—I know what it's for. I think—I'm ready—to use the floor. [*He takes the key and chain in both hands, makes a noose, takes off the hat, and experimentally tightens the keychain around his neck. He stoops over the hole and brings the end of the chain down to the hook, finding it's long enough. He straightens and loosens the noose. Then he pulls the sheet across the hole, smoothing it all around so that it hides the hole. Going to the duffle, he rummages and produces his alarm clock, which he sets ringing, while running to the edge of the hole. He snatches up and puts on* LANLOR'S *hat.*] Come on! I'm ready. I'm going to use the floor! For the time being. The time being! The time being!

LANLOR: [*Enters through right "wall" pulling out his watch, which is sounding ping-ping-ping* (pause) *ping-ping-ping* (pause) *at great volume. He stalks up to* HOBOB *slowly, portentously, his robot character very apparent. He is wearing* HOBOB'S *hat. When the watch is held to his ear,* HOBOB *tears the watch and chain away from* LANLOR, *at which* LANLOR *goes limp.* HOBOB *slips the noose over* LANLOR'S *head, tightens it around his neck, and, simultaneously, kicks the stilts off, which slide along the floor.* LANLOR'S *hat, which is* HOBOB'S *hat, falls off on the sheet, both of which plummet down the hole. In the scuffle the alarm clock, still ringing, falls in the hole.* HOBOB *forces* LANLOR *to bend over so that he can tie the end of the keycord to the hook.* LANLOR'S *arms are slack, and he makes no resistance. It's as if he were already lifeless, a dummy figure. The effect is of a hanging in effigy. He falls, swinging by the neck from the hook under the floor, as*

HOBOB *says.*] Use the floor, Old Man. For the time being. [*blackout*]

Scene 4

[*Lights come up almost immediately, and* HOBOB *is seen with stilts on, tall hat on, duffle on his shoulder, open watch in his hand, now sounding its ordinary ping-ping-ping* (pause).]

HOBOB: The time being 9 P.M., Sunday, December 12, 1965.* [*The glint of the heavy key and the white top of* LANLOR'S *head can be seen where he hangs in the black aperture, as* HOBOB *clicks shut and pockets the watch, turns his back, and strides on stilts through the right "wall."*]

Finis

*Substitute actual time and date at the moment this speech is made for each performance.

IV
Letters to Elizabeth Bishop

Yaddo
October 11, 1951

Dear Elizabeth:

It's a dreary, rainy day here—and I am quite unable to write when it rains. It has been raining quite a bit the last two weeks so my "output" has been meager. However, I have written six new poems (three good I think, three awful I'm sure). The mansion is closed now, but the music room there is getting a paint job—the painters are listening to the World Series on a radio they brought with them, so very incongruous sounds come through the stained glass windows as one walks by. The water has been drained out of the big fountain (the one with the statue) and the goldfish removed, but hundreds of crayfish no one knew were there till now are dying for lack of water, sprawled in the mud or tottering sluggishly on their stilt-like feet—they got in with the goldfish, grew up with them, but now, poor orphans, have been left stranded. Bill Robinson[1] and I scooped up two buckets full and poured them down the waterfall, but we had a time avoiding their claws—they look like a lobster, but smaller, are brown and gray and ugly—miniature monsters. There are really too many to save them all. Well, we decided, they should have foreseen their fate and practiced birth control.

The leaves are not so vivid in color as last fall, in fact everything seems a little duller than last year. However, I'm enjoying every minute and have put on three pounds to prove it. The people left here now are:

Nancy Wilson Ross, who wrote *The Left Hand Is the Dreamer* and *I, My Ancestor.* She is very nice, too. Hyde Solomon, a nonobjective painter (whose nonobjects I have learned to like, having

---

This selection of letters is taken from the May Swenson Papers, Washington University Libraries.

1. William (Bill) Robinson, a fiction writer in residence at Yaddo from September 7 to October 27, 1951.

had the time to enter into them). He stutters, but this doesn't stop him from talking more than any of us, and he's a wonderful comedian, keeps us laughing all the time. The last sunny day we had (about a week ago) Hyde and I played tennis. He had never played before and hit every ball over the fence, mostly into the patch of stinging nettles, so that in recovering them we got a rash on our legs that still hurts when you take a bath. Michael Carver is the painter I play chess with in the evenings but I haven't beat him yet (I *almost* did last night). No one can beat him at anything—not Ping-Pong, Chinese checkers, anagrams.

Then there's Bill Robinson, who is part Indian, part Negro, part Portuguese, French, Irish—everything but Spanish, he says. Curiously, he looks quite Spanish (or perhaps Mexican), is very good-looking—he has black black silky Indian hair. His first novel is to be published by Viking next year, and, upon leaving Yaddo, he's going to Paris on a Whitney fellowship. Last, but not least, is Betty Smith,[2] whom you know from last year. Tonight Betty is going to make potato latkes with sour cream in honor of Clifford,[3] who is leaving tomorrow. Cliff is on the edge of being accepted for a fellowship at Huntington and Hartford in California, where he hopes to be painting for six months. This is a new colony (you probably know of it) financed by the president of the A&P, I believe. Oh, I forgot, Jorun Birkeland, a woman writer (Norwegian name) who has a federal job in Washington and who gets up at six and works till breakfast. She's very nice. In fact we are all extremely congenial. We had a masquerade party, and Clifford made masks for us. Mine was a unicorn—quite beautiful. We played charades, and the funniest one was what Bill got: PLEASE ADJUST CLOTHING BEFORE LEAVING (sign in men's john). He, of course, made every gesture but the obvious one—it was side-splitting.

Did I tell you Otto Luening set a poem of mine to music? Yes, I think I did. Well, Howard Swanson, another composer who was here earlier, set two of my poems to music that he found in ND

2. Betty Smith, a painter in residence at Yaddo from September 4 to November 3.

3. Clifford Wright, a painter.

12,[4] and I got a letter from a music company in New York saying I would collect royalties (!).

During the rainy season I have been preparing the material necessary to apply for the Guggenheim and am now almost through typing all the copies required. The deadline date has been extended to November 1, thank heaven, so I guess I'll get it in in time. I would like very much to put you down as a sponsor, Elizabeth, if you are sure you won't mind. It was terribly nice of you to offer to. You'd be my star witness, and I'd be eternally grateful, truly. Others who have agreed to sponsor me—bless their hearts—are: Malcolm Cowley, James Laughlin, Otto Luening, Alfred Kreymborg, David Morton, Kenneth Rockwell, and Elizabeth Ames.

Actually, I know, you don't know my work very well, and so will you mind if I send you a copy of the stuff I'm preparing for the committee so that you can have some background on which to base an opinion? And, if after reading it you decide not to stick your neck out, just forget about it. . . . I won't be mad. I'll send you the stuff under separate cover tomorrow—just discard it when you've glanced through it as I'll have other copies.

Hope you are feeling good and enjoying yourself, and that this reaches you before you sail for South America. I do hope you'll drop me a card so we can keep in touch. I read your Dickinson letters review in the *New Republic*—it was very fine—and will watch for the Marianne Moore review and the Fowlie review—and, of course, *Concordance,* which Polly[5] and I are both so excited about. You know, I just remembered, I dreamed about you two nights ago. You were playing with a big yellow beach ball (we were on the beach), and it kept slipping out of your fingers and was carried out by the waves, and I said, "Sit still, I'll get it for you," and started running through the breakers after it and then remembered I couldn't swim—and you were laughing and hollered from the shore, "Never mind, the tide will bring it back." But meantime it got smaller and smaller going farther away, but I thought maybe it just *looks* so far out because I'm nearsighted (which I actually am) and I hollered

4. Swenson's abbreviation for *New Directions.*

5. Polly Hanson, a poet and the assistant to Elizabeth Ames, director of Yaddo.

"Can *you* still see it?" and you just laughed. And the waves did bring it back—right to where you sat, and I felt ridiculous. Let's see—Eye on the Ball, Eye-Ball, I-Ball, On the Ball? Well, I'd rather not go any further into *that.*

With love, and best regards
from everyone at Yaddo.

Tues. March 10, '53

Dear Elizabeth:

I loved getting your letter and so much news about you on one soft, thin page. The blue of the paper, I decided, must be the color of your Toucan bird's eyes. I looked him up in the dictionary, and the drawing shows a plump bird with a short fan tail and a stupendous beak, almost the length of the body, curved down at the end. He eats fruit and is brightly colored, it says. [. . .] So glad you are "plain happy" there.[6] I'm glad for your comments on the egg and the butterfly poems.[7] The egg has been revised since I sent it—shortened—"keel me oval" is still in, though. This is supposed to give a droll sensation—maybe it's too obvious. I will work on the butterfly again with your reaction in mind. I sent these two, plus one called "By Morning" (about a snowfall in the city), to Howard Moss,[8] and [the] *New Yorker* took that one—which seemed like a triumph until he said it probably won't appear until next winter, as it's unlikely to snow anymore this year. Do they pay on publication or acceptance, I wonder? I felt it would be too ungrateful to ask him. Also, he asked to punctuate it—which is alright—but also wants to change [the] title to "Snow, by Morning." This does seem to me to spoil it somewhat . . . oh, well. I've assembled a book, or rather three. I guess when I wrote you it was one big one, "Another Animal," but all the poems didn't fit together sensibly in one, so [I] made three smaller vols. of 30 to 40 each. "Thing and Image" and "Sky-Acquainted" are the other titles. I

---

6. Bishop had last written to Swenson on February 12, 1953, from Samambaia, Lota Soares's home in Petrópolis, Brazil.

7. Swenson sent her poems, which became "At Breakfast" and "Was Worm" in *A Cage of Spines* (1958).

8. Howard Moss, a poet and the poetry editor at the *New Yorker.*

took them to Twayne, and Jack Steinberg there said he would send them on to [John] Ciardi, and they would let me know in two weeks. Steinberg called next day and said he personally liked them. But Cecil Hemley, who recently started the Noonday Press and is bringing out Jean Garrigue's collection this year, tells me that Twayne has some gimmick about one's getting 200 of one's relatives and friends to pre-subscribe before they publish a book of poetry—how horrible, if true—but he says this is standard practice with many these days. I thought of sending a copy to the Houghton Mifflin fellowship committee and wrote for their application. Also might take it to Farrar Straus and Young, as Stanley Young has seen some of my work. I submitted twenty poems to the Poetry Center Contest (John Malcolm Brinnin is head of it), which is to be judged in April. It would mean $300 to the winner. I haven't a job yet but must have in next two weeks, as my savings are about gone—it will probably be another dictaphone job[. . .]

I do appreciate your writing. Hope I will have more interesting things to tell you in my next letter. Let me know if I can be of any use to you, sending books or something—I will be your representative in "the States."

Blackie[9] sends her best love,
as I do, too.

September 14, 1953

Dear Elizabeth:

Forgive me for not replying immediately. I've now found the June 27 *N[ew] Y[ork]er.* "Gwendolyn" is a beaut of a story. I liked the part about the dusty marbles—this is what illuminates the difference between a child's and an adult's feelings (or maybe not the difference—but adults wouldn't admit it) with regard to *attraction:* Objects and persons can equally intensely possess it. Or rather, either one can be as well invested with it by imagination. Persons become like objects and objects have personality, aesthetically. The handling of detail is so perfect—there are such clear colors, such *primary* sensations.

I'll be ever so happy to type all the stories, following instruc-

9. Pearl Schwartz, Swenson's friend and partner at the time.

tions as you outlined.[10] Did you say in [a] former letter that November was when you'd need them done? I'm not sure I can get it all done by then, but will try. My mother and Dad are coming to visit next month, on their way to Sweden, and I expect I'll not get much "homework" done during that week or 10 days. However, I *may* be able to do some at the office[. . .]

I see your points about "The Even Sea"—It is a fragment and barely, or is it nearly? misses being sentimental it seems to me now. The nonpunctuation, I'm afraid I'm committed to, in spite of everything against it. It doesn't make things easier, certainly. An extra discipline is imposed in the manipulation of language in such a way as to do without it, without apparent strain. You say no punctuation limits one's range, but I've found that frequently an effect can be gotten from the absence of punctuation itself, that adds to the particular quality of a poem. And it causes one to work for exactness and compactness, the whole burden being on the *words* and how they are combined. The reader is induced to concentrate a little harder, too—must drop his "for granted" attitude, can't skim over the surface so easily. Doesn't it lure him deeper into it—force him to follow more subtle clues to understanding? And provided the reward is genuine, might it not give him an extra satisfaction in finding it? Of course there are other ways to snare the reader—I mean, one does want to capture him and make him like it. I remember, though, how opposite my earlier defense was—something about poetry must be so clear it doesn't need guides. Maybe this inconsistency in argument proves not using punct. is only a conceit. You've made me think about it at any rate. Don't you like *some* of [e. e.] cummings—and some of [Kenneth] Patchen (more of cummings naturally)? I shall send you a more "complex poem" one of these times and see whether your objections can be proven upon it.

"The Shampoo" I like *very* much—after many rereadings. [11]Es-

---

10. Bishop paid Swenson to type her manuscript of seven stories for submission to Houghton Mifflin. These included: "In the Village," "The Baptism," "The Farmer's Children," "Gwendolyn," "The Hanging of the Mouse," "In Prison," and "The Sea & Its Shore."

11. Bishop sent this poem to Swenson, saying that the *New Yorker* and *Poetry* had rejected it: "I can't figure out why—it seems perfectly clear to me, and rather pretty. So please tell me exactly what *you* think."

pecially now, as I just read it, it sort of gently assembled itself for me. It feels right, but I would have a deuce of a time saying why. It's *not* intellectual, and at first I tried to bite too hard into it and worry a meaning out. I felt I didn't quite get it. Well, I still don't specifically—that is, I wouldn't hazard a decision that it means thus and so and can't possibly mean something else. It's beautifully made. I'm willing to accept *precipitate and pragmatical* now which annoyed me at first reading, as a hippity-hop in the rhythm, and sort of inconsistent with the affectionate tone of the rest. I find it's alright read aloud, though, and *precipitate* has an important double meaning, I guess. Then I like *pragmatical* and *happened* near each other—the sounds. In a way I don't care to figure out what it "means"—one enjoys the way it's put together—the unexpectedness that the images as well as the rhythm have. It's pretty tightly organized and regularly rhymed, which comes as a surprise because it *sounds* so casual, spontaneous, unpretentious. I'm dead sure it's a good poem. I like it very much, but can't really grasp it—that is, it feels like something has been left out—but this makes it better, in a way . . . a mysteriousness, although the expression is perfectly straightforward. I dislike Dali for the most part but this poem reminds me of those paintings of his where a piece of landscape becomes the head of a woman and changes back again. But that's not the point—just incidental. I remember a poem of yours about "his green gay eyes" that seemed even more mysterious in the same kind of way. I felt the emotion or impression being expressed but couldn't seize an outline of what was behind it—what was engendering it. Guess maybe I try to read symbolism or special significance into this, when it's simply a comparison between someone's hair streaked with gray and the lichen on a cliff. No, that's not all—it's a kind of tribute to someone—and it's also a regret about old age—but the observation that it comes gradually and like the passage of time cannot be seen happening, only realized afterward—or the wish that a person could change or age as slowly as a cliff—or that this person *has* that kind of foreverness—or that by washing her hair in the old basin of the moon, you could confer it upon her.

Well, it certainly has *occupied* me, hasn't it? It's ridiculous to try to say in reportorial fashion what a poem "means"—but I so frequently never find out whether other people receive the same basic associations I think I've put into something—they will never tell you in so many words what they think it is saying. I like *flocking* in [the] last stanza echoing *rocks and shocks* in the first—and the way the poems comes round at the end—satisfying. In sound it's very agreeable, and I like the dependable construction, which isn't stiff—still maintains a naturalness[. . .]

I would adore, naturally, to have a copy of *North and South*—only if it doesn't cost you anything. Some in it that I love are "Iceberg" and the one about the chiming air, and the toy horse with a dancer on its back. Then the Big Fish—and the Cocks—and the one about the hobo with the shotgun, I remember vividly. When I was at MacDowell last summer, did I tell you?, we listened to you reading the Big Fish in the Library of Congress recording. You couldn't ruin it, even with that awful reading that sounded like a stock market report.

With love

23 Perry St., NYC 14
December 11, 1953

Dear Elizabeth:

Your letter and enclosures of the 3 stories came the other day, and typed copies have now gone forward to you Airmail. These include: "Farmer's Children," "Hanging of Mouse," "Baptism," and "Sea & Its Shore"[. . .]

I think all three of these "new ones" are fabulous (literally for two of them). I have tentatively concluded that you are a blend of Lewis Carroll, Kafka, and Jean Genet, laced with some home-distilled Presbyterian bitters. "The Sea & Its Shore" is my favorite—*such* a lovely[. . .]

Marianne Moore (I know I always spell it wrong) was splendid on the podium at the Y. She read from her translated *La Fontaine Fables,* with numerous interpolations of whatever came into her head. Seemed extremely at ease. A disappointment: She read only about an hour and [the] audience clapped and clapped for more but she did not come out. Afterward, as is the cruel custom, she had to autograph her books for whoever could shove their way to the table. The mob pressed and craned around her exactly as if she were an accident case. Looked well in dark velvet—sort of seal-brown. I didn't accost her, although I wanted to[. . .]

I saw the new *P[artisan] R[eview] Reader* with your two poems—both beauties. I was reading them surreptitiously, though, in a bookshop . . . must go back and go through them more leisurely. "Anaphora" I believe I remember from somewhere else—it is so wise. The other long one I want to read carefully again—exotic[. . .]

A few (possible) corrections on mss.: I wonder if, on the first page of the Baptism, where it says . . . "When the snow grew too deep—it grew all winter, as the grain grew all summer, and finally wilted away, etc.," one *grew* should not be eliminated to read: . . . "as the grain in summer . . ." This is a beautiful comparison but spoiled for me a little by three *grews.*

In Sea & Shore, page 3 (of the mss.), where it says: "Sometimes he would put a match to this file of papers . . . as if they were his paid bills . . ." since file and not papers is the subject, and is singular, shouldn't it read something like: "as if *it* held his paid bills"?[. . .]

I'm reading a very amusing book: *Epitaph of a Small Winner* by Machado de Assis—do you know his work? He's a landsman of yours, that is a Brazilian who wrote about Rio. It's published by Noonday. Also, was very taken with a book of short stories by Nadine Gordimer, about South Africa, called *The Soft Voice of the Serpent.*

Well, a Merry Christmas to
you, and much love

Monday, January 25 [1954]

Dear Elizabeth:

Sorry I've waited so long to answer your last letter but I sort of expected to get any day in the mail [the] rest of [the] corrections for "In the Village." I don't see how there *could* be any, really, as to me it seems quite perfect—I say this very carefully—it moved me tremendously, emotionally and aesthetically—art and *feeling* are welded in it, a very rare thing[. . .]

Do you know either of two poets named Harry Duncan and Murray Noss? Well, they are going to be my bookmates. The book will probably be called *Three New American Poets Today* and will come out from Scribner's in September. It is to be the first of a series of such volumes, of three full-length volumes in one.

If a smaller house were doing it I'd think it a shabby idea, but since Wheelock[12] tells me they intend to promote it well and make a "distinguished" volume out of it maybe it will turn out o.k. and open the way for a second volume of my own later on. I hope so.

Did you see Miss Moore's Fables in the current *Partisan?*

I am reading Coleridge's *Biographia Literaria,* and it is simply fabulous. I want to send you a copy of the notes I intend to keep on it. (But that's silly—you must have read it ages ago—I never had until now.) [. . .]

I'm looking forward to some new stories, and will type "In the Village" as soon as I get your corrections—I've noted the one in your last letter[. . .]

With love

May 18, 1954

Dear Elizabeth:

[. . .] I hope your weather is past its wet stage now and that your asthma is better, too. It was amusing to hear about Tobias[13] and his footprint on the bathtub rim after his dive out the window. We do look forward to the picture when it's ready. You were right that I was correcting proofs *just then*—the galleys have been returned for quite some time and I'm expecting the page proofs any day. I will make at least a couple of people read them before they go back. I didn't do it with the galleys because I think it's cruel. Wheelock is writing the introduction to the three-poets volume and a portion of it, he tells me, is to appear in the May 23 Sunday *Times* Book Section with a mention giving it some advance publicity . . .

It's extremely nice of you to offer to stick up for me with the Guggenheim again—I do intend to apply in late September or October, and am allowing myself to hope that a copy of the book may give some weight.

I went to a cocktail party at Noonday Press for Louise Bogan

---

12. John Hall Wheelock wrote the introduction for *Poets of Today* (New York: Scribner's, 1954), which included Swenson's first book *Another Animal.*

13. Bishop's cat.

the day her *Collected Poems* came out. There was a great jam, of course. It's a very handsome printing job. It seems that she quit Scribner's because they were reluctant to publish this book, but Wheelock told me the reason was that she had only two new poems in the collection and the rest had been previously published with Scribner's. Noonday was very glad to get her as they believe she is in line for the Pulitzer and possibly other prizes next year. Politics and poetry make a ludicrous pair, don't they[. . .]

I'm somewhat less discontented with my job now[14]—I think it was partly the winter that made things seem so monotonous—I feel better now, the sea is blue outside the window and Battery Park is green. I really ought to stick [with] it until the middle of August and collect my vacation; then *if* I stay to the end of the year I will get about a $300 bonus which I ought to do but I don't know. I applied to MacDowell and was accepted for Sept.–Oct. and may go there.

With love

June 1, 1954

Dear Elizabeth:

[. . .] I'm sorry you and Lota[15] have both been having afflictions—I do hope you are both feeling well now. So glad *Cold Spring* is to emerge in the Fall—(won't you have to change it to "Fall"?). I would certainly be glad to type your new stories and articles—please call on me at any time. The way it looks now I'll be here most of the summer, maybe all of it—definitely to the middle of September when I may go to Peterborough, but I'm not sure of that yet. I had a stroke (of fortune) the other day when "Discovery" bought a story[16] for $250—also, in the same week the *New Yorker* bought two poems to total about $100, so I am in the chips. I must tell you sometime about the long-drawn-out hassle I had with the *New Yorker* about things they wanted changed—it's funny and not-so-funny. I feel that poetry should

14. Swenson was working in the office of the United States Steamship Lines in the Battery.

15. Lota de Macedo Soares, with whom Bishop was living in Brazil.

16. "Mutterings of a Middlewoman," which appeared in *Discovery 5.*

be immune from revisory suggestions by editors—it should either be taken in one chunk, as is, or rejected totally. Prose is a different proposition in this respect, and can be hacked or patched or stretched or shrunk without cracking its spine entirely, at least sometimes. But trying to make poetry *fit*—into or for anything—is dangerous.

I happened to be listening to the radio last Saturday (WNYC) and heard your name. You were elected to the National Institute of Arts and Letters—congratulations! [Archibald] MacLeish gave a speech on the same program that was awfully well said—about poetry and science being two different species of animal that needn't be enemies but couldn't be lovers. (That isn't what he said, but that's what I concluded from what he said) [. . .]

As ever

November 8, 1954

Dear Elizabeth:

It was good to get your letter of October 15—about receiving *Poets of Today*,[17] about the two-month fog, and about your Brazilian translations. You must have mentioned these translations in a former letter but I can't recall what they were—is it something of yours into Portuguese? Please tell me more about it [. . .]

About reviews of the book, there haven't been any, hardly, and may not be, for all I know. The only thing that remotely resembled one was in the *N[ew] Y[ork]er* which I'm afraid you have seen, by Louise Bogan. Rumors and promises: John Ciardi did one for the Sunday *Times* which he was paid for, but it hasn't appeared so far. He let me know that it praised my end of the book; one is to come out in the *Saturday Review of Lit.* (someday), and in *Western Review*, in *Perspectives*, in the *New Leader* (!) [. . .]

The book has sold about 500 copies (1,500 was the first printing). I feel Wheelock used poor judgment in selecting Noss's book, and I somewhat resent the fact that Duncan's book is 3/4 translations, good as they are [. . .]

17. Published September 14. In her letter of November 14, 1954, Bishop indicated her favorites in the volume: "Feel like a Bird" and "Horse and Swan Feeding."

Well, I've resigned myself to indifference (without admitting that I deserve *this* much) and am trying to forget it and concentrate on new poems and prose. Oh, one "bright spot" (maybe) that I forgot: Edward Weeks of *Atlantic Monthly* invited me to send some poems to him since he liked *Another Animal*—so I did the other day, but of course he may not like what I sent him. And something else (I'm glad it's in the far future)—the Poetry Center has asked me to read on a series to be called "Twelve Contemporary Poets" in the spring, for which I'm to earn $35 for an hour and a half reading and discussion. I'm not working now (hope to hold out until January 1). Weather very dreary and quite cold here, much rain, but today was nice. I'm reading Virginia Woolf's diary—have you read it? Almost *forgot* (important) to tell you I applied for the Guggenheim and sent in everything October 15, and I listed you as a sponsor, the others being: Mark Van Doren, Malcolm Cowley, Wheelock, James Laughlin, John Ciardi, Elizabeth Sergeant,[18] Louis Untermeyer, Otto Luening, Karl Shapiro—a total of ten! which ought to club them into giving it to me, if anything can.

With love

New York, August 24, 1955

Dear Elizabeth:

Well, here is a day at last when I'm able to read your book (again) and write you about it. I'm so very glad to have *North and South* as well as *A Cold Spring,* for I never did get hold of the first one, and right off I must tell you I think the volume itself is lovely: cover, quality of paper, print, etc., and the dust jacket (so slick and clean and *un*dusty) exquisitely designed. Did MacIver[19] have in mind, I wonder, a Ginkgo leaf? It is that *color* and something like the shape. The white is North, the blue South, and the green, peculiarly yellowed, is The Cold Spring. I was excited to see Richard Eberhart's review in the *Times* (which was certainly respectful). Of the new poems I had formerly read only eight (and

18. Elizabeth Sergeant, an editor at the *New Yorker* and the sister-in-law of E. B. White.

19. Loren MacIver, a painter.

they seemed new in their new setting and read *now*) so that there were ten entire surprises, a wonder-full package. "At the Fishhouses" for me is perhaps the most *moving*—by that I mean that most of your poems (among the eighteen) are *not*—they engage something else than the emotions. What is it? Something else, and something more important. They are hard, feelable, as objects—or they give us that sensation—and they are separate from the self that made them, rather than self-effigies as poems easily tend to be. Not to say I don't like "At the Fishhouses"—I do, very much—only it reminds me of your stories, for instance "In the Village," partly because there is a you pictured in it. The line "Cold dark deep and absolutely clear, element bearable to no mortal . . ." by itself has carved a groove in my mind, I'll bet, forever—that music, that evocation, alone, is worth ——. That many poems by as many other writers.

Everyone of the eighteen is excellent in my opinion, with the possible exceptions (for me) of the Four Poems, and "Varick Street." I don't understand the Four Poems, that is I get their *mood,* but I can only imagine what they're talking about—my imagination goes pretty wild and comes back with strange answers, none of which fit exactly. It's like smelling a strong odor, or hearing a keen sound and not being able to discover what it comes from. Didn't "While Someone Telephones" used to have a different title? At any rate, now, as part of this group it takes on another "meaning" than when I read it in—was it *Partisan Review*? Reading these four poems I have to furnish them with "meanings" from my own experiences because you've left yours out (their labels)—you had to, I suppose, to get them said at all. This makes them non-objective, which I sense is necessary for you are trying to say—not say, but record—what can't or isn't ordinarily recorded. And an originality occurs that way. So I'm left outside here, sniffing and listening, and no use pounding on the door[. . .]

August 29th [1955]

Got side-tracked, and a weekend went by. Sunday we went to the ocean—Riis Park in Far Rockaway—the water was very rough and beautiful. Friday I walked around in Central Park and wrote a poem, not a very good one, but I haven't finished anything for so long that pushing through like that and getting one done in one day made me feel hopeful. I quit my job again about two weeks ago in order to go to the Breadloaf Writers' Conference in Vermont, but changed my mind about going, one reason being that Blackie (Pearl) has to have a small operation on her throat; she has a node on one vocal chord that has been affecting her voice for some time, and which the doctor says might grow and cause further trouble [. . .]

Back to *A Cold Spring*: Poems new to me, and full of delights: "Over 2000 Illustrations . . . ," "The Bight," "A Summer's Dream," "Cape Breton," "Insomnia," "Faustina," "Letter to N.Y.," and "Invitation to Marianne Moore." The latter I discover especially lovely to read aloud, when all the "ings" come out, like triangles being struck at the back of the orchestra. It's all glittering and full of light and the excitement of taking off, everything being seen from above, and M. M. elevated to where I distinctly see her making the trip by herself through the air, upright, not even needing wings let alone a plane. The part about the Library Lions following up to the reading room is magical, of course, by itself—and in many of the poems there is such an enfolded, unexpected prize, or more than one. In "A Cold Spring" they are the bullfrogs sounding "slack strings plucked by heavy thumbs" and the petals of dogwood "burned, apparently, by a cigarette-butt." This poem, too, comes out entirely only when read aloud—you *think* that you hear it all in the head, reading silently, but find you haven't. Some of the more regularly-formed ones, though, I found hard to read *right,* aloud: "Letter to N.Y.," "Insomnia," "A Summer's Dream"— They need a particular control, and careful timing, because they're built like steps, or a ladder, and haven't such a smooth, level flow. The end-line of "Insomnia" is so startling that it almost scares you. I think *it* is tremendously good. But I want to go back to collecting nuggets: Sometimes it's an improbable juxtaposition of things that leads to a nobody-ever-used-it-before-rhyme, like "extraordinary geraniums" and "assorted linoleums," or it's a person improbably in the setting: the preacher "carrying his frock coat on a hanger" in the bus in "Cape Breton"; the seal, "a believer in total immersion" in the serious and sonorous setting in "At the Fishhouses" and "Miss Breen" in

"Arrival at Santos." [Richard] Eberhart already picked out the prize in "The Bight": "the water . . . doesn't wet anything, the color of the gas flame turned as low as possible." There are some shorter poems that are simply *all* like that, from first word to last, the whole chunk—like "Insomnia," "The Mountain," "Letter to N.Y.," and "View of the Capitol." "Unceasingly the little flags / feed their limp stripes into the air" is a thing so perfectly seen and said; it reminded me of a description, but, in comparison, long-winded, in Virginia Woolf's diary where she says: "The one pleasant sight I saw was due rather to the little breath of wind than to decorative skill; some long tongue-shaped streamers attached to the top of the Nelson column licked the air, furled and unfurled, like the gigantic tongues of dragons, with a slow, rather serpentine beauty"—which I remembered underlining when I read it, and just now had to look up to see how it compared. "Gigantic" is wrong there, isn't it?—spoils it, somehow. I also looked up the copy of "The Shampoo" you sent me once, to see if any changes had been made, and none had. It's curious how a thing in print becomes more positive, enters the mind with less conflict, than in typescript. "The Shampoo" seems entirely filled out and complete to me here in the book. It has a hard-to-define mood, or tone, as has "Argument" (which, at first, I couldn't find enough in to get hold of) but read aloud, a special tone or vibration comes from it giving the import that is beyond the words. And this I get, too, from "Varick Street" read aloud—this is probably the most terrible poem here—I mean in its import—worse than "The Prodigal," even, because there the terrible is more on the surface. The ones, I guess, that give me most *pleasure*—each a different kind of it—are "At the Fishhouses," "View of The Capitol," "Insomnia," "The Mountain," "Invitation to Miss M. M.," and "A Cold Spring." How nice to have the whole gallery of them, the first and second one both, to examine and enjoy whenever I want. Thanks very much for having it sent to me. Not to need illusion—to dare to see and say how things really are, is the emancipation I would like to attain, as you have—but I guess you don't need to try, you just do see that way, being you [. . .]

With love, as ever
and love from B.

October 28, 1955

Dear Elizabeth:

[. . .] Thanks very much for sending "Early Sorrow."[20] Please *don't* turn against it; I think it's special—a different vein for you in poetry, going into the far past, instead of taking things from the present. Now, it might not be that at all; maybe it's something seen recently, but for *me* it has that almost surrealistic feeling of some room way down deep in memory, or in a dream, that's been dark, and suddenly the light is turned on and every detail is seen, as on a far away stage, tiny but very clear. It's hypnotic. It's wonderfully organized, and yet so casual in tone. What do you call it when a set of the same words are used to end the lines in each stanza? I never studied prosody. The "small hard tears" that "dance like mad on the hot black stove, the way the rain must dance on the house" is one of the best metaphors—one of those things that, when you read it, you know that *you* have made the same comparison (seeing or listening to rain hit a hard surface, and its whiteness and sound like steam) but at some level of the brain just below thought or word-making. Then I think the "moons" falling out of the almanac is wonderfully surreal, as well as the house the child draws inside of the house she's in. I get a strange effect of *color* out of the poem, apart from the actual colors of things in it; it comes from the repetition of vowel sounds. Mostly it's black on white (like playing cards), [a] little red and a little yellow. All the *ō* sounds seem to make these black spots; the *ā* sounds seem to make white; the *e* sounds yellow; and the vowel in such words as "h*ea*rt-less" and "m*a*rvelous" is the red; but there's so little red, like a pack of cards mostly spades and clubs. Of course, *moon* is a very black word, and *equinoctial* frighteningly black. Does all of this sound ridiculous to you? Well then, I'll give you a chance to get back at me with the enclosed: "Looking Uptown", which I just finished—if it is.[21]

B. is much better now; her voice has come back nearly to

20. Titled "Sestina" in *Questions of Travel.*

21. Bishop responded that this poem had some of Swenson's "best lines" in it.

normal, although she is still seeing the doctor once a week for exercises to improve the flexibility of the vocal cords [. . .]

On Saturday I am going to hear Marianne Moore read, and I will write you about it.

Love, as ever

December 9, 1955

Dear Elizabeth:

[. . .] I was up to see Howard Moss at the *N[ew] Y[ork]er* today—to "explain" some poems that they might take—and he gave me a copy of this week's issue containing your "Filling Station"—which I love. The "dirty dog, quite comfy" and the "big dim doily draping a taboret" are little marvels, for instance, of humor, exact description, and language-play (and several other things I feel but can't catch hold of in words just now). It's wonderful how the poem is funny and serious both, how it points up the foolishness and squalor-trying-to-be-homey features of the people living there, and at the same time is so indulgent of them. The last line is remarkably thought-provoking, making us ask—(B. and I were just discussing it and she thinks the line means the people believe in god just like they believe in doilies, hairy begonias, etc., and I said, no, it means just as the person who waters the plant, etc. loves it, *somebody* loves these people (the poet, as an instance) and, by extension, somebody loves the poet, he being part of "all") which meaning, straight or satirical, shall we take? And the answer, of course, is *both.* I'll bet James never wrote a sentence as Chinese-boxy as that (the above). Howard also showed me the "Sestina" set up for proof, and a beautiful long one that I could not read properly while he chatted. These you must have written all since the book; I think that's wonderful. Also, he said one of yours came out last week, and I must try to catch it in the library. He has two of mine waiting to go in next summer, and if he takes these two I'll be very pleased (with the check)—one is rather long; the other is "Looking Uptown," which you liked, and I took your suggestion about "something scaly" instead of "some scaly thing," as well as took out "as" in stanza 6, as you suggested. (Thanks) [. . .]

I would not expect you to send me the *Complete Rhyming Dictionary and Handbook of Poetry* for Christmas—it would cost a great deal of postage—but I am going to get a book dealer friend of mine to find one for me. Could you give me publisher and date of last printing? When I get hold of it perhaps I'll learn what a PANTOUM is, which sounds very exciting.

Gad, it *is* wonderful "living on my awards" as you put it. Of course, they—rather, it—comes in little chunks (once a month) which barely meet the chief bills, but so far I've managed on it, and on a check for something sold once in a while. Also, I take part-time temporary jobs when they're offered. I did an Election job—that is, wrote down people's names in the registration books and worked the voting machine on Election day, and for a week's work got $69. Right now, I'm doing three hours of dictaphone work for Bob MacGregor of New Directions every day, in the late afternoon, by which time I've done all the writing I'm apt to do anyhow.

Miss Moore still looks capable of riding a merry-go-round. When I heard her at the "Y" she wore a long blue—I think, linen or cotton—dress, with a bouquet at her belt; it had (the dress) white Quakerish cuffs and collar. She looked very rosy and well, had much poise, and the audience loved her. Alas, she doesn't read well—that is, it's hard to distinguish her words—enunciation is not good. I went home though, and read all the poems she read, and enjoyed them more for having heard them with her inflection. A couple of nights later I heard a perfectly wonderful male voice read her poems on "Limited Edition," a WNYC broadcast—they really brought lumps to my throat, they were so splendid, and read so well. I tuned in in the middle and didn't get the man's name. I waited to shake M. M.'s hand after her reading, but she was a little glassy-eyed from all that she'd gone through shaking so many admirers' paws and having to show appreciation for their compliments, so that I only said a couple of words to her. I mentioned that I had heard from you recently, and she was pleased to hear your name. She is such a country-looking person. I like her looks. (This was the first time I'd seen her so close up.) [. . .]

I'm sending you the *Paris Review* containing a "piece of prose"[22] I did—rather juvenile, I'm afraid. I have another, longer one (a city setting) which I'm going to send them hoping

22. "Eclogue."

they might buy it. By early summer I should have a new collection of poems done, which Scribner's is "interested in seeing" of course, but it may go no further than that. When is your book of stories to be out?

Merry, merry Christmas from
May (and B.)

January 31, 1956

Dear Elizabeth:

[. . .] The reading at the "Y" went off alright. Delmore[23] could not be located until the last minute, and when he did turn up was in poor condition so that he asked to read first, and briefly, with the result that I had to take up most of the time. The audience was not very big, but they were interested. Since there was time at the end and I had finished my prepared poems—guess what?—I read three of your poems from the book, and three of Howard Moss's from *The Toy Fair*—and under separate cover I send you the large bag of applause collected from your "View of the Capitol from the Library of Congress," "Insomnia," and "Letter to N.Y."

I'm glad the reading is over with, which I worried about much too much in advance.

Is the translation done by now? Did you find a title?

Best love to you, and I will
write again soon.

February 29, 1956

Dear Elizabeth:

[. . .]Thanks very much for your evaluation of "The Centaur." I'm afraid you are right about its being overemphatic, and that it could be cut. If only I had had the wit to see this before it was published. Yes, I did send it to Howard Moss first, but *he* wanted to chop off the last two stanzas, and I felt sure that wasn't right. Before it appears in a book—if ever—I'll try to make it better with your feeling about it in mind. Well, I got this tearsheet when I went to the *Nation* today to talk to Robert

23. Delmore Schwartz and Swenson gave a reading at the YMHA Poetry Center in New York City.

Hatch about some reviewing—this not-very-impressive-just-kind-of-a-*Nation*-type-poem[24] will appear in next week's issue. I do wonder whether you would mind giving me your estimation of one I'm working on, called "Something Goes By." Only if it doesn't bore you. I don't know whether what I mean comes through in it. I guess it doesn't, or I'd not have the question. Also, is it interesting enough as a poem? Be tough with me, if you do decide to comment [. . .]

Again on "The Centaur": the constructions of "cut me a long" and "filled me a glass"—I used them as Westernisms, they came naturally, this being the way we used to talk out there when I was little (they still talk like that in my state). The knife is there to point up that she's doing something tomboyish, which her mother objects to. I did used to carry around my brother Roy's knife, whenever I could sneak it away from him, to play mumblety-peg with, or cut willow switches. I liked your interpretation of "ghostly toes in the hall"—one I didn't have consciously in mind, but which fits as an extra meaning. This was one of those poems that I didn't have much control over while writing; it came very quickly, and it seemed that certain details simply *had* to go in. I'm sure a Freudian would find all the symbols of an open-and-shut case, but I don't mind [. . .]

With much love

July 6, 1956

Dear Elizabeth:

Your radio is going forward by air today with a New Directions label marked Books, but my name as sender. I do hope it gets to you without a hitch. As it turned out, I got you a Philco because after asking a friend who knows about appliances and consulting *Consumer's Guide* I found that it is considered among the very best (Magnavox isn't, particularly) and also because I could get it through a wholesale house at a discount including case with carrying strap and two extra batteries. It's retailed priced at $75 without case but I got the whole for $59.69 [. . .] Now I wonder if you wouldn't rather I send books and Scrabble by regular mail because I estimate that this heavier package (I

24. "Cause and Effect."

had to pad the inside to keep pieces from rattling) might cost as much as $10 by air? Maybe you could let me know this right away. I will be leaving for the Colony at Peterborough in a week.

I'm sorry the radio is not a dark color but it can be cleaned with a damp cloth and I think it's quite simple and esthetic looking. (This is the only color Philco makes in a transistor.) [. . .]

I'll be off to the P.O. now and jot down cost of the airmail before sending this.

Peterborough, Sunday August 5 [1956]

Dear Elizabeth:

You've no idea how fascinated I immediately became with your two gifts—the *Rhyming Dictionary* and the *Oxford Nursery Rhyme Book*—which reached me few days ago done up in lovely wrappers with gold paper ribbon inside of outer wrapper and gift card signed Elizabeth in a clerk's handwriting. I would never have bought the *Dictionary* myself, would have been scared to—because of the information on writing formal poetry and feeling that it makes it (poetry) *calculating* to use an aid of this sort, and now at this late date I find out how idiotic that attitude is. I've had great fun (and hard work) doing two poems "inspired" by the *Dictionary!* One of them's pretty good I think. What happened too is that I made longer poems which has always been hard for me. I didn't use any of the "forms"—in fact I haven't looked at that part yet—but made up a form for [the] first stanza and followed it through the others. I will show you this attempt sometime. Just have dipped into the *Nursery Rhymes* so far but can see there's a delicious mine, to explore and recollect, in it. I think you must have meant the Riddles section especially for me. You are very nice to have had them sent, here and at this time. They both came like lucky pieces. I wonder if the radio *did* arrive? It should certainly have reached you before your card (with the Christ) dated July 22, if not before your letter of the 16th. I'd feel awful if it didn't because I didn't put books around it. The scrabble and pocket books were sent regular mail just before I left New York July 15. Hope they reach you before your summer does. So strange to hear of the cold where you are and imagine yours and Lota's "little white hands" freezing as you lug stones for the new fireplace. Well, here in my studio I have a tremendous fireplace made of boulders, lots of pine and birch logs are supplied, and on a rainy day it's cozy to have a blaze. Were you ever at MacDowell? I think you would like it better than Yaddo in the sense that there's vast territory to wander in outdoors, beautiful woods, so many kinds of birds and animals—hares, deer, woodchucks, porcupines (I saw one), red fox—mosquitos the size of dragonflies almost and deerflies, of course, but if you wear a hat and have arms and legs covered you get along. The best thing is that the studios are very far apart and you really have privacy. There's electricity in them now so you can work at night if you want [. . .] The food is unimaginative and not Yaddo-style. There are more people here than one is able to get to know well, and maybe that's an advantage. Peterborough is a mile down the hill. There's one bar, Gatto's. Otherwise you can't be served a drink anywhere unless you buy a meal with it. There's one liquor store, somewhat *out* of town but fairly near the Colony. There's the Peterborough Players, a movie house, square dancing, an outdoor swimming pool in town. Tennis court, badminton, Ping-Pong, croquet on the grounds, and golf course at country club available to Colonists. Don't know why I'm furnishing this brochure. Guess I hope to tempt you away from your mountainside and HiFi set and bring you back to the States, at least for a visit [. . .]

I have a cat—gray tiger type with triangular white bib and white chip on his nose (so I call him Chippy)—that was lost and followed me to [the] studio one day. He's very entertaining and grateful for the mush and milk I bring him from breakfast and the horsemeat I buy him (canned). There's a little stairway leading to a platform, a pulpit-like place, and that's his kennel. From there he can leap onto a ledge that runs around the room just under the peaked roof, so he has a promenade all to himself where moths and flies and spiders can be played with. He's very fastidious and either goes to toilet outdoors or if it's raining, on the pine needles in his kennel (this if the fire is going—if it's not he uses the fireplace). [He] has a singed spot on one hind paw where he squatted on a hot cinder one day.

I interrupted this to go to dinner, which is served at 1 P.M. on Sundays instead of in the evening, and on my way back through the rye field I saw two butterflies mating—well, courting and then mating—both yellow with brown-orange rims on their wings, the male smaller and deeper yellow. Wherever she went, making scallops of flight up and down, he fluttered right above her so that it looked like one four-leafed butterfly.

I saw in *Times* Book Section that you had won a *Partisan Review* prize or fellowship. Congratulations! Does it mean money—I hope so and that it's a lot. There are hardly any periodicals available here except *Life, Time, Harper's,* and *Atlantic.* Is it like the *Hudson Review* or *Kenyon Review* grant? (But I don't know much about them either.)

I'm sure you are right about "sea-thing" in the Woolf poem.[25] What I meant was the whorl-shape and not to suggest a creature, which of course it does *also,* and so it's certainly inexact. As I work with the idea of collecting "another" book I notice the blunders I've let remain in quite a number of poems that have been put in magazines, and certainly the ones farther back in *Another Animal*—it's as if I've been composing by ear, never troubled to learn to read notes. One can only go a limited distance that way and it's forgivable only in a youngster. I only hope to work to become a poet; so far it has been play and exercise, and it's past time that sort of thing should be supplanted. Not to be more *serious* but to be more sure of what one is doing, and why. This little excoriation has done me good—to put it down instead of just hazily feeling it—so don't feel you must be nice and contradict it [. . .]

Love to you, as ever

Monday, October 15, 1956

Dear Elizabeth:

I feel badly about not writing you right away. I've been putting my book together—doing all the typing on it, and deciding about an arrangement, and what poems to leave out—and have been absorbed in that. Now, it's done, and I have an appointment at Harcourt, Brace, on Wednesday, with Margaret Marshall. It will be a great stroke of luck if they do take it. If not, I have a couple of other leads—but not as promising as this one.

---

25. In "Frontispiece" Bishop had objected to Swenson's use of the word *sea-thing.*

It's a damned shame about the radio. I felt so certain it would get to you; I thought that the New Directions label, the "professional" way it was packed, and the fact that the package looked and weighed as if it were Books, would get it there without any trouble. Now I see that I made a mistake: it should have been imbedded in paperback books as you suggested, even though this would have made a much bulkier and sloppier package [. . .] Somehow I assumed that, sent airmail, it wouldn't go through hands that would have a chance to steal it.

Here is what I would like to do: (I hope that you will not object—you will, at first, but think it over—from my side particularly—and do try to agree). I would shop around, with the aid of a friend who knows about discount and wholesale houses, and find a radio, a good one of whatever make, that can be got as cheaply as possible (new) and send it to you, declare it as such, and you could pay the duty on it. I'll find out what the duty would be approximately, from the post office. Or, if there is the chance that you'll be coming to N.Y. this winter, you could take it back with you, couldn't you? I just sold some more poems to the *New Yorker,* and am due to get some fat checks, and I really mean it when I say I can afford it without feeling the slightest pinch. The motive is selfish, believe me—to make up for my stupidity. Really it is quite awful that you should have entrusted me with $75, and because I didn't follow your instructions it was lost. Please see it my way and don't raise an objection [. . .]

I am back at New Directions now, working from three to six each afternoon. They simply let the manuscripts pile up while I was away—the ones for the Annual, that is—and the antique cradle in which unread mss. are kept was overflowing onto the floor. Deadline for *N[ew] D[irections]* 16 has been put forward again—to December 1—with publication scheduled for April; this because Laughlin has kept postponing his reading of the held manuscripts and making decisions on them [. . .]

Two plays seen lately, at little theaters—*Uncle Vanya* at the Fourth Street (which was rewarding, but the balance between comedy and tragedy was tipped a little too far to the tragic side by the actors, so it sagged somewhat); *The Iceman Cometh* at Circle in the Square—a five-hour play on hard seats—O'Neill treated with more reverence than this effort deserved. He could have proved how weak people waste their lives, in three hours just as thoroughly, and the result would have been a stronger play not reflecting the egotism of the author [. . .]

Much love . . .

November 15, 1956

Dear Elizabeth:

I haven't heard from you about the jeans, and dare not buy them without knowing sizes. I think *you* would wear probably a 26-in. waist—didn't you say you weigh about 118 lbs. in a letter recently? But please confirm this, and let me know L's waist size and weight. They always make the legs too long but they look best folded up anyway. WRANGLERS are the kind I like (zipper in front) but if you want other brand, please mention [. . .]

Blackie (who has been renamed Jessie) and I have tickets to hear Bogan read your poems at the "Y" next Tuesday. I'll tell you how it comes off. I have to read there in January along with Donald Hall and Alistair Reid [. . .]

Oh, and I had a letter from *Beloit Poetry Journal* saying they're having an issue devoted to celebrating Robert Frost next year, inviting me to write a poem in tribute to him—which sounded like a silly idea, but all of a sudden I did one very quickly, with double meanings and rather wild. I don't know him personally so felt free to say whatever I wanted. Don't know if I'll send it. They may think it impertinent. (Enclosed)

And got a letter from Katharine White (E. B.'s wife) on the *New Yorker* saying she admired my poems and did I have any prose to send. Golden opportunity! I sent her a nonstory called "From the Window" but of course it was not for them so now I have sent her another, maybe closer to their wants, but not close enough I'm afraid. And have to do a review of four not-so-good, I'm afraid, books of poetry for *Poetry* in Chicago which is to be in by Dec. 15, but it will mean a bit of money. What do you think of this very formal "theory" poem which nobody will buy? (Enclosed: "Order of Diet.")

My book at Harcourt has not been heard from.[26] I'm told one

---

26. Swenson had met with Margaret Marshall of Harcourt, Brace about her new manuscript. On January 6, 1957, she wrote Bishop that it was not accepted: "It's a good thing, because I now see that it needs to be 'weeded.' "

has to get Big Names to contact the higher-up editors and urge publication in order to get them to risk it where a lesser-name poet is concerned. Very nasty situation. Of course I sent them the good parts from reviews of *Another Animal* but probably this doesn't count for much. Margaret Marshall, to whom I submitted it (by the way, I think I'll change the title from "Shadow-Maker" to "The Promontory Moment and Other Poems"),[27] liked it very much—she told this to a friend who told me, but she hasn't contacted me yet—but she is one of the smaller wheels at Harcourt . . . so all is in the lap of the giddy gods. Do you, by any chance, know Denver Lindley there, who I believe is the man who makes decisions?

Well, the election was a sorry thing. I guess a general, with or without stomach, is what the masses want here. That it should have been the landslide that it was is very discouraging [. . .]

When are you coming to N.Y.?

Love to you

March 27, 1958

Dear Elizabeth:

Here it has been raining for four days, the city is gray and slimy. On the first day of spring we had a big snowstorm and strong winds, then rain and slush, and more rain—very depressing, since just before that it had been warm and sunny, temperature in the fifties. Two weeks ago in the botanical gardens in Prospect Park we saw crocuses and the buds looked ready to crack open on the Japanese cherry trees. We even saw two robins—besides a cardinal, bluejays, chickadees, and juncos. All but the robins, of course, stay around there all year.

I've been intending to write you ever since finishing *Helena Morley*—and since your letter, which it shocks me to see is dated January 15. Well, much has been happening. I've taken on a number of little things in order to earn extra money [. . .]

But what a good luck is that Rinehart accepted my book and it is scheduled for end-of-September publication. I am having to do a lot of "business" in that connection, too, writing for

27. In her next letter Bishop expressed her dislike of both titles but did not offer any alternative ones.

permissions to editors who have published many of its poems, getting up a list for their pre-pub. announcement, conferences with them, etc. Naturally I'm very relieved that it will come out this year. I don't like the title much,[28] but *could not* think of a better one, somehow—and the poem from which it's taken, I hope, will invest it with some sense—but maybe not. They are printing 1,500 copies, and it will be something like 125 pages. I had to cut some poems out—am not sure if I took out the right ones. The only other house that saw it was Harper's—except Harcourt Brace, which considered it over a year ago—and Harper's liked it but said they couldn't do it this year, *maybe* next. The royalty deal with Rinehart is a steal for them: 5 percent on the first thousand copies and 10 percent "thereafter." On the advice of people who ought to know (Louise Bogan for one) I agreed to this. Others said I should grab the chance without any royalties at all—that these days poets, even those with reputations, are entering into share-expense deals with publishers because the latter won't risk it otherwise. Anyway, for good or ill, my contract is now signed. I accepted an invitation to do two readings at the Poetry Center in San Francisco when we will be out there next fall—end of November. And a friend of mine at Washington U. wants to fix up a reading for me in Seattle. I can also maybe get readings at other places (Iowa U. and Chicago for instance) to do on my way back—which would help pay for the trip out and back. The idea scares me and I don't know how far I ought to go into that sort of thing. I'm afraid it would mean I wouldn't *write* anything for a long time. Of course Rinehart thinks it a good idea because it will help sell the book. Wish I had a pile of money and could say the hell with all that, and go where I like and stay where I like and write. If wishes were fishes we'd all be in the swim.

Now I want to talk about *The Diary,* which I enjoyed so very much—and yes it did take me back to my childhood (and made me think of the diary I used to keep—the difference being that it was only about me, me, me—the "genius" of this one is that it's about all the people around her, and events outside of herself). What a *tremendous* job you did, and what a lot of detailed, patient, thorough work over a *long* time you had to do on this

28. Swenson had revised the title to "A Cage of Spines."

translation, I could only realize after finishing it. It's so natural in the style that one forgets it wasn't written in English—completely lifelike, immediate, and right in tone all through—and not a strained page or a dull one in it. All the little footnotes are marvelous just by themselves. I was awfully impressed—even more than I expected to be. Of course you did have a rare mine of material (diamonds) to work with, and you were the very *one* to do it—still, sustaining such a big task, keeping within the mind of this youngster so consistently in order to choose the right expressions in another language—making it *build* in interest to the end—that proves great power on your part. You've made it a delicious book—one probably alone of its kind. I think it ended very appropriately, but I was sorry it didn't go on and on [. . .]

Did I tell you that we have a kitten whose name is Z. B. (because zebra striped)—and part Siamese and part alley. He's over four months old now—a deep voice which he uses a lot—eyes owl colored, very yellow. Ears too big and hind legs seem too long at this age. He can leap up five times his length, and gets into and on top of everything in the apartment. He perforates all my papers by putting his teeth into them—but he's fun.

I hope I thanked you for writing the Guggenheim again. I'm sure I'm not among the chosen, though, or I think I'd have heard by now.

Rinehart wants me to get—or, rather, they suggested that *they* would write to a few contemporary poets of note that know my work and ask for jacket statements. I felt that review statements from the Scribner book ought to be enough (there were a few fairly good ones) but in addition they suggested you, and [Richard] Wilbur, at least. One time in a letter to me you wrote: "Your poems make one sit up and take notice. I find their tone so admirable, brave, energetic and open—such a relief after the attempts at infinite knowledge, wisdom, experience and oh-the-weariness-of-it-all of so many contemporary poets." Maybe that would do, do you think? You also wrote a statement when I submitted to Harcourt, Brace—but I think I like this one better. If Rinehart were to send you a mss. copy (or galleys) would you rather read, and say something else? Or would you rather *not*—either one? I think it is all a lot of hooey and would rather see a dust jacket *bare* except, say, for a printed pattern of specks of dust.

Well, I shall end. At any rate before the year is up I'll be able to send you a copy of a book-to-myself. I'm glad of that.

All best love to you—and to Lota.

May 22, 1958

Dear Elizabeth:

Thanks so very much for your letters—both of them—and for the new note about my poems, which I think is *stunning*—in its simplicity and accuracy of aim. (I hate those statements that are full of big soft words, like a marshmallow dish, mostly sugar and air.) Bill Raney[29] liked it very much too, he told me today. I had just finished correcting the first galley proofs and brought them to his office. It is discouraging, but they have used a cramped type that I don't like at all—and of course several poems had to come out (including, by the way, the "de Chirico," which you liked—because it was too long). The jacket is not what I want, either. In an effort not to be old-fashioned they have made it bold and blaring. They are all very nice, in their manners, but terribly tough and unyielding in action. I hope you did not destroy the "criticism letter" you wrote—please let me have it, if you can. I very much *need* to be criticized. *No one* takes the trouble to do it, and I confer only with myself about my work—unhealthy and misleading. Thanks for listing the ones you liked.[30] [. . .]

As ever

June 24, 1958

Dear Elizabeth:

I do, very much, appreciate—and might even benefit from—your long letter about my poems. I've taken so long before

29. Swenson's editor.

30. Bishop's favorites were: "Almanac," "The Promontory Moment," "The Poplar's Shadow," "Hypnotist," "Water Picture," "Early Morning: Cape Cod," "The Tide at Long Point," and "De Chirico," followed by "The Centaur," "The Red Bird Tapestry," "Fountain Piece," "At Breakfast," "By Morning," "Frontispiece," "Looking Uptown," and "To the Statue."

answering partly because I've been busy—but mainly because I thought I'd better let it soak in, and then reread, trying to be objective. Which I think I can be, pretty well, now. Galleys and page proofs have been corrected; the book should be in print (advance copies) in about a month or so, I imagine. Nine poems were removed, leaving a total of fifty-seven—still too many, I'm afraid, but taking out more would have made sequence-gaps that seemed disturbing, or made an imbalance between the sections. (I'll confess to you that I'm by no means sure this book is even as good as my first—this has nothing to do with what you said, or what anyone else may say—has to do with my own limitations.) You were generous, honest, and thorough in your comments, taking the time and the labor to analyze and set down. It's a great help and an illumination, like being given a mirror when you've never had one before. You said, truly, that I'm old enough to know what I'm trying to do. Well, I don't always know what I'm trying to do until I start doing it. *It* does *me.* And you said one should experiment, but not all one's life—one finally has to settle down with one's own style. These are things that have bothered me, sporadically—now I see that I should get serious about it. Not because I'd swallow what you'd think, but because a self-suspicion is given added weight.

I feel that I want to go through your points, and answer them. (1) Possibly too many city-poems coming together in last section: Well, the general plan of the sections was to have in part 1 "something-to-say" poems, in part 2 "riddle poems," and in part 3 descriptive poems. As it stands, now, there are seven city-poems, four sea-poems, and eight country-poems in part 3. One or two were dropped from that section. (2) Yes, those "little things"[31] that you list are very important, and they can wreck a poem, and one you didn't mention that's worse than "echoes of other people" is echoes of oneself—letting the mind go into worn grooves of association and getting into the poems, not necessarily *same* effects but, effects *like* ones that have worked before. I'm guilty of it. (3) My typographical arrangements: They are conceits, and not necessary to the poems. True, and I

31. Misuse of words, overuse of some words, echoes of other people, lack of grammatical clarity, and bad meter.

will only explain what I guess has made me do it. It's part of my compulsive eye-mindedness. I want to make the shape attractive on the page, and occasionally varied—avoid monotony for the eye. In none of the poems here (eight in all, I think) except the first "Fountain Piece" does it "illustrate" anything—in the latter it could illustrate cascading water. In "R. F. at Breadloaf" the words are broken in order to get double meanings—to describe the opposing facets of him (his charm and his crustiness) at once. You're right about numbers for stanzas, I agree. They do have the effect of separating, though, and they change the appearance—eye-mindedness, again—but a superficiality.

From the very beginning I came at poetry backwards. I never studied prosody; I never acquired a background in what had already been done by others. In the few cases where I've approached the traditional in my work it's happened accidentally—to date I've never followed a predetermined form, either one of my own or in imitation of others. The form develops as the poem grows; I try to impose consistency and an inner logic for each poem—but a *total* consistency or a pre-arranged logic, or following a strict form, that doesn't work for me—I don't *enjoy* that. Of course, I don't think that you are suggesting that I work that way, but my approach to writing, since the beginning, has been sort of irresponsible—playful, not scholarly—I have excused my ignorances, I've been lazy and easy on myself, never *trying* very hard. The poems that I think are worth something (a few) that I've done have *come* to me, from somewhere—it hardly feels as though I made them. I tooled them, of course, but not very strenuously. And I've not found how to *make* good ones come. They come through *living* (how else?) and the truth is I may already have nearly used up that source because it often seems to me I haven't *lived,* really, very much, as old as I am. And will I, in the future? I don't know. Depends on what the future *brings.* (I hate that. You can see how passive an attitude that is.) You mustn't think that this dolorous tone is brought on by your letter (I'm only using *that* as an excuse to pour out to you what I have thought before to myself) and I don't want you to allude to it or try to buck me up. It's a mood that's good for me to express to someone besides myself for once—and having written it down maybe it will cause me to reform.

Now, your point (4)—My use of anatomical words in the poems. An udder *does* cringe. When you let go of it, it retracts, wrinkles up. I don't use these words "to startle and make the poem strong"—it's not deliberate. It is, or has been, a can't-help-it. The physical is the beautiful to me—it's awfully strong in me—and then I don't see, logically, why *buttock* is an uglier word than, say, *thumb*. Or that *groin* is an ugly word, or image either. It depends on the poem's intentions, of course. The effect of all words, I grant you, comes from their associations. I guess I like physical associations. Worse, there is almost a compulsion to employ them. Your mention made me go through the poems and count the number (I'd no notion they were so frequent—not only the "unmentionable" body parts but many others relating to the body and the senses). I think my taken-for-granted belief is that, as human animals, we have *nothing but* our sensual equipment, through which all impressions and expressions flow: thought and philosophy, reason and the spiritual, all included. That is an extreme view. It's not a *view,* really—an indelible *feeling.* Still, you are right that too much of any effect overbalances a poem, and turns it toward the ludicrous. I am going to keep a controlling eye on this trait in future work. (Then, too, there are ways of saying something strongly without using the *obvious* terms—yes, I do see your point.)

(5) In "A Lake Scene" *thwart* means a place of crossing—the rock I lean on is as round as the lowest hill across the lake in the wedge of the other hills that form each side of the far shore and, if I have to draw diagrams, it means it's a wrong word. Also, I guess it can't be used as a noun here, very well—it does get mixed up with *obstruction.* In "Working on Wall St."—with *figurines* I intended only the change to smallness and fragility from *slabs,* suggesting tall, heavy, thick. I used the word to mean "little shapes" not seeing them curved especially, or modeled. (And no irony was intended.) In "Promontory Moment"—yes, I'm lying on my stomach, resting on elbows, facing away from the sea, and with a half-turn of the head, can see the cove with swimmers to the left, the rock jetty with fishermen to the right (beyond that, the sailboat). Gull is close ahead of me on the beach. The pencil, stuck in sand, is under my eye, casting its shadow. I guess this is alright—unless it makes the reader's neck stiff.

Yes—obstacles. The Stravinsky quote[32] is a very good one for *me* to remember. I'm too easy on myself, lazy—and I think my worst danger is that of self-repetition. "Inventiveness" (superficial kind) becomes an evasion, a substitute for determining a main style. The apparent nonrepetition (experimentation) is really self-repetition at the source. Main style arises out of knowledge of motive and sticking to the motive. Motive, with me, has been left pretty much up to accident up to now. I write as I eat and drink: for the taste. There's a self-centeredness, too, in my work that keeps it limited.

I don't think you were at all hard on me. Rather, the contrary. What I expect is that the book will get scant attention one way or another from *critics.* I don't know if it's in me to write *important* poetry. I don't know if my life will turn out to have been important, except to myself. (Significant poetry comes out of a significant life.)

However, I am going to try to abandon my conceits and superficialities in my coming work (or, if I can't, at least see that they're less obvious). My first book was entirely unpunctuated (except for the question mark)—one conceit that I've largely got rid of.

I have ego enough, I think, not to get upset or be unduly influenced by whatever reactions there could be to the poems. On the other hand, there are a few people whose opinions *count*—yours in particular—and I'm thankful to you for being explicit. It constitutes a real help—as I say, a needed mirror, one that doesn't merely flatter [. . .]

Love to you, and to Lota

March 18, 1959

Dear Elizabeth, and Lota:

It is a very clear, brisk day out—with a slam-bang wind—and I have a cold that's been with me for a week—otherwise,

---

32. "The more art is controlled, limited, worked over, the more it is free . . . my freedom thus consists in my moving about within the narrow frame of what I have assigned myself for each of my undertakings. . . . It will be so much the greater and more meaningful the more I surround myself with obstacles."

"financially, morally, mentally," I've nothing to complain of. No, you had not sent us the Petropolis card with statue of the emperor before. Those several kinds of palms around the statue, and the lush lawn—it looks tropical but cool and fertile at the same time. The other day a letter came from Amy Lowell's trustees which offered me that traveling scholarship of $2,000, which must be spent outside North America and last one year and cover traveling expenses too. Of course that is nearly impossible but I am casting about to get information on where it would be cheapest to go—Spain? Italy? Puerto Rico, maybe? and considering whether I could save enough money by September (when the grant would start) to pay back and forth fares and perhaps have a bit extra so as not to feel too insecure. Maybe I will write them and ask whether it can be postponed in starting for six months or so, then I could save more money. They pay it in $500 chunks, so it occurred to me that when, after eight months, the fourth check would arrive I could use that for passage home (cheating a little bit by spreading it over less than a year, thus having more to spend per month). It hasn't made me as happy as I ought to be because of the strings attached—then too, it makes me aware of how unprepared I am to take off to a foreign land—alone—and stupid about any other language except English. As a matter of fact, I don't think I'd want to go alone. Well, I must let them know by April 1.

I just finished doing an article on the painter, Milton Avery, for *Arts* magazine—which was pleasurable to do and earned me $60. It recently changed hands, has a new format; the editor, Hilton Kramer, is a friend and let me do it in my own way—not pretending to be an art critic. At the first of the year the *New Yorker* offered me their $100 a year arrangement to have first look at my poems (which is very nice of them) and I bought a new typewriter with the money. It is a Royal Portable "Futura" and has everything but tail-fins (they have made it look as much like a little automobile as they could—when you touch the emblem "Royal" on the front, the hood flies up for changing the ribbon or cleaning the keys). I had a hard time finding one that wasn't pink, green, or blue—it's two-toned gray [. . .]

April 21, 1959

Dear Elizabeth (and Lota):

Well, it never pours but it avalanches, and I *did* get a Guggenheim Fellowship! The announcements were in the *Times* and *Tribune* yesterday and I was notified a few days ago. What is so lucky is that I had previously asked for the Amy Lowell grant to start in the spring of 1960, which they agreed to, and so the two good fortunes won't be running concurrently and I can have both!—the Guggenheim for this year and the other for next. Of course I am walking on the ceiling and feel very strange, with mixed reactions of "Do I deserve it?" and "Can I live up to it?"—then "Never mind—I like it—it feels *good.*" So this makes Europe very possible, for both me and Pearl. But we probably won't be going until next spring, and I will take a course in French in the meanwhile, and we will make very careful plans on just where and how to spend a year abroad. We'll disembark at Naples, perhaps, travel south all around the Boot and up north into France during the spring (beginning about the middle of April), spend some of the summer in England and maybe Scandinavia, and for the winter come back down into Spain, where, on the Mediterranean side, I'm told we can settle down (Valencia?) and live cheaply for six months or so. Then, after all the adventure, I could get some writing done. These are very general plans as yet. But we want to get passports and make tentative reservations very soon. If you get a sailing in the "thrift season" it's much cheaper, I hear, and we plan to move in the opposite direction to the summer tourists. Well, it will all be great fun just *planning* it for the next year. How will I be able to hold on to the Guggenheim money ($3,600) for that long? Easy, I think—I'm so used to scrimping that it's a habit. I'd rather do it this way and have a fat sum to spend comfortably over a year for the two of us abroad. I'm so glad Pearl will come with me because it wouldn't really be enjoyable alone.

So your hunch in your last letter was correct, Elizabeth—I was so very glad to get it, and all your good advices. What I would *really* like to do (but I'm afraid it's not financially possible) is to go to Europe for the first half and Brazil for the winter of next year. I know—or feel—that I'd like South America, its wildness and differentness from the museum that Europe is. It was wonderful of you to suggest you would welcome us there near you—I wish I could do it—am dreaming of it, but the fare, either boat or plane, is awfully steep. We'll have $5,600 to spend between us for a year—maybe we can work out some sort of freighter trip to S.A. Anyway I am going to investigate it [. . .]

Haven't really answered your letter, as don't have it before me. But it made me feel so good, coming when it did. And *you* had an awful lot to do with my astonishing good luck—directly, and in many indirect ways. There is no way of *thanking*—but I wish I could. Will write again soon.

April 10, 1961

Dear Elizabeth:

I have two letters of yours to reply to—and two poems! I wish I were an eager letter writer—I wish that intentions were deeds, and etc., etc. I am sitting in an upset apartment—the painting was halted in the middle by our monstrous landlord—I won't go into all the ludicrous details but he is trying to force us to move so as to replace us with richer tenants. We are not going to do it, of course.

Yesterday (it being sunny though chilly—it's pouring today) we got into our Simca with two friends who live on Bank St. and went to Jamaica Bay, near the Rockaways, where we tramped around and spotted a number of birds: the kildeer, piping plover, horned grebes, a number of ducks including the coot, scaup, bufflehead, ruddy duck; and then the American egret and the snowy egret. There were redwings and horned larks there, too. We intend to spend our weekends camping (as soon as the weather warms up) in upstate New York and Connecticut. I plan to go Yaddo for August—having been invited by Elizabeth Ames.

My book is going to be done by Holt, it appears. It probably won't come out until spring 1962, though. I send you a poem, "How to Grow Old," which came to me in the Tuileries in September as I was waiting on a bench below Maillol's statue in honor of Cezanne, waiting for Pearl to come out of the Louvre. (The place had nothing to do with it—just my mood.) It is one of those "given poems"—sometimes, but quite seldom now, I have them, and can't change them hardly at all from the first version.

I'm wild about your "Song for a Rainy Season" and so glad you sent me the copy. It is just tremendously good—so easy, and so free as if it were singing itself, coloring itself, floating under its own power—telling so much symbolically. *Not* sad, in spite of the ending—a poem of realization, so triumphant—all is done with such a light touch. Did it happen this way, or was it tough to work out? "From Anthony Trollope's Journal" doesn't appeal to me so much—its content doesn't happen to touch me—but the rhyme scheme and construction are so good I have to admire *that* [. . .]

April 24, 1962

Dear Elizabeth:

[. . .] You are more than good—and *reckless*—to say you'll put your name to it[33] *before* reading . . . should you change your mind I'll not blame you a bit. I have numerous doubts about the collection in its present form—I *know* it's not right—but I've fooled around so much trying to fix it right that now I just don't know. My opinions and feelings vacillate so much, and I've selected and deleted and arranged so many times that I'm tired of the whole deal. I have twice the number of poems in that ms., written since my last book, and I'm not even sure I've chosen the "best ones." I wonder if the whole seems too artificial, and if those typographical notions for some of the poems should be abandoned. I would be glad to improve simply by eliminating (if I could decide *what*)—make it smaller—three instead of four sections for instance—and if a possible sequence could still be had, after elimination. God, it's all such a headache and a bore. If it just *occurs* to you, during reading, and you don't have to work at it, could you give me any suggestions or reaction you get, please? I will honestly not be hurt by *anything* you say—but will be helped—even if you say: "Wait, don't publish another book yet." [. . .]

It's interesting that [Robert] Lowell is going to visit you in June. I heard a recording over WBAI the other day in which Lowell read his poems and a commentary about them was given

33. Bishop had agreed to read and endorse *To Mix with Time.* In a letter of April 3, 1962, she offered detailed criticism of the book.

by a West Coast professor (I forget the name). He read "Memories of West Street and Lepke" and that whole group, including the one "for Elizabeth Bishop"—"Skunk Hour." Of course I think he is splendid, and he read beautifully, too [. . .]

A new, in fact unidentified, bird is visiting our garden this spring. I was watching him this morning—a pair of them, male and female, in the ailanthus branches (which are just beginning to bud). He would be a crested flycatcher except that the color is wrong. About the size of a redwing blackbird, black head with a crest, black to brownish chest and wings and back, a white patch on back just above the tail; tail wags like a flycatcher and has white rim on its squared-off tip; the startling feature is that the whole rump under the tail is vermilion. None of the flycatchers have a red behind, but that's the only species it resembles by shape, size, action, and "song"—it makes an aggressive *chirk* with the *rrrs* trilled. The female is just like the male but a little smaller and more brownish than black. I saw a female yellow-bellied sapsucker, too, this morning, going up one of the trunks—and there have been flickers, jays, juncos, chickadees, and ruby-crowned kinglets. We get quite a lot of birds in the spring and then they move north as soon as the heat sets in. We were at Jamaica Bay last weekend and had a good water-birding time. We didn't find the Marble Godwit, though, although some of the Brooklyn Bird Club people had seen it. We nearly lost our boots tramping through the ooze on a kind of island of mussel shells and fragmite stubble, while the tide was out at Broad Channel. We were waiting for Godwit but he didn't show up.

[. . .] I hope you realize how grateful I am for your willingness to read through my book—I hate to ask it—it's a chore—please just do [what] you're able, and there's no hurry. (I'm working on a few *new* poems and I am placing my hopes on *them.*)

Love to you

May 21, 1962

Dear Elizabeth:

Thanks ever so much for your letter received today—saying you got the spectacle wipers. On the day I received your long, careful, and extremely helpful letter about my poems I would have liked to reply instantly . . . if only everything I had to say could have streamed out simultaneously with my *thinking* it, a telepathic ribbon that would appear before you—a ticker-tape kind of thing (like the news strip around the NY Times Building)—of course, and visible only to you. But I have been in quite a swirl since then, and I wanted to be able to report the result of my "machinations" when I answered you. It's not *quite* settled—that is, I haven't signed the contract—but it appears certain that Scribner's instead of Holt will be doing my book, and it will appear on their spring 1963 list [. . .]

I've been doing research for the writing of an introduction to a new edition of *The Spoon River Anthology* by Edgar Lee Masters that Collier Books asked me to write—which has a close deadline. Well, I've got all my material now (it took me a good while to read the anthology itself—about 250 poems) and have eight days to do the article in—I promised to deliver by the end of the month.

I found your comments and your *grading* of the poems in *To Mix with Time* very canny—I admit I'm inclined to trust you nearly all the way—You point out the weak spots in several poems that make me feel I can maybe rescue them. I've already tried, with "Distance and a Certain Light" and with "Pigeon Women." [. . .] It appears there are only five poems you didn't like at all—which I know is too generous of you. The only one of those that I had high hopes for is "How to Be Old"—but maybe it's partly the typographical handling that keeps it from doing what it should. In fact, before hearing from you I had revised it somewhat—I have another version that I'll send to you sometime. (I know I sent this to you in a half-baked version when I had just written it. Probably it's not finished *yet.* It's probably too obvious—and I can't see that yet.) *Hudson Review* the other day accepted "God," "The Universe," and "Night Practice," and Frederick Morgan[34] called me up and said he liked them very much. Well, *now* of course I will do some hard thinking about what to keep in and what to drop and what to make better—and I do have a few new ones and one or two other old ones that might get in instead of the weaker ones presently there. (I know I'll want to revise some of the poems I intend to select from *A Cage* and the first book—some have already been revised—and I'll

34. Frederick Morgan, a poet and the editor of the *Hudson Review.*

be glad of the change to present corrected versions. In looking them over swiftly the other day, it seemed to me I could be quite definite about what to *omit* from those volumes—I don't have the indecisiveness I had with the present book, thank God.)

You gave me seventeen stars. After the depression and doubt I had been in about the whole thing, I felt tremendously encouraged and relieved to have your evaluation. You are most wonderful to take the time and care and interest to look the ms. through so thoroughly. Yes, I see what you mean about putting a few *ands* into "At the Museum of Modern Art"—I agree with all except the one in the last stanza. And about leaving out certain adjectives, unless absolutely exact ones can be found—yes, I'll apply that. What I have resolved—and wonder if I can stick to it—in my future work, is to *stop* comparing things and depend on *precision,* on emphasizing the uniqueness of things, their *un*likeness to other things—can it be done? Not entirely, maybe, but it's healthy to try. (*You* solve this problem by absolutely unused comparisons, when you use them—startling ones—startling because they fit so well at the same time as they seem far-fetched, being shown for the first time.)

I can tell you now which ones in the collection I've decided definitely to drop so far—there may be others as well: "The Wish to Escape," etc., "A Boy and Big David" (unless I can fix), "11th Floor W. 4th St.," "Trinity Churchyard" (unless can fix—This is expanded version of shorter poem that might have been better in the first place), "On the Terrace," "What Did I Dream," "Swimmers." I'll take out the phrases naming each section, which seem to be unnecessary now, and I'll arrange the poems in a free-er order—bury God and the Universe somewhere where they'll be less conspicuous (if I can't bring myself to throw them out). Fact is, I have a larger group of poems "on the same theme" that got written last winter (1961, I mean) for some reason—the others are no good at all—but one of them called "3 Models of the Universe" got sold outright to Steuben Glass for $250—like a painting, without right of reproduction.

You're right, of course, about *meet* in "The Pantheon"—damn it, it's ridiculous to have let that stay. In many places you've put your finger on the essential blot—I hope will be able to fix those places suitably as soon as I can settle down to it with undivided concentration.

I'll defend "From the Office Window" just a little bit: *Evacuations* after all simply means a letting out—and in this case it is very white smoke, which ought to "keep it clean"—well, I'm laughing a little about it in the poem, I guess. Besides, I think the *sound* of that word is very nice. "Caning the sky" refers to the contrail of a jet plane—a white line that, when the plane turns, begins to make a curved handle (or it did, as I was looking at it)—and then I superimposed on that the sound of the sonar boom, so *caning* has a double meaning. But I can see that possibly this is too fanciful, and gets to be tricky and obscure.

Still, I don't think I will change it. Maybe you didn't get "The Contraption" if you read it just as being about a rollercoaster (did you?)—it's supposed to be a kind of ironic life-and-death metaphor—too elaborate, forced, not evident enough?—and the "car" becomes a number of things, finally a coffin. That's why day and night come into it, the sudden unforeseen ups and downs, the sense of not knowing where you're going, or being able to see the shape and plan of the crazy thing because you're in it and can't get above it, etc. I had a whole other stanza ending this poem that made its intentions clearer, but someone—I think it was Howard—thought it was overstressed so I cut it. (I'll send you a clipping of the other.) *Undippered* means that the car is shaped like a dipper and feels like that as it holds you just before dropping from the top of the slope—and, if you were dumped out, you'd fall through the air without a dipper (emptiness).

I guess I'll remove "The Totem"—that bulky Empire State poem—it really doesn't work and I've realized it in a shadowy way all along—the tone isn't right, too melodramatic in language, and now you've pointed out little other things that are inconsistent and make it ludicrous. The "cubes and cones" do look like a "chaos of knives" when you're looking at the Wall St. district from the top of Empire State and the sun is striking their metallic or glass parts—but, no, it's careless description and generalized. (I might make "11th Floor" better and omit "Totem," which is repetitious and overambitious—it's actually an old poem, going back about ten years.)

"Astonishing others out" in "Fireflies" means making them come out, become visible, too. Howard said this was the one poem in the collection he just plain didn't like—and didn't say why. "Warts of water" in "Seeing the Frog" are on my hand when

I bring it up out of the pool not having caught him when he dived, and I'm left looking at my grabby hand and *it's* shaped like a frog. This is an involved poem that tries to get at something subconscious and I'm not sure I could entirely justify it logically—yes, I could, but won't try here. I'm sorry you don't like the rose and bee poem—it's one that came all in a rush from a visit to the Brooklyn Botanical Gardens about three years ago (on June 1st!) and I always love the little ones that come flowingly—they're becoming rare with me—and then I thought the many *O* sounds in it were so musical. With such an old-fashioned subject can't one be excused for Freudianizing a bit? *Mademoiselle* bought this long ago and as far as I know have never printed it—I'll have to ask them to use it before the book comes out if I decide to include it. (I probably will.) I think I may leave out "When You Lie Down the Sea Stands Up"—it's not very important, and yes, you're right, the position of the viewer is not too clear: it's lying on your back parallel to the waves on a slightly inclined shore, with head turned to the water so you get almost an upside-down view if you roll your eyes upward. It helps if you have just waked up and are squinting besides. I did at one time know that there was an echo of you in the title—I'm glad if you don't mind—And "The Crossing" came to me at Bread Loaf—no wonder it's Frost-saturated. I can fix the little hitches in it that you point out, I feel pretty sure.

I shouldn't be boring you with my rebuttals to your notes this way.

I'll be very glad to have your statement—and there's no hurry over it—I already bragged to Scribner's that you're doing one for my book [. . .]

Love to you,
and so many thanks.

June 19, 1962

Dear Elizabeth:

Thanks very much for your card. Of course I know John Clare.[35] At least, I've read the half-dozen poems of his included

---

35. Bishop had told Swenson that her fresh observation of things reminded her of the nineteenth-century English poet John Clare.

in a fat anthology of English poets that I have—and like him very much. If I'm accused of being like him in my work I'd be pleased. I think my *attitude* is something like his—getting it from the source (which is nowhere but inside oneself) rather than *learning* from somebody else. If I've been influenced by other poets it's been unconscious—I hope I haven't, too much. And then I'm not very educated, and I don't mind. Poets that drag all of history, mythology, whatnot, into their poems bore me. I think a poem should isolate the present moment, vivify it—it's alright to use the future, too, because *that* belongs to the imagination, and to intuition—the present belongs to the color of one's feelings, and to one's point of view (a particular way of squinting at things). The past is all so settled, and trampled over. It's no fun unless you stand on the end of the diving board, alone, naked, not thinking of "how" or "why" or the best technique, but just the sensation—let impulse do it, instead of heavy knowledge. And not to care whether anyone's watching or not is very important.

I had lunch with Mitchell[36] the other day and signed the Scribner contract. He is being very nice and is going to let me help plan the format for the hardcover book (so it can fit the poems)—the paperback however, will have to be standard and go by the size and looks of the first edition (Robert Creeley's *Selected Poems*) that they've already put out—because it's planned as a series to appeal to teachers and students. I'm putting the new poems together now, and choosing the ones I'll include from the other books—the whole to be finished by August 1 [. . .]

Mitchell is very pleased that you are going to say something about the poems for the jacket. He suggested I ask you if it could be received before August 1. We both thought that it should go on the back, and be the only "endorsement"—and, if you feel so inclined, it could be up to 300 words—or as long as you like, for that matter. (It's easier to write something longer than shorter, isn't it? It is, for me.) But let that be just as you wish [. . .]

Love to you—and to Lota.

36. Burroughs Mitchell, Swenson's editor at Scribner's.

January 24, 1963

Dear Elizabeth:

I finally sent the perch-scrapers off to you today—I'm sorry I've been so long about it—and unless you have been away from Rio (or are still away) you must have received the Robert Johnson record (I sent that about two weeks ago). Both packages went Air Mail and were marked *Presente—under $5.00,* so I hope they get there all right. I was very glad to do these little shoppings for you. Please forgive me for being slow about it [. . .]

It was fun to visit the Belmont Pet Shop (where a large toucan was giving out with a sharp "wolf-whistle" so that women passing by in the Plaza corridor turned around to see *who* was taking such insulting notice of them)—and we did play the *Delta Blues* just once before I sent it off, and decided it was "the real good old stuff"—especially the second side. Please let me know anything else I could send you, and I promise to be more prompt [. . .]

Advance copies of my book are being mailed now, my editor tells me. When you next write please let me know if you got yours. Although I asked them to, they probably didn't sent it Air Mail. It looks fairly respectable—although the colors on the jacket didn't turn out as dark as I would have liked—the black should be really black, the green deeper olive—instead, in the quantity reproduction the colors washed out somehow. Well, I am really grateful to them for doing it *at all. The Carleton Miscellany* later in the year is going to print a poem of mine (new one) called "Motherhood"—that I'll send you. Howard [Moss] liked it a lot, he said, but didn't take it [. . .]

A couple of years ago Steuben Glass bought a poem of mine (called "Models of the Universe") and now they have made a "glass sculpture" out of it. This was shown, along with six others, in a "screen presentation" at the annual dinner of the Poetry Society of America at the Hotel Astor last week—while the poems were *intoned* in a most artificial way by somebody named Arnold Moss, connected with Steuben. It was all very weird—but the members were deeply impressed. The glass thing they made (I've no idea of the size) was supposed to be inspired by details in the poem, but their artist put a naked man floating in the middle (supposed to be God, I guess)—and I never intended such an interpretation, obviously. There's going to be an exhibition in April at the Glassworks (Steuben's) on Fifth Ave. and next year they're going to show them at the World's Fair—they say—in the meanwhile, sell them in reproduction, I suppose—while pushing the pitch of supporting poetry and the arts. [Robert] Frost was not at the dinner this year, being in hospital. Marianne M. did come—but late, after dinner and while the prizes were being given out—a young man handed her inside the door, and everyone rose and applauded her to her seat on the dais. She looked pretty chipper, and later on was asked to say a poem in front of the mike—which she did—something about four lines long, very fast, with the word *fen* in it, which she began to explain and then changed her mind, said it didn't need explaining, and sat down.

Let me know how Zephyrino[37] enjoys having his perch scraped. You know, when I first read your request I thought you meant *fish*-scrapers—for *perch*—something to get the scales off easily. I guess those little wire brushes could do that, too.

Love to you, and Lota—
and love from Pearl

April 16, 1963

Dear Elizabeth:

Just now I have been to Saks Fifth Ave. and bought your bathing suit, and had it sent to the APO name and address you gave me. I'm sorry to have been so long in getting it done—my free mornings seem to have become swamped with things to do and it doesn't look as though I'll ever catch up. *I fervently hope it fits.* It is exactly the one shown in the ad, and was the only one of that material and style they had left. In fact I had a little trouble getting them to remove it from the model—that's how it happened still to be there—it was on a model—and it may be a little shop-soiled—but I tried it on, it seemed O.K., in fact it fit *me* and I'm bigger than you, so I predict it should be right for you—maybe a little large [. . .]

We spent last weekend at Bennington and Dartmouth and Saratoga and enjoyed ourselves, although it was rather a strain.

37. Bishop's recently acquired orange canary.

The readings went off without any serious hitch. There was a blizzard going on at Bennington where I read in what used to be a coach house, and the wind was slamming the roof so noisily that I had to shout, practically. In the Tower Room of the Baker Library at Dartmouth their sonorous college chimes tolled 9 P.M. as I began a short poem—I found myself saying the words *between* the bell tones so that it sounded like a dialogue: "Out of an hour I built a hut . . ." BONG. "And like a Hindu sat." BONG. There was barely concealed hysteria because the last bong struck exactly after the last word of the poem. We stayed at the Eberharts, who were very nice to us, fed us a big ham dinner, and there was a lively party afterward. (I'll send you an extra of the Dartmouth paper showing me in the pulpit. Will send it along with the magazine that's got my "Motherhood" poem in it. Under separate cover.) The best part of the trip was relaxing with Jane and Leslie[38] at Grand Stand on Saturday and Sunday. Snow almost gone in Saratoga and buds breaking out. We saw golden crowned kinglets, nuthatches, brown creepers, and some downy woodpeckers on a tramp through their woods.

I saw and greeted Marianne Moore at the press preview of that Steuben Glass exhibit yesterday. She was dressed up charmingly—big-brimmed hat—and was very sprightly. We told each other our complaints about the crystal *things* they had made of our poems. She said she didn't like the way her monkeys had been treated, but that the giraffe looked pretty good. If you haven't got a copy of the anthology with the photographs of these objects—most of them are mistakes in one way or another—and if you'd like one, let me know, I'll send you an extra I have. Steuben has a new building now, you know—across the street from where they used to be—an icy-looking rectangle all glass—and when you walk in, although you sink over the ankles into the plush floor, everything else around you is glass—shelves, tables, cases of it—and now these poems that they've literally crystallized, displayed in red velvet cubicles in an inner room like a mausoleum. My thought was, "I wish I were a bull . . ."

Weather has been delicious the last few days—clear, quite

38. Jane Mayhall and Leslie Katz, Swenson's lifelong friends after their meeting in 1950.

warm, and excitingly springy. Magnolia is in bloom in the garden—hyacinths and jonquils up—the ivy reviving, and the privet is already green-sprigged. This is not a proper letter. There was much in yours I wanted to comment on—will try to remember to in my next.

Love to you, and Lota.
And from Pearl, too.

July 12, 1963

Dear Elizabeth:

I'm back on Perry St., and so glad to get your last letter, noting that you finally did get *mine,* sent from the Colony at Peterborough.[39] (I may not have put enough airmail on it, and that's why it took so long.) Came home in the middle of a heat wave (99 degrees) to a mess of manuscripts at the office, and piled-up correspondence—and to a house that needed a thorough cleaning, window-washing, etc.—so have been very busy trying to restore some sort of order. Haven't been able to sit down to my own typewriter yet. And Pearl has been suffering with Tennis Elbow (not from playing tennis)—from working too hard on her job. Little motions that you have to make all day when writing interview reports in longhand cause the tendons in your arm to become painful, and it can become chronic. But when she remembers not to be a piston, and to take more frequent breaks and relax, as her doctor tells her to, it gets better for a while. She gets a vacation in August and we'll spend a week or more at Wellfleet, beginning Aug. 17—we'll be camping near the ocean [. . .]

I guess it's because you endorsed my book that reviewers have decided I'm following in your tracks—a foolish conclusion to jump to—the other foolish notion is to lump women poets together, or connect them in some way. Well, *categorizing* is the first (and often only) duty of the reviewer, it seems. But there is coming in *The Nation* (I saw the proof) a good review by Richard Moore, one I really like, and he considers the book without having to compare me to anyone—and says some

39. Swenson had been at the MacDowell Colony in June.

canny things. I hope they print it *all*—it's quite long, and more probably will be cut. I'll send you a copy when it appears. I've tentatively accepted a reading tour through New England colleges for next April that will earn me at least $500—for five readings. It's so far away that it doesn't worry me, yet [. . .]

Back to you, me and Marianne Moore: the fact is I *have* been influenced by you a lot—not as to method, but as to attitude. I'd like to be more so. But when I write I find I can't do just as I intend to—it goes its own way. I would like to find the casual and absolutely natural tone that you have in your poems—they are never overcolored or forced the least little bit—they are very honest, and never call attention to their effects. Their brilliance is inside, and not on the surface. And they are subtle—not obvious. I think my greatest fault is being obvious—and I never know it until the poem's been printed—quite long after that, and it's too late. It comes from a poor education, and from being a loner, and never letting anyone else in on what I'm doing—not having the benefit of better judgment than my own. Up at the Colony I began to "make a study" of Marianne Moore—her *Collected Poems*—something I've never done before—I've never studied anyone's thoroughly. (And didn't finish—but I will as soon as I get straightened around.) I found so much to marvel at—I tremendously enjoyed reading her aloud. I have the feeling I *know* how to read her. It bores me to read critical articles, but I'm going to look up critiques of her work and check whether anyone has found the key-points to her method in the way that it seems I can sense them. *Syllabic verse* doesn't mean anything—or is a mere superficiality. She has a texture that is absolutely unique. And she has a philosophy that's solid, self-made, and applicable, but she keeps it unobtrusive so that when you *see* what she means it's a fine surprise, and true, and something that was hard to express is perfectly expressed. She is a very rich poet. I don't think your work is like hers—except, again, maybe in *attitude*. It's more of a personality thing than a craft thing [. . .]

I made several poems at the Colony—must work on them further. Two or three I have hopes for.

Love to you and Lota, as
ever—and from Pearl.

June 17, 1964

Dear Elizabeth:

[. . .] Cal Lowell will be having his play, called *The Old Glory,* produced at the American Place Theatre in September. I hope to observe some of the rehearsals, since I may be connected with this repertory group under my Ford grant[40]—which I'm taking up a month from now, but have been assigned first to the Lincoln Center Rep. Theatre—their temporary stage is right on Washington Square. I'll be separating at last from New Directions in about two more weeks. *That,* I'm convinced, is a good result of my getting this crazy grant.

My mother came from Sweden and visited us for almost a week the end of May. We took her and her traveling companions to the World's Fair—which she very much enjoyed. Then we had the apartment painted—a big upset, from which we have now almost recovered. I'm to do a reading at Middlebury College, Vermont, on July 6, and another at Wagner College July 8. In August we've planned to go to Martha's Vineyard for perhaps two weeks—we'll camp there [. . .]

It would be quite wonderful if we could look forward to seeing you here on your way home from abroad. You could stay with us. Our place is quite presentable just now. Foxy is nearly as big as ZB by now![41] Has a magnificent long thick fluffy tail. He's devilish, very active, and in contrast ZB has become retiring and dignified—in fact, well-behaved.

As ever

October 2, 1964

Dear Elizabeth:

Forgive me for neglecting to write for so long. It's a gloomy wet day. Trucks are going noisily over the slimy cobbles on Seventh Avenue. We're finally getting some rain after an unusually dry summer. We had our last camping trip of the season last

40. As a result of receiving a Ford Foundation Grant, Swenson wrote a one-act play, *The Floor.* Robert Lowell had received a similar grant and produced *The Old Glory.*

41. Swenson's cats.

weekend—at Montauk. Very windy and chilly there but sunny most of Saturday so we could walk on the beach at least and watch the eternal rollers [. . .]

The week we spent on Martha's Vineyard in August was a good one, although it was cold and we didn't get into the water very much. We had a camp between Oak Bluffs and Edgartown and went to the beach around Gay Head as well as exploring most of the island in the car. The only other time I was there, years ago, I had no car and saw only the part around Menemsha. I wrote a poem about the Flying Horses (an old merry-go-round at Oak Bluffs) and some other poems. Also at Truro during the second week I got some poems done. One called "Out of the Sea, Early" (about seeing the sun rise out of the ocean) will be in the *New Yorker*—which now has five poems not yet printed. (I just talked to Howard [Moss] on the phone and he said to send you his love. A play of his is going to be produced at Theatre South soon—he promised to send me an announcement [. . .])

I'm not with New Directions anymore. I quit in the middle of July and have been living on my Ford Grant, attending rehearsals at the Lincoln Center Repertory Theatre almost every afternoon. They are rehearsing *The Changeling* (which will open Oct. 29) and also the new Miller play *Incident at Vichy*. It's fun watching Elia Kazan handle the actors—they seem to be crazy about him, and he seems to have almost full control of their strings, with their consent. If somebody hadn't already done it I'd write a play called *The Rehearsal.* So far, aside from several wild ideas, I have done no solid work on a play. I think I'll have to switch my whole creative attitude—from looking to listening, for instance—and I'll have to infiltrate into the feelings of other people. Don't know if I can.

[. . .] I'm enclosing a little article I wrote for Marianne Moore's Birthday Book—principally because I'm not sure it'll be printed, and you maybe be the only reader. Tambimuttu[42] asked me to do it—and asked for material from a number of people—since he wants to print a sort of anthology honoring MM on her seventy-seventh birthday in November. But he's quite a sloppy and undependable sort, and, although he called

42. Thurairajah Tambimuttu, a Ceylonese poet, who was active in the New York literary scene from 1942 until the late 1960s.

me the other day and said part of the text was on its way to press, I sort of doubt it. I don't think my essay is very good—I did it in a hurry.

Much love to you, and Lota.
Pearl sends love.

December 2, 1964

Dear Elizabeth:

A pleasure to get your last letter. Several days ago I went to Ginza on Eighth St. and picked out two lanterns as close to your specifications as they had. They seemed not very sturdy to me—I'll bet they are inferior to the ones you bought before—but these are the kind, the only kind they have now. There are a couple of other Japanese shops in the Village that I investigated and they carry the very same thing. I do hope these are going to be usable for you. (They didn't cost very much, and please let them be a Christmas present from me. Not a very satisfactory one, I'm afraid.) The shop didn't want to bother with wrapping and mailing them, so I did it myself—sent them just ordinary mail to the APO address.

Lowell's three plays, *The Old Glory*—as you must know—are getting extraordinary praise from reviewers and almost everybody else (except from Ruth Herschberger in the *Village Voice*). Somehow I've lost the issue with her first letter—but maybe you've seen it?—it implied in quite a nasty way that Lowell has fascist or racist tendencies and that the plays show evidence of this. Poor Ruth, she's apparently really going off her nut. . . . I've seen all three of the plays, and they are very good. I thought *My Kinsman* was given the best *production*—the way it was staged is the most original and fitting. The dramatic realism of *Benito Cereno* wasn't managed as well by the director, seemed to me, and the night I saw it it had draggy sections, a too-slow pace at times, with no action, just stretches of dialogue. *Endicott and the Red Cross* was given just a dramatic reading, with props but not costumes, on an evening by itself, and then afterward in front of the audience, Lowell, [Stanley] Kunitz and others discussed it as a panel—the question being whether to expand it or contract it, since it's not in balance as yet. The *language* of all three of these plays is first-rate—and the probes they make into the nature of patriotism are sharp and profound. Lowell has made these grim and violent slices of American history into living experiences—he shocks the audience into examining its own conscience. The beauty of his technique is awesome. . . . And I'm having a wonderful experience reading *For the Union Dead.* Did I tell you that I'm to be an NBA [National Book Award] judge along with Howard M[oss] and Allen Tate? Roethke's and Lowell's books of poems are obviously, I think, the important ones published this year. However, Tate proposed and Howard and I agreed that authors who have already received the NBA award should not be entered in the competition. I don't know whether the NBA Committee will go along with this or not—but chances are it will, since it's Tate who made the suggestion. He thinks the Pulitzer committee, for instance, made itself ridiculous by giving the prize three or four times to Robert Frost.

Friday, December 4—

[. . .] I'll bet "The Burglar of Babylon" is the biggest space the *New Yorker* has ever given to one poem—a serious poem. I was surprised by it, and very moved. It's a sociological exposé in ballad form and the tragic biography of an outlaw. But the real point is that its language is beautiful and that it makes one *see* and *feel* so vividly everything that you tell about in it. Someone who knows and has lived with it, as you have, should compose a tune for this bitter story-poem. You must have been working on it a very long time—without letting out a peep about it. The hills of Kerosene, Skeleton, Astonishment, Babylon—what a tremendous refrain they make! I wonder if their sounds are as powerful in Portuguese?

[. . .] I'm working much harder, it seems to me, than when I used to go to work—without getting much of significance accomplished. I've gotten hung up with "business" of all sorts—I won't go into it, it's too boring—and I never catch up on my correspondence anymore. If I can only get through this Ford Foundation year (which has *not* proved productive up to now) maybe I can get back to my natural state and start fresh. What I need is a big patch of irresponsibility and anonymity to wade around it—no goals, just expectations. This makes me think of the lucerne field that used to be across the road from our place in Logan—where, when I was little, the lucerne grew higher than I was, and I would make a cave in it, and had secret paths to it, and pretended that, if I couldn't be seen from the house, I couldn't hear them call me . . .

Love to you, and to Lota.
From Pearl, too.

23 Perry St., NYC 10014
June 30, 1965

Dear Elizabeth:

[. . .] Do you remember that quite long ago when you were telling me about the *Bicos de Lacre* in your letters I began work on a poem in which I used word-for-word quotations from your letters? I sent you a rough copy once when it was still a mess. Well, I finally finished it and sent it with a batch of other poems to the *New Yorker,* and Howard [Moss] now wants to print it—he took several others as well. Since it really amounts to an inadvertent collaboration on your part, and *your* descriptions of the birds is what made me want to write it—they're what give it any distinction it may have, I think—it's necessary to have your approval to print it I should think. Besides, Howard says that technically they ought to have permission to use your quotes. He's going to put it into proof—since I said I was rather sure you wouldn't object—but if you let me know it's not O.K. I'll withdraw it of course. Howard also wants me to add, under the title in parenthesis, "A Reply to Elizabeth Bishop in Brazil"—which I will do, if that's all right with you. If there's anything not factually correct—or anything at all you object to—maybe you would mark it on one of the enclosed copies and send it back? I say this with trepidation—but never mind, I mean it[. . .][43]

Love to you & Lota

---

43. Swenson and Bishop's correspondence about this poem appeared in the *Paris Review* 131 (summer 1994): 171–86.

Feb. 23, 1966

Dear Elizabeth:

I wonder how you are liking it in Seattle by now?[44] I hope it is not too hard and that they are treating you well. I note your book is up for the NBA [. . .]

I finished a one-act play (called *The Floor*), which the American Place Theatre may put on this spring along with two other short plays, one by [Lawrence] Ferlinghetti. Scribner's wants me to do "a book of poems for young people"—teenagers. I told them I couldn't write anything specifically like that, so we have agreed to make a selection from my "riddle poems" for the purpose—possibly to be illustrated with photographs (if not too expensive) or drawings that won't give the "riddles" away too obviously. They're anxious to have it out by fall—whereas my book of new poems can't be until next year [. . .]

23 Perry St., NYC 10014
May 1, 1966

Dear Elizabeth:

I've just answered Robert Heilman's letter asking me, at your suggestion, to do a term at the U. of Washington at—it comes out to $600 per week! The letter floored me at the time—then I got obsessed with my play, rehearsals for it are now going on, and had to attend to other things, and I just now got around to answering him. It's beautiful of you to have thrown me such an opportunity—maybe they'll ask me again later on. Of course I've already signed to go to Purdue this fall and also for spring semester next year [. . .]

Wish you could be here during the run of my play, *The Floor*—but realize you can't. It's to have fourteen performances at the American Place beginning May 11. Working on it with the director and the actors has got me completely hypnotized—it's almost taking the place of *living*—and I'm glad it'll soon be over. Then I've been busy also with getting the manuscript done for a selection of poems to be called *Poems to Solve* that Scribner's Juvenile

---

44. Bishop had accepted a teaching post for the winter and spring at the University of Washington.

Dept. made me do—coming out in October—and with the ms. of *Half Sun Half Sleep* that I've got a deadline for July 1 [. . .]

Love

408 South Grant,
West Lafayette, Ind. 47906
Nov. [?], '66

Dear Elizabeth:

A big thrill to see your handwriting again, on a card from London, which came this morning. A year and a half from now I hope to be there—or abroad somewhere; money saved from what I'm doing here is going to help bring that about, I hope. I'm in a little old-fashioned house with a peaked roof on a dead-end street near the railroad tracks—can walk to the campus (about five blocks north)—having the pavement to myself, since everyone is in cars. There's a big new power house almost across the street, a grassy hill with trees on its property; the power house, especially at night, is the best and most exciting building around here—all of glass, in big squares, which let various colors of light through, *pastel colors*—gladioli shades, or sweetpea—a big high stack on one side has red blinker lights that flash in alternate rhythm to the airport beam fanning back and forth about a mile to the west. I walk up there quite often before going to bed—to the power house—and sometimes the doors are open (they slide up) and I can see the weird contraptions inside, metal tubular things on platforms, a balcony with other peculiarly shaped generators, or whatever they are—this ground floor part in a cold cathode light, a mixture of hummings heard, smooth sounds not very loud—and not a human anywhere in there—it seems to work by itself. Well, once I did see a watchman strolling on the balcony in an olive uniform, his hands and face greenish in the light.

I can see the studs in Orion's belt on clear nights. About the best thing out here is clear air, smell of grass and evergreen, and all the time now burning leaves. There are juniper bushes around the house and yard and they have a wonderful odor. The house doesn't get dirty—or my nails and hair—and that's nice.

The campus is rather ugly—flat, spread out—it looks like a manufacturing plant—and is. The only building with any grace on the campus is an old Main (not used for that anymore) with a little tower—French style architecture—and they've remodeled the inside so that it's boring inside. Near it is John Lafayette's gravestone, a short thick round-topped slab in the center of an oval hedge enclosure.

My "teaching" is going all right by now. The class meets each Tuesday afternoon for three and a half hours—a break for smoking in the middle. I have thirteen students, upper and undergraduate, ranging in age from nineteen to about forty-five—about half men. There are two (mail—I mean male) who may become writers. Some of them are nuts about me—or just plain nuts—and becoming flagrant about it. It is Squaresville here by the Wabash, and gossip is the sport, second only to football. Ladies may not put an elbow on a bar in this town—in fact, to *find* a bar takes underground connections—but there is a good Negro bar called Al's on the shady outskirts, that's got a juke and a colored TV and best spareribs I've ever eaten. There's a roadhouse too, where you can get fried catfish—Friday nights there is a good place for camping—at least I haven't seen anyone from the English Dept. there yet [. . .]

And so, I guess I'll survive into the spring— May 31 is the magic date I'm due to be sprung. I've had three other offers to "residence" and "teach"—one from Robert Heilman in Seattle. I've let him wait a long time without decision—I'm pretty certain I'll say no. How did it go for you? Was it worth it? I heard indirectly that you became ill. I didn't try to find out more. I thought that, if you wanted to, you'd write and tell me—and if you didn't, then there were reasons.

I hope you're well—and that Lota is, by this time.

My love as ever

73 Boulevard
Sea Cliff, N.Y.   11579
October 27, 1969

Dear Elizabeth:

[. . .] I was in N.Y. on Friday to see the dentist and my editor, and I bought $10 worth of Beckett—mostly his plays, but one novel, *Watt,* in paperback. I've been reading him; he fits my mood. I used not to be able to identify with him at all.

Too bad about *Watat* (typo)! though: it starts out so profoundly and I was fascinated; the mix of humor and hopelessness so true—and then, before the middle, starts to fill up the pages with mindless repetitions and cataloging. Maybe it comes back to itself in the last half—so I will persist. His play *Film* I found marvelous.

Iconographs, my next book, is in production, slowly, but getting quite a factory handling—and I've given them a problem with my typographical "shapes" and "frames"—I should probably never have done it this way. You'll probably hate it when you see it, but I'll send you a copy anyway. I doubt that it will be out before February. I made a long poem "First Walk on the Moon" (not to be in book) and sent to Howard [Moss] recently along with three other new ones. Didn't you like, a lot, Howard's "Ménage à Trois" in the *New Yorker* of Oct. 11?

I hope you are happy, and working, and well. I love you a lot, you know.

73 Boulevard
Sea Cliff, N.Y.   11579
October 21, 1970

Dear Elizabeth:

Boobs, bubbies, tits, dugs, headlights, knockers . . . I am boxing your prudish ears with 'em all—and which would you substitute (in the Bond movie) if you don't like the first? Never mind, and don't be mad. So good to have your letter. I'd heard you were at Harvard temporarily, in Lowell's place—[. . .] And then Howard leaked it to me the other day that you're poetry reviewer for the *New Yorker* now. But I had sent *Iconographs* before I knew that, so that isn't why I did. Of course I just wanted you to have a copy. It came out a year later than promised—Aug. 21—and Scribner's has given it exactly one tiny mention in a general ad. However, it's sold 1,300 copies in the two months, I was told.

[. . .] Have you read [W. D.] Snodgrass's latest, *After Experience?* It's so fine. And I'm reviewing it (along with seven others—ugh!) for *Southern Review*'s January issue [. . .] Someone wants me to do translations of a Swedish poet, Tomas Tranströmer.

Have you ever heard of him? Maybe I will, if I like his book—haven't seen it yet—he's getting some prize or other from the International Poetry Forum in Pittsburgh.

It's so fine that you took the NBA Award. Belated congratulations [. . .]

Love, as ever

December 2, 1971

Dear Elizabeth:

I just now read your translations of two Brazilian poems in last week's *New Yorker*—and I love them very much—especially "Sonnet of Intimacy." To have managed to give them such perfect form—with meter, rhymes, and all—along with transferring the content so naturally—What persistence it must have taken. And love. And luck. I saw your "Crusoe in England," too, some weeks ago. Wonderful, and sad, and absurd, and true. The one of a kind, the explorer, marooned, mateless—who chose uniqueness, invented his survival equipment, and lived on his own world—only to find in the end that he's no *exception* to the common fate of all those others who never ventured . . . A great and remarkable poem, on all its levels—there are at least three levels that I see [. . .][45]

Thanks for your long letter explaining your feelings about the Ann Stanford anthology.[46] She wrote me that she heard from you, and now understands your point of view. Of course, I do, too. I mean, I agree about nonsegregation and equal rights, for heaven's sake, for *every body* in the whole of nature! [. . .]

I got the 100-page ms. of the Tranströmer translations in to Pittsburgh Press the other day. However, Tomas now wants to drop some of the poems, so it'll probably be a smaller selection. Such a lot of business and correspondence has been necessary with this, and I've been at the project a whole year. It's about

45. In her next letter Bishop thanked Swenson for "so beautifully" getting the point of the poem.

46. Swenson had unsuccessfully urged Bishop to reconsider her refusal to be in Stanford's collection *The Women Poets in English.*

worn me out. The translating itself was enjoyable—but I'll never do it again.[47]

We plan to be in Florida from the 24th to about Jan. 4th. We'll be looking for a house.

Maybe, somehow, after the New Year we can get together. We'd love to see the Blue-Footed Boobies on your slides, and hear about the Galapagos Islands. What luck to have been there!

870 Hilgard Ave.
#218
Los Angeles, Ca. 90024
December 2, 1978

Dear Elizabeth:

[. . .] By now, if you're back in Boston, you'll have received your own copy of *Things Taking Place*.[48] It would have been even thicker, more "fearful," had I not, fortunately, been asked to reduce the original manuscript, which otherwise would have been too expensive to produce. When in future I attempt a *Collected,* maybe I'll be able to skin way down, and call it *Contracted Poems* instead. It's worth a great deal to me, Elizabeth, to have your good opinion. I gave a sort of lecture-reading at the Guggenheim recently on "The Education of the Poet" and said: "I didn't *know* anything and so had to invent everything." There's to be a review of *Things* in *Parnassus* along with an interview with me taped last summer. I've been asked to read at the U. of Texas in Austin, and may do it, since the pay is good. And have a few readings (for peanuts) to do here around L.A [. . .]

The bookstores in Westwood here are stocking my book in both paper and hardbound, but it's irritating to see it placed *next* to [May] Sarton's on some shelves. It bugs me to be confused with her. One May S. is a weak poet with a big rep.; the other is the opposite. Eight years went by between this book and the one before. Scribner's kept me dangling about a new one while let-

---

47. The book was nominated for the National Book Award in March 1973.

48. In a letter of February 24, 1975, Swenson told Bishop that Scribner's had let her books go out of print, so she was assembling a *New & Selected.*

ting the others go out of print. Little, Brown took almost two years to produce my *New & Selected* after *asking* for the manuscript. All of this was discouraging. Also, for certain personal reasons my powers went into hibernation. But they are warming now—they are coming back. I'm working. I've never had enough *chutzbah* to push for attention. Maybe this book will win a prize, and I'll win back my identity. And maybe not. Doesn't matter. *I* know who I am. "I'm the one who'll be with me for the rest of my life." That's a quote from a poem now in the works.

A sunny, breezy day here. We're so glad to be out of the snowy east. I think you like snow and nippy red cheeks, do you? The winter knocks me on my rear because of my allergy. Zan[49] and I might take a cruise boat down to Mexico after New Year: Mazatlan, Puerto Vallarta, Ixtapa, Acapulco, and back. (I've never been to Mexico.) If we get our projects well under way so as to deserve it. Zan has a contract for a novel—an adult book this time. She has several juvenile sports books in print.

It was just lovely to hear from you, Elizabeth.

Love, as ever. Kisses. Thanks.

Los Angeles Feb. 12 '79

Dearest Elizabeth:

It is wonderful luck for me that I've been made a Fellow of the Academy and gifted with $10,000! I know that *you* had much to do with it. If only I could make you feel my joy and thanks! Although I have several friends among the Chancellors—bless them—your influence is immense and without your nod I'm sure this could not have happened for me. Please know that I love you—always will . . .

May[50]

---

49. R. R. Knudson, whom Swenson met during her teaching appointment at Purdue and with whom she lived from 1967 until her death in 1989.

50. Elizabeth Bishop wrote Swenson two last postcards, dated March 22, 1979, and April 12, 1979, and Swenson wrote one last letter, dated March 28. Bishop died on October 6, 1979. Swenson's elegy for Bishop, "In the Bodies of Words," written at Bethany, Delaware, October 13–15, 1979, is contained in *In Other Words* (1987).

UNDER DISCUSSION
David Lehman, General Editor
Donald Hall, Founding Editor

Volumes in the Under Discussion series collect reviews and essays about individual poets. The series is concerned with contemporary American an English poets about whom the consensus has not yet been formed and the final vote has not been taken. Titles in the series include:

Charles Simic
edited by Bruce Weigl
On Gwendolyn Brooks
edited by Stephen Caldwell Wright
On William Stafford
edited by Tom Andrews
Denise Levertov
edited with an introduction by Albert Gelpi
The Poetry of W. D. Snodgrass
edited by Stephen Haven
On the Poetry of Philip Levine
edited by Christopher Buckley
Frank O'Hara
edited by Jim Elledge
James Wright
edited by Peter Stitt and Frank Graziano
Anne Sexton
edited by Steven E. Colburn
On Louis Simpson
edited by Hank Lazer
On the Poetry of Galway Kinnell
edited by Howard Nelson
Robert Creeley's Life and Work
edited by John Wilson
Robert Bly: When Sleepers Awake
edited by Joyce Peseroff
On the Poetry of Allen Ginsberg
edited by Lewis Hyde
Reading Adrienne Rich
edited by Jane Roberta Cooper
Richard Wilbur's Creation
edited and with an introduction by Wendy Salinger
Elizabeth Bishop and Her Art
edited by Lloyd Schwartz and Sybil P. Estess